angles on

child psychology

Cheltenham: Nelson
Thornes, 2001

0748759751

dedication

This book is dedicated to Clare.

angles on child psychology

Matt Jarvis with Emma Chandler

Series Editors: Matt Jarvis Julia Russell

Published in 2001 by:
Nelson Thornes Ltd
Delta Place
27 Bath Road
CHELTENHAM
GL53 7TH
United Kingdom

01 02 03 04 05 / 10 9 8 7 6 5 4 3 2 1

A catalogue record for this book is available from the British Library.

ISBN 0 7487 5975 1

Illustrations by Oxford Designers and Illustrators
Page make-up by Northern Phototypesetting Co. Ltd

Printed and bound in Great Britain by The Bath Press

contents

part 2 cognitive development

acknowledgements

I would like to thank all those who have worked on this project. Rick, Carolyn and Louise at Nelson Thornes have been – as always – consistently warm, helpful and positive. Julia, as series editor, has provided invaluable advice throughout. I would also like to thank Cara Flanagan for her expert advice, and those who have taught me what I know about child development, particularly the department of Child Psychotherapy at the Tavistock Clinic and Maggie Linnell at Portsmouth University. I am extremely pleased to introduce Emma Chandler, a major new talent in psychology.

The authors and publishers are grateful to the following for permission to reproduce material:

- *The Guardian* for extract (p. 97 – author, Sarah Boseley)

- *The Independent* for extract (p. 26 – author, Elizabeth Nash; pp. 184–5 – author, Cherry Norton)

- *Journal of Autism* for diagram, "The triad of impairments" by Wing and Gould (p. 209)

- Nuffield Provincial Hospital for "Marcia's adolescent types" from *Psychology a New Introduction* by Gross et al. (p.120)

- *The Observer* for extracts (p. 48; p. 117 – author, Paul Harris)

- Routledge for extracts from *Relationships in Adolescence* by Coleman (p. 123) and for extracts from *The Nature of Adolescence* by Coleman and Hendry (p.125)

- Routledge for extract from "The inner life" from *Forms of Feeling* by Hobson (p. 81)

Every effort has been made to contact copyright holders and we apologise if anyone has been overlooked.

Photo credits

- Bettman Corbis (pp. 2, 129)
- John Birdsall (p. 119)
- British Psychological Society (pp. 10, 23)
- Sally & Richard Greenhill (p. 167)
- Angela Hampton/Family Life Picture Library (p. 73, 192)
- Michael Howe (p. 182)
- Kings College London (p. 14)
- Kobal (p. 218)
- National Autistic Society (p. 207)
- Rex Features/Laurence Kiely (p. 57)
- Wellcome Trust (p. 200)
- Stephen Wiltshire (p. 208)

Coverage of examination board specifications

Chapter	Topics covered	Edexcel	AQA A	AQA B
1 Social, personal and emotional development	Freudian theory Social learning theory Behavioural genetics Social constructionism	Psychodynamic approach Learning theory Genetic influences	Personality development	Psychoanalytical approach
2 Attachment	Attachment formation Bowlby's theory Ainsworth's theory Culture and attachment Critiques of attachment Theory and research	Bowlby's theory Attachment types Cross-cultural studies Criticisms of research	Development of attachments Individual differences in attachment Cultural variations	Development of attachments Functions of attachment Measuring attachment
3 Deprivation and privation	Short-term deprivation Long-term deprivation Privation	Short-term deprivation Long-term deprivation Privation	Short-term deprivation Long-term deprivation Privation	Short-term deprivation Long-term deprivation Privation
4 Friendship and play	Friendship development Popularity of individuals Culture and friendship Types of play Theories of play Play in therapy	Developmental trends Popularity of individuals Cultural differences Categories of play Theories of play Therapeutic value of play		Age and sex differences Popularity of individual
5 Development of identity	Self concept Self esteem Theories of gender		Theories of gender	Aspects of the self Self esteem Theories of gender
6 Adolescence	The adolescence construct Theories of adolescence Ethnic identity Relationships with peers and parents		Culture and adolescence Identity in adolescence Relationships with peers and parents	
7 Piaget's theory of cognitive development	Piaget's theory Application to education Neo-Piagetian theory	Piagetian theory Application to education	Piagetian theory Applications Information processing approach	
8 Alternative theories of cognitive development	Vygotsky's theory Bruner's theory Application to education Theory of mind	One alternative to Piaget Application to education	Vygotsky's theory	Vygotsky's theory Bruner's theory
9 Development of intelligence and abilities	The intelligence construct IQ testing Origins of intelligence Gifted children		Cultural differences Origins	Gifted children
10 Development of moral reasoning	Cognitive-development theories Gender differences Prosocial reasoning Family context		Cognitive-development theories Gender differences Prosocial reasoning	Cognitive-development theories Gender differences Prosocial reasoning
11 Autism	Symptoms of autism Theories of autism Intervention with autism			Symptoms of autism Causes of autism Treatments of autism

1

Theoretical approaches to social, personal and emotional development

what's
ahead?

In this chapter we will be looking at four major approaches to explaining individual personal, social and emotional development in children. We begin with the psychodynamic approach, developed by Sigmund Freud, and move on to examine the learning approach, with a particular focus on Albert Bandura's social learning theory. Psychodynamic and learning perspectives remain important in explaining personality development, but our understanding has been enhanced in recent years by behavioural genetics, which has given us an understanding of the importance of how genes affect personality. We also need to consider the importance of culture in children's development. In *What's new?* we will introduce a new and rapidly growing perspective on the study of child development, the social constructionist approach.

The psychodynamic approach

The psychodynamic approach is based on the following ideas.

- Our behaviour and feelings as adults (both normal and in cases of psychological problems) are largely rooted in our early childhood experiences.

- Relationships (especially those with our parents) are of great importance in determining how we feel and behave.

- Our behaviour and feelings are strongly affected by our unconscious mind, i.e. mental processes of which we are not consciously aware. These unconscious influences come both from past experiences and also from instincts, with which we are born.

Sigmund Freud's theory

Sigmund Freud

There are a number of psychodynamic (or *psychoanalytic*) theories of personality development. In this chapter we will concentrate on one theory, that of Sigmund Freud (see Jarvis *et al.*, *Angles on Psychology* (2000) in this series for an account of alternative psychodynamic theories). Freud, who wrote from the 1890s to the 1930s, remains the best known and perhaps the most argued-about psychologist of all time. He developed a collection of theories, which have together formed the basis of the psychodynamic approach to psychology. Freud was a therapist and his theories are based on what his patients told him during therapy, together with reflections on his own life. Freud wrote on a wide variety of topics, but here we are concerned with his views on child development. It may make things clearer, however, if we briefly overview how Freud saw the person. According to Freudian theory we have a number of aspects to the self, including the *id* or *it*, which is present at birth and is driven by powerful *instincts*. We are born as pure *id*, but through experience develop an *I* or *ego*, which is logical and copes with the demands of the outside world, and a *superego* or *above-I*, which gives us our moral sense. We have no conscious awareness of the *id*, although we are influenced by its wishes. We are largely aware of the *ego*, and become aware of the *superego* when we make a moral decision and experience pride or guilt.

One function of the *ego* not usually available to consciousness is the use of *psychological defences*. Defences shield us from having to experience unpleasant emotions such as anguish or guilt. They include *repression*, in which memories are blocked from consciousness, *denial*, in which we refuse to admit an unpleasant truth to ourselves, *regression*, in which we revert to behaviour typical of a younger person, and *displacement*, in which we redirect an emotion such as anger on to a third party (for example coming home in a bad mood and kicking the cat). In this chapter we shall look at Freud's stage theory of development, during which the various aspects of the self are acquired. We can also look at the acquisition of psychological defences in childhood.

Stages of children's development

Freud (1905) proposed that psychological development in childhood takes place in a series of fixed stages. These are called *psychosexual stages* because each stage represents the fixation of *libido* (roughly translated as sexual drives or instincts) on a different area of the body. If this sounds slightly odd, it is important to realise that Freud's use of the word 'sexual' was quite broad in meaning, and he did not mean that the child experiences these instincts as 'sexual' in the adult sense. Libido is manifested in childhood as *organ-pleasure*, centred on a different organ in each of the first three stages of development.

The oral stage (0–1 year)

In the *oral stage* (the first year of life), while the child is breast-feeding and being weaned, the focus of organ-pleasure is the mouth. As well as taking nourishment through the mouth, children in the oral stage are taking comfort and their knowledge of the world via the mouth. Freud proposed that if the child experiences a trauma in the first year they can become fixated in the oral stage and continue to display oral characteristics into adulthood. Oral habits can include thumb-sucking, smoking, preferences such as for oral sex and attitudes such as *dependency* on others (as a baby is dependent) and *gullibility*, which represents the unquestioning taking in of information as children do in their first year. Oral personalities also tend to have difficulty in delaying gratification – like a baby that, being all *id*, wants immediate satisfaction of its needs.

The anal stage (1–3 years)

In the *anal stage* (years 1–3), the focus of organ-pleasure now shifts to the anus. The child is now fully aware that they are a person in their own right (i.e. they have an *ego*) and that their wishes can bring them into conflict with the demands of the outside world. Freud believed that this type of conflict tends to come to a head in potty-training, in which adults impose restrictions – for the first time in the child's experience – on when and where the child can defecate. The nature of this first encounter with authority can determine the child's future relationship with all forms of authority. Early or harsh potty-training can lead to the child becoming an *anal-retentive personality*, who hates mess, is obsessively tidy, organised, punctual and respectful of authority. Alternatively, the child may turn out an *anal-expulsive personality*, who is messy, disorganised and rebellious.

The phallic stage (3–6 years)

In the *phallic stage* (years 3–6), the focus of organ-pleasure has shifted to the genitals, as the child becomes fully aware of its gender. This coincides with a growing awareness of the child's exclusion from some aspects of its parents' lives, such as sleeping in the same room. The resulting three-way relationship is known as the *Oedipus complex*, named after Oedipus, who, in Greek legend, killed his father and married his mother (not realising who they were). In the Oedipus complex, a rivalry relationship develops between the child and the same-sex parent for the affection of the opposite-sex parent. Freud believed that on an *unconscious level*, the child is expressing instinctive wishes to have sex with his mother and kill his father. This is not to suggest that children possess a conscious awareness of sexual intercourse or death in the adult sense. One of Freud's case-studies, Little Hans (Freud, 1909) illustrates Freud's ideas about the Oedipus complex.

classic research

a case of the Oedipus complex?

Freud, S. (1909) Analysis of a phobia in a five-year-old boy. *Collected Papers, vol. III,* *149–295*

Aim: Little Hans, a five-year-old boy, was taken to Freud suffering from a phobia of horses. As in all clinical case-studies, Freud's most important aim was to treat the phobia. However, Freud's therapeutic input in this case was extremely minimal, and a secondary aim of the study was to explore what factors might have led to the phobia in the first place, and what factors led to its remission. By 1909 Freud's ideas about the Oedipus complex were well established and Freud interpreted this case in line with his theory.

Case history: Freud's information about the course of Hans's condition was derived partially from observation of Hans himself, but mostly from Hans's father, who was familiar with Freud's work, and who gave him weekly reports. Hans's father reported that, from the age of three, Hans had developed considerable interest in his own penis or 'widdler' and that at the age of five his mother had threatened to cut it off if he didn't stop playing with it. At about the same time Hans developed a morbid fear that a white horse would bite him. Hans's father reported that his fear seemed to be related to the horse's large penis. At the time Hans's phobia developed his father began to object to Hans's habit of getting into bed with his parents in the morning. Over a period of weeks Hans's phobia got worse and he feared going out of the house in case he encountered a horse. He also suffered attacks of more generalised anxiety.

Over the next few weeks Hans's phobia gradually began to improve. His fear became limited to horses with black harnesses over their noses. Hans's father interpreted this as related to his own black moustache. The end of Hans's phobia of horses was accompanied by two significant fantasies, which he told to his father. In the first, Hans had several imaginary children. When asked who their mother was, Hans replied 'Why, mummy, and you're their Grandaddy' (p.238). In the second fantasy, which occurred the next day, Hans imagined that a plumber had come and fitted him with a bigger widdler. These fantasies marked the end of Hans's phobia.

Interpretation: Freud saw Hans's phobia as an expression of the Oedipus complex. Horses, particularly horses with black harnesses, symbolised his father. Horses were particularly appropriate father-symbols because of their large penises. The fear began as an Oedipal conflict was developing around Hans being allowed in the parents' bed. Freud saw the Oedipus complex happily resolved as Hans fantasised himself with a big penis like his father's and married to his mother, with his father present in the role of grandfather.

Discussion: The case of Little Hans does appear to provide support for Freud's theory of the Oedipus complex. However, there are difficulties with this type of evidence. Hans's father, who provided Freud with most of his evidence, was already familiar with the Oedipus complex and interpreted the case in the light of this. It is also possible therefore that he supplied Hans with clues that led to his fantasies of marriage to his mother and his new large widdler. There are also other explanations for Hans's fear of horses. It has been reported for example that he saw a horse die in pain and was frightened by it. This might have been sufficient to trigger a fear of horses. Of course, even if Hans did have a fully-fledged Oedipus complex, this shows that the Oedipus complex *exists* but not how *common* it is. Freud believed it to be universal.

Freud believed that the phallic stage was the most important of the developmental stages. When boys realise that they have a penis and girls do not, their unconscious response is *castration anxiety*; the belief that girls have already been castrated and the fear that they might share the same fate! Their response is to repress their desire for the mother and identify with the father (in much the same way as we might identify with a bully and become like them in order to overcome our fear of them). It is this identification that gives rise to the *superego*. The *superego* is essentially the mental representation of the feared same-sex parent. Freud was somewhat perplexed by how girls dealt with the Oedipus complex on an unconscious level. He speculated (Freud, 1924) that when girls discover they lack a penis they feel that they have somehow come off worse, and are left with a sense of *penis envy*, the wish to have a penis. Penis envy is later sublimated into the wish to have a baby, and eventually relieved by actually having a baby.

Feminist writers have objected vigorously to Freud's speculation that women are motivated by feelings of inferiority because of their lack of a penis. If Freud is to be taken literally then this is quite justified. However, the later French psychoanalyst Lacan (1966) has suggested that the idea of penis envy is not intended to be taken literally, but rather to mean envy of the penis as a *symbol of male dominance* in society. From Lacan's perspective, penis envy is not envy of the penis itself, but of men's position in a male-dominated society.

A balanced appraisal of Freud's psychosexual development comes from Brown and Pedder (1991). They suggested that Freud's labels of oral, anal and phallic were too narrow to describe what occurs in these stages. They suggested that we should think of the oral stage as a stage of complete *dependency* on the caregiver(s), the anal stage as a period of *separation* from the caregiver and the phallic stage as a time of passionate emotions in which a *rivalry* may form between the child and the same-sex parent for the affection of the opposite-sex parent. The concepts of dependency, separation and rivalry are extremely useful in understanding the developing relationship between a child and its parents. Moreover, Fischer and Greenberg (1996) have reviewed studies of the oral and anal personalities, and concluded that there is moderately good evidence for their existence as distinct personality types, though not for links with early experiences.

Interactive angles

Psychologist Richard Wiseman has discovered that we can classify people into oral and anal-retentive personalities based on their use of their bank accounts. Oral personalities tend to use their cashpoint cards often, regularly withdrawing small amounts of cash (in the same way as a baby requires regular feeding). Orals also tend to impulse buy (difficulty in delaying gratification) and go overdrawn. The anal-retentive personality, on the other hand, tends to keep as much money in their account as possible (in the same way as a harshly potty-trained child retains faeces), and are thus good at saving money. They are cautious in spending money (as the harshly potty-trained child is cautious in going to the loo), and do not go overdrawn (perhaps because of the anal-retentive's fear of authority).

Questions

1 Think about how you use your bank account. Would you be classified as an oral or anal personality?

2 Even if we accept that two types of people exist, which we can call oral and anal, we are left with a problem in linking them to childhood experiences, as Freud would say should be possible. Design a study to test whether bank account use can be linked to childhood experience.

Freud suggested that of all the psychosexual stages the most critical is the phallic stage, and that Oedipal conflict is important in affecting the child's later gender and moral development, their mental health and their future relations with males and females. We shall revisit the Oedipus complex in discussions of gender development (p.104) and adolescence (p.118), but we can briefly summarise modern research findings here by saying that Freud vastly overstated its universality and importance in development. Interestingly, though, it may well be that something important in children's sexual development does take place in Freud's phallic stage. A longitudinal study by Okami *et al.* (1998) followed up 200 children who had been exposed to scenes of parental nudity and/or sexual activity prior to 6 years and assessed them at the age of 17–18 for several measures of development including self-esteem, quality of relationships and sexual relations. Few effects were found, but it is interesting to note that girls exposed to nudity/sexual activity were more likely to become pregnant or infected with a sexually transmitted disease than others. Boys, on the other hand, were significantly *less* likely than their peers to impregnate a girl or contract an STD (sexually-transmitted disease). While this study does not directly support Freud's theoretical views on the Oedipus complex, it does support his observation (controversial in itself) that parental sex is an issue for children under six.

media watch

My parents still have sex

I'm 11 and I was looking in my mum and dad's room for something and found a packet of condoms – with two missing! My mum and dad are both in their 40s. I have this horrible feeling inside. Please help me feel better.

Depressed Mizz fan

Imagining your parents having sex gives some people a funny feeling. It does come as a bit of a shock, but it's a good sign. It shows they still love each other and enjoy being together. And as they're using contraception, they're probably not going to surprise you with a new brother or sister!

You're becoming more aware of sex now – whether it's in books, films, TV or your own family. This is normal. It's only when you imagine your parents getting close that things get difficult. Relax. People have sex a lot later than their 40s! Give your parents a break – and some privacy.

Mizz Magazine, 2000

Questions

1 What explanation might Freud have given for this 11 year old's discomfort?

2 To what extent would you consider that explanation a credible one nowadays?

The development of psychological defences

Psychological defences are an important part of our personality, and affect powerfully our everyday behaviour. Psychological defences were systematically described by Sigmund's daughter Anna Freud (1936). She proposed that the tendency for defensiveness was acquired in childhood as a result of traumas, especially with regard to relationships with parents, and that different defences were associated with relationship difficulties at specific ages. Defences are also triggered, according to Anna Freud, by conflicts between instinctive impulses and societal disapproval (i.e. *id–ego/superego conflict*). Support for this idea comes from Griffith (1999), who looked at the use of *denial* in different categories of prisoner in relation to their crime. Those who were convicted for sex offences – which carry particular conflicts between individual impulses and disapproval from others – were more likely to exhibit denial than other prisoners.

While there is little evidence for associating particular defences with events occurring at particular ages in childhood, there is considerable evidence that the tendency to use psychological defences is acquired in childhood. Silver-Aylaian (1999) looked at the responses of 54 adult cancer patients to their condition. Those with a strong tendency to deny the severity of their condition (i.e. they displayed the defence of *denial*) tended to have had a number of early traumas. This suggests that they had developed their use of denial as a way of coping with trauma. Perhaps the most direct support for the development of defences in childhood comes from Myers and Brewin (1994). In a study of memory, they found that women who had had particularly poor childhood relationships with their fathers tended to have great difficulty recalling unhappy memories, although they had no difficulty in recalling happy memories (suggesting repression).

for and against

Freud's stages of child development

+ Freud was probably correct to say that our early years and our early relationships with our families are extremely important in affecting our development. He is also probably correct that the themes of dependency, separation and rivalry can be important aspects of the child's development.

– It seems very likely that Freud overestimated the importance of body parts and the 'sexual' nature of children's development.

– Freud's emphasis on the phallic stage and the Oedipus complex appears to be misplaced. Although rivalry relationships certainly do develop sometimes, they are not universal and probably rarely as significant as Freud believed.

+ There is reasonably strong support for Freud's ideas about psychological defences, including the idea that they are acquired as a consequence of childhood experience.

The psychodynamic approach in the rest of this book

Whenever we look at an area of child development with an emphasis on the impact of family relations or the emotional significance of events, we are adopting a psychodynamic approach. Although we shall be looking at Freudian theory in several chapters you should not make the mistake of confusing Freud's ideas with the psychodynamic approach as a whole. Attachment theory (Chapter 2) is a psychodynamic theory (a much more modern and popular one than that of Freud), and the effects of deprivation and privation (Chapter 3) can be seen as *psychodynamic influences* on development. The psychodynamic perspective on play (Chapter 4) emphasises its emotional significance, and it is possible (though this is a highly controversial idea) that psychoanalytic theory can help us understand gender development (see Chapter 5).

where to now?

The following are good sources of further information about psychodynamic approaches to psychology:

▶ **Bateman, A. and Holmes, J. (1995)** *Introduction to Psychoanalysis*. **London: Routledge** – a detailed but relatively clear account of a variety of psychoanalytic theories, including their links to mental health and therapy

▶ **Jacobs, M. (1992)** *Sigmund Freud*. **London: Sage** – a neat overview of Freud's major contributions, along with rebuttals of the major criticisms that are made of him

▶ **Lemma-Wright, A. (1995)** *Invitation to Psychodynamic Psychology*. **London: Whurr** – written for the layperson as well as the student, this book discusses well the issue of human relationships and in particular the importance of the first relationship.

The learning approach

The learning theory approach is based on the following ideas.

● Our environment influences behaviour. We can best understand the ways in which the environment influences behaviour by the concept of *learning*.

● Humans and animals learn behaviour in very much the same way, so we can study the acquisition of behaviours in animals and apply the results to understanding human behaviour.

- The systematic study of learning can generate general laws about learning, which can be applied to understanding, predicting and controlling behaviour.

The learning approach is concerned with the mechanisms by which we acquire behaviours. These include classical conditioning (learning by associating two events together) and operant conditioning (learning by reward and punishment). Of particular importance to child development is social learning.

Social learning theory

Social learning, by definition, depends on the presence of other individuals and the role they play must be more than merely incidental. Being surrounded by others may enhance learning by increasing competition or reducing fear, but this is not *social*. For social learning to occur, one individual must acquire a new behaviour by imitating another, the *model*. This model need not be aware of their role, although in tutoring the model alters their behaviour to maximise learning opportunities. So a hunting lioness may act as a model for cubs to imitate, whereas a mother cheetah that repeatedly catches and releases her prey for the young to observe is tutoring them.

Albert Bandura

When will observational learning occur?

According to Bandura (1977) there are four requirements for observational learning to occur.

1 **Attention:** the observer must be paying attention to the model

2 **Retention:** the observer must be capable of retaining a memory of the observed behaviour

3 **Reproduction:** the observer must be capable of performing the observed action

4 **Motivation:** the observer must be motivated to generate the learned behaviour either in return for an external reward or because of some intrinsic motivation generated by the model (hence individuals differ in their power as models).

For humans, we must be watching or listening to the model to attend. As schoolchildren we may remember the plaintive cry of 'Pay attention or you won't learn anything' and even earlier than that we may have heard 'Watch how mummy does it'. Having seen the model in action, we must then be able to remember their behaviour. This is sometimes more difficult than it sounds. I may have carefully watched the way the mechanic at the garage assembled my new windscreen wipers and be perfectly capable of repeating the actions myself, but completely unable to remember what to do.

What features might affect the modelling process? As indicated by the findings of Bandura *et al.* (1961), same-sex models are more effective than opposite-sex models for increasing aggressive behaviour in children. Other key attributes of effective models include power and likeability: hence popstars and sports personalities as well as parents are potent models. In animals, as well as in people, status affects the likelihood of being copied. Pennington (1986) identifies three types of variable that affect imitation, the characteristics of the observer and of the model, and the consequences of the behaviour for the model. These features include the age and status of the model, and the observer's level of self-esteem. Models who are of similar age and also high in status are more likely to be imitated. For example, young people who perceive drug-users as high in status may be drawn into drug taking because the sight of high-status people taking drugs is more influential than the threats their parents make.

classic research

will children copy violent behaviour?

Bandura, A., Ross, D. and Ross, S.A. (1961) Transmission of aggression through imitation of aggressive models. *Journal of Abnormal and Social Psychology, 63, 575–82*

Aim: To investigate whether aggression learned through observation of the aggressive acts of others would generalise to new settings where the model was not present and to investigate the effect of gender on such modelling.

Method: Children aged three to six years (36 boys and 36 girls) were first scored for initial level of aggressiveness, being rated by a teacher and an experimenter for physical aggression, verbal aggression and aggression towards objects. The children were divided in groups matched for initial behaviour; a control group who did not see a model and two groups that were exposed to adult models who behaved in either aggressive or non-aggressive ways. Half of each group saw a same-sex model; the others an opposite-sex model. The children were then tested in different situations to ascertain the extent to which they would imitate the aggressive acts of the model. The experimenter took each child to a playroom, meeting an adult (the model) who was invited to 'join in the game'. The child sat at a table offering potato printing and coloured stickers to play with, while the model sat at another table with Tinker toys, a mallet and a 5-foot-high inflated Bobo doll. In the non-aggressive condition, the model assembled the Tinker toys for ten minutes, while in the aggressive condition this lasted only one minute after which the model attacked the Bobo doll. The sequence of behaviour was identical each time: Bobo was lain on its side, sat upon, punched on the nose, picked up and hit on the head with the mallet. It was then thrown up in the air and kicked about the room. This sequence was performed three times over nine minutes accompanied by aggressive comments such as 'Kick him' and 'Pow'.

After exposure to the model, all participants were put in a situation designed to frustrate them, to increase the likelihood of aggression being displayed. They were taken to a room containing attractive toys such as a fire engine and a doll with a wardrobe (remember, this is the 1960s). After a short opportunity to play the children were told that these toys were for other children and were moved to another room. This final stage offered non-aggressive toys such as crayons, dolls, a ball, cars, a tea set and plastic farm animals, and aggressive toys including a Bobo doll, a mallet and dart guns. The children were allowed to play here for 20 minutes and were observed by the experimenters using a one-way mirror. Records were made of aggressive acts that replicated the model's behaviour (both physical and verbal), other aggression with the mallet and non-aggressive behaviour. These were then compared.

Results: Children exposed to violent models imitated their exact behaviours and were significantly more aggressive than those children who did not receive aggressive modelling. This effect applied to both physical and verbal aggression. The increase in aggression for boys was greater than for girls, although girls were more likely to imitate verbal aggression and boys physical acts. Boys were also more likely to imitate a same-sex model as, to a lesser extent, were girls. The effects of non-aggressive modelling, however, were inconsistent, with some behaviours being reduced compared to the control group but others not.

Conclusion: The findings demonstrated that observation and imitation can account for the learning of specific acts without reinforcement of either the models or observers. In this case it is possible that seeing an adult's aggression suggests to the child that such behaviour is permissible, reducing their inhibitions against it and increasing the probability that they will perform aggressive acts in the future. Same-sex modelling may have been more effective for boys than for girls because male aggression is more culturally typical, so carries the weight of social acceptability.

for and against

For and against social learning theory (SLT) as an explanation of human behaviour

+ SLT can explain the acquisition of behaviours, such as aggression, through observation.

+ SLT can explain why children follow role models and are influenced by the media.

– SLT cannot account for the acquisition of new behaviours that have not been observed in a model.

– SLT emphasises the importance of learnt behaviour at the expense of thinking and feeling. It is thus more useful in explaining some aspects of child development than others.

The social learning approach in the rest of this book

Social learning becomes important when we are interested in how a child behaves as opposed to how they think or feel. It thus features in Chapter 5 when we come to look at how children learn gender-specific behaviour.

where to now?

The following are good sources of information on social learning in children:

▷ **Leslie, J.C. and O'Reilly, M.F. (1999)** *Behaviour Analysis*. **Amsterdam Harwood Academic Publishers** – an advanced text on learning theory in general. Chapter 6 has a good account of social learning

▷ **Durkin, K. (1995)** *Social Developmental Psychology*. **Oxford: Blackwell** – Chapter 1 has a great section on social learning theory and the ways in which this can be applied to understanding child development.

The behavioural genetics approach

The behavioural genetics approach is based on the following ideas.

- Genetics is a pure science, and psychologists taking a genetic perspective tend to see psychology as a science and to be highly scientific in their approach.

- Our genetic make-up, i.e. our individual collection of genes, is of considerable importance in determining our individual characteristics, abilities and behaviour. This is not to say that the environment is not also important, but the environment acts on us all in slightly different ways according to our genetic make-up.

- Our thinking, behaviour and feelings (both normal and abnormal) are strongly affected by biological factors such as brain structures and neurochemical levels, which are influenced by genes.

Genetic influences on personality

One of the most important developments in psychology in the last 20 years has been the recognition of the importance of genetic influences on individual differences between people (Plomin *et al.*, 1997). You may have noticed that, just as some families have a number of very tall or redheaded members, some psychological characteristics also appear to run in families. There are thus families in which there are an unusually large number of

Robert Plomin

highly intelligent or particularly bad-tempered individuals. One way in which characteristics can pass from one generation to the next is through genes. *Genes* are units of DNA, which contain the information required to build biological structures. The reason that as humans we share so many characteristics is that we share 99.9 per cent of our genes with one another. It is relatively simple to understand how a characteristic like eye-colour can be under the control of genes because eye-colour is obviously physical in nature. The question of how genes might affect psychological characteristics is a more complex one. It appears that genetic differences between individuals produce biological differences between people (sometimes very subtle) that, in combination with their environment, lead them to develop into unique individuals.

Behavioural geneticists are interested in genetic and environmental influences on individual differences in people. However, in real life it can be quite difficult to study genes and environment separately because people in the same family tend to share a similar set of genes and a similar environment. There are, however, various circumstances under which we can investigate the relative importance of genes and environment, including cases of twins and adoption.

Twin studies of personality

We know that identical twins (properly called monozygotic twins or MZs) share 100 per cent of their genes. We also know that fraternal twins (properly called dizygotic twins or DZs) only share 50 per cent of their genetic material. These facts give us the basis for twin studies.

In one type of twin study, we can compare the similarity of identical twins who have grown up in the same family or in different environments and see whether those who have grown up together are more alike than those who grew up apart. The fact that MZs reared apart show more differences than those reared together demonstrates the role of the environment, but the fact that even separated identical twins tend to be much more alike than two unrelated people demonstrates the importance of genes. Table 1.1 shows the similarity in personality of identical twins who have been reared together and apart. The correlations in the table represent how similar the twins were, with 0 meaning no relationship between the scores of the two twins and 1 being a perfect correlation between them.

Twin type	Correlation	
	Extraversion	**Neuroticism**
MZs reared together	0.51	0.46
MZs reared apart	0.38	0.38

Table 1.1 Similarity in personality between identical twins reared together and apart. From Loehlin (1992)

The term *extraversion* refers to how impulsive and sociable the twins were. *Neuroticism* refers to how anxious and moody they were. Looking at Table 1.1, you can see that, although the twins reared apart are distinctly less similar than those reared together, they are still much more similar than we would expect if their genetic similarity were not a factor. Of course, this assumes that personality can be measured with sufficient accuracy to show up differences between different pairs of twins. Not all psychologists would accept this.

Twins studies provide a powerful argument for the role of genes in affecting individual differences among us with respect to personality. However, there are problems with twin studies. In the case of separated identical twins, researchers must rely on data from a small group of people who have been separated at various ages and in a variety of circumstances. Some 'separated' identical twins may have spent considerable time in a similar environment *before* separation or they were 'separated' but actually lived in very similar environments. They may also have been reunited for a considerable time before their personality and intelligence were assessed, so that they had a chance to share their later environment and hence to become more alike. When researchers compare the environments of MZs and DZs reared together, they make the assumption that MZs and DZs grow up in equally similar environments. In fact, because MZs look more alike than DZs, people may treat them in a much more similar manner and hence give them a more similar environment as well as the same genes. This means that when we compare the similarity of MZs and DZs we cannot know to what extent we are seeing the influence of genes and to what extent the effect of environment.

Temperament

For many years psychologists thought of babies as 'blank slates' on which experiences would act to produce the individual personality. However, most parents with more than one child will tell you that each child has a distinct personality, apparently from birth. It is these aspects of the personality that appear to be present from birth that are collectively called the *temperament* of the child. Because temperament is present at birth, it is generally assumed to be under the control of our genes. In a classic piece of research, Thomas and Chess (1977) sought to develop a way of classifying children by their temperament. They questioned parents about several aspects of their babies' behaviour, including their level of activity, their regularity of eating and sleeping, their curiosity towards new situations, their emotional reactivity and their tendency towards good and bad moods. Using this information, they classified children into three temperament types.

- **Easy babies:** comprising 40 per cent of the sample, these children were characterised by good mood, regular eating and sleeping, and the ability to adapt well to new situations.

- **Difficult babies:** comprising 10 per cent of the sample, these children displayed bad moods, irregular eating and sleeping, and they became very stressed in unfamiliar situations.

- **Slow-to-warm-up babies:** making up 15 per cent of the sample, these children were rather moody and slow to adapt to new situations, but did not display the same extreme distress as the difficult babies.

Out of the babies in the Thomas and Chess sample 35 per cent did not neatly fall into a temperament type because their behaviour was not sufficiently consistent. The relevance of temperament type to social development is clear. Easy babies are, as the name suggests, easy to get on with and relatively easy to parent. They will find it easy to have successful interactions with carers, and they may not require particularly sensitive parenting to thrive. Difficult babies are by no means *doomed* to a less successful social development than easy babies, but they might need more sensitive parenting in order to get on as well.

The idea of temperament is important in understanding the individual development of young children. However, although temperament is present at birth and is presumably influenced by our genes, it is not set in stone and can be modified by the environment. In one study, Belsky *et al.* (1991) followed the progress of difficult babies from three to nine months, in order to see whether the temperament remained constant and whether any changes in temperament were associated with particular environments. They took measurements throughout the six-month period of the quality of mothers' interactions with the baby, and of the quality of the parents' relationship with each other. It was found that where the parents had a good relationship and the mother was highly skilled at interacting with the baby, there was a good chance of increasing the 'easiness' of the baby.

Because temperament can be modified by experience, we cannot use temperament alone to predict later social development. However, the idea of temperament is extremely useful in reminding us that not all children are equally easy to parent, and that we should not jump to the conclusion that a bad-tempered and unsociable child is the result of a failure on the part of the parents.

for and against

the importance of genes

+ It seems certain that babies do display individual differences in personality from birth. It seems likely that these differences are at least partly due to genes.

+ There is a large body of evidence, for example from twin studies, to show that differences in genes do influence individual differences in characteristics such as personality.

+ An understanding of temperament has freed parents of difficult babies from the assumption that they are necessarily to blame for the child's behaviour.

– It seems likely that for many children, temperament is less important than their early experiences. You should bear in mind that genes provide a starting point for an individual's development. They are then influenced by their environment.

Genetic influences in the rest of this book

Behavioural genetics becomes important whenever we consider the extent to which an aspect of human development is influenced by environment or when we consider individual differences in children's responses to their environment. Temperament is an influence on the formation of attachment (Chapter 2) and on children's differing responses to deprivation (Chapter 3). In Chapter 5 we consider the extent to which psychological differences between boys and girls are under genetic control, and in Chapter 9 we look in detail at the evidence for a genetic component to intelligence. In Chapter 11 we consider whether autism has a genetic component.

where to now?

The following are good sources of further information regarding behavioural genetics and temperament:

▷ **Plomin, R., DeFries, J.C., McClearn, G.E. and Rutter, M. (1997)** *Behavioural Genetics*. **New York: Freeman** – a state-of-the-art account of the field of behavioural genetics, including chapters on molecular genetics and genetic influences on intelligence and mental disorder.

▷ **Rose, S., Kamin, L.J. and Lewontin, R.C. (1984)** *Not in our Genes*. **Harmondsworth: Penguin** – puts well the case against the overriding importance of genes in behaviour. This is well worth reading as counterpoint to the positive attitude expressed here towards behavioural genetics.

Cultural and cross-cultural perspectives

'Culture' is a word we often hear, but it is widely misunderstood and therefore worth exploring a little here. *Culture* is a set of beliefs, values and practices that characterises a group of people. Culture varies between people from different parts of the world, between different ethnic and religious groups living in the same region, between socio-economic groups, between men and women, and even between families. There are traditionally two major ways in which culture is studied in psychology. The *cross-cultural* research tradition compares beliefs, values and practices in different human societies. In this context, a *society* means a group of people living together. When you read of cultural variations and cross-cultural comparisons, it is important to remember that this is not simply comparing two groups of people, but the culture of those societies. We can study cultural variation equally well by comparing the beliefs, values and practices of people in different historical periods of a society, males and females, etc.

The *cultural psychology* tradition has rejected the idea that we can understand the importance of culture by simply comparing different societies. Instead the emphasis is on how different cultures allow for the same human needs – what Super and Harkness (1986) have called the developmental niche – and how the beliefs, values and practices of a society are transmitted from one generation to the next (this is called *cultural transmission*). A good example of cultural psychology is in Vygotsky's theory of cognitive development, examined in detail in Chapter 8.

Cultural and cross-cultural traditions of psychology are closely linked to the growing social constructionist perspective (see p.19). One way of examining whether a concept like adolescence or intelligence is 'real' or whether it is just a social construct is to look at how it varies between different cultures.

Culture in the rest of this book

The importance of culture is highlighted in several of the topics examined in this book. In Chapter 2 we look at cultural variations in the formation of attachment with infants and in Chapter 3 we consider the different meanings accorded to friendship in different cultures. In Chapter 6 we consider cultural variations in adolescence. Culture is also important in cognitive development, and in Chapter 8 we consider a cultural theory of cognitive development. In Chapter 9 we look at cultural variations in what is meant by intelligence, and variations between different societies in performance in different mental abilities.

where to now?

The following are good sources of further information about culture and child development.

▶ **Valsiner, J. (2000)** *Culture and Human Development*. **London: Sage** – very advanced stuff, but gives very detailed accounts of the role of culture in a number of areas of child development

▶ **Woodhead, M., Faulkner, D. and Littleton, K. (1998)** *Cultural Worlds of Early Childhood*. **London, Routledge** – again, quite advanced material, but useful in appreciating both the importance of cultural variation and the ways in which culture is transmitted.

what's new?

the social constructionist perspective on child development

This is a new and radical perspective on child development, growing rapidly in influence in the 21st century. Social constructionists look at what social, cultural and historical factors might have led us to look at issues and construct theories of child development as we have done. For example, in Chapter 2 we will look at theories of attachment that have emphasised the importance of attentive mothering. From a social constructionist viewpoint it is no coincidence that this approach first became popular in the 1950s, following the Second World War when the British government was facing mass unemployment of demobilised military personnel, many of whose traditional jobs had been taken over by women (Burman, 1994). Attachment theory was used to return women to their pre-war status as housewives by presenting working mothers as harming their children.

Social constructionism differs from other psychological approaches in questioning the scientific and non-political nature of psychology, traditional research methods and the very nature of reality itself. A good starting point to understanding the social constructionist position is the term 'childhood'. Before studying psychology we probably all have no doubt that there is such a thing as childhood, and we are all capable of identifying a child when we encounter one. However, social constructionists remind us that childhood is regarded quite differently in different cultures, and that the modern Anglo-American view of the child is historically relatively recent. Only 150 years ago, British children worked extremely long hours under brutal conditions in factories and mines. This is entirely incompatible with the dominant view of childhood in contemporary Britain, where it is regarded as essential that children are nurtured and educated.

Social constructionists disagree with the traditional view of psychologists that our job is to make objective and unbiased observations about people. In fact social constructionists do not believe that it is possible to be objective or make unbiased observations because we can only see the world as it is represented in our culture. Thus, many of our ideas about child development that we often take as 'fact' are, rather, products of culture. Thus, in Victorian Britain when industry required child labour there was no real concept of the child as essentially different from a small adult.

Social constructionism is often intentionally political. Whereas most psychologists would see their work as uncovering scientific knowledge, social constructionists instead see their role as more to uncover and challenge social inequality and injustice. Social constructionist explanations of psychological phenomena look at social and historical reasons why ideas might have emerged, with particular regard to power-relationships between groups. For example, traditional assumptions about gender include the idea of women as submissive, gentle and caring. A social constructionist would probably say that femininity has been constructed in this way, so that women will serve the needs of men without challenging the male-dominated society. Similarly, by defining a group such as the middle classes or white Americans as 'more intelligent' than other groups, by virtue of the fact that they tend to score more highly on IQ tests (which are of course biased towards the knowledge and skills of white middle-class people), white middle-class Americans strengthen their own power relative to other groups in society.

where to now?

The following is a good source of further information on the social constructionist perspective on child development:

▶ **Burman, E. (1994)** *Deconstructing Developmental Psychology.* **London: Routledge.**

Conclusions

We have examined three major psychological perspectives on the development of individual differences in personality. The psychodynamic perspective emphasises the role of parenting and family dynamics in affecting the developing personality. The best-known psychodynamic theory of child development, that of Sigmund Freud, sees development as occurring in a series of psychosexual stages. This notion of infant sexuality remains highly controversial, although Freud used the word 'sexual' in a much broader sense than we do today. Most contemporary psychologists would challenge Freud's developmental stages, but not the general psychodynamic principle that parenting and family dynamics are important in children's development. The social learning approach of Albert Bandura also sees parenting as very important, but Bandura has explained this in terms of how children learn behaviour by modelling and the effects of reinforcement.

There is a growing awareness in psychology of the likely influence of genes on our personality. This is not to say that learning and family dynamics are not important, and behavioural genetics research has indeed supported the importance of these environmental variables. None the less, most psychologists now believe that our genes are one of the major influences on individual differences. As well as considering three important perspectives on individual personality, we have looked at the social constructionist perspective on child psychology. Like psychodynamic, social learning and behavioural genetic approaches, this is a general approach to psychology that can be applied to numerous topics in child development. It differs, however, in that it seeks to explain not so much child development itself as what psychologists have said about child development.

what do you know?

---

1 Outline Freud's anal stage of development.

2 Suggest one piece of evidence for and one against Freud's Oedipus complex.

3 Describe in detail one study showing that children acquire behaviours by social learning.

4 What is temperament? How might it affect our development?

5 What is culture?

6 What is social constructionism? Give an example of how the view has challenged traditional child psychology.

2

Attachment

In this chapter we will be looking at the importance of our earliest relationships; how they come about and how they can affect us in later life. Having briefly examined the process of attachment formation, we can go on to look at the work of John Bowlby, from whom many of our current ideas about attachment come. We shall also look in depth at the work of Mary Ainsworth, who extended Bowlby's theory with the idea that children can be classified as having different attachment types according to their behaviour towards their primary carer. We examine research, looking at the later consequences of attachment type, both with regard to intellectual and social development, and consider what factors influence attachment type. We then look at attachments across the world and consider the different meanings attachment might have in different cultures. In *What's new?* we will look at a recent development – the discovery of atypical or *disorganised* attachments associated with neglect and abuse. Finally, we shall look at the social constructionist view of attachment and the social implications of emphasising the mother as the major influence on children's development.

What is attachment?

An attachment is a two-way emotional bond in which people depend on each other for their sense of security. Attachment is characterised by proximity seeking (wanting to remain close to each other), distress at being separated and pleasure at being reunited. Although we form attachments throughout our lives, psychologists are particularly interested in the attachment that forms between babies and their primary carers. Note the term *primary carer*. Psychologists normally only use the word 'mother' if they are referring to the biological mother, and 'mother' is generally used in this book when we are looking at studies that have looked in particular at biological mothers.

It is generally accepted that the infant-primary carer attachment develops over time. In a large-scale study, Schaffer and Emerson (1964) followed up 60 Scottish infants from birth to 18 months, regularly interviewing their mothers about infants' attachment behaviour, particularly their protests at being separated from the primary carer. Schaffer and Emerson observed four distinct stages in attachment formation:

1   **The asocial stage** (0–2 months); from birth, infants respond to human faces and voices, but initially they do not form attachments. They may recognise their primary carer or carers but they readily accept comfort from strangers.

2   **The indiscriminate attachment stage** (2–7 months); at this point infants are highly sociable and can distinguish between familiar and unfamiliar adults. However, they are not anxious around strangers and will accept comfort from them.

3   **The specific attachment stage** (around 7 months); for a time infants tend to show one strong attachment. They show joy at reunion with the primary carer and are wary of strangers.

4   **The multiple attachment stage**; very soon after the formation of the first attachment, others follow.

Psychologists now tend to be quite wary of stage theories, because the idea of fixed stages implies that all children will go through precisely the same sequence of events at the same ages. However, although there is some individual variation in the development of attachments, Schaffer and Emerson's stages have stood the test of time. Until the 1950s, most psychologists believed that babies become attached to their primary carer because they associate them in some way with being fed. However, the work of John Bowlby changed that view.

Bowlby's attachment theory

John Bowlby's (1951, 1958, 1969) theory of attachment remains the dominant explanation in psychology today. There are several strands to the theory, and we shall restrict ourselves here to looking at four areas in particular:

● maternal deprivation hypothesis

● the evolutionary basis of attachment

● social releasers and instinctive parenting responses

● internal working models.

John Bowlby

Maternal deprivation hypothesis

The most fundamental of Bowlby's ideas was that the development of an attachment in early life is an essential aspect of a child's development. Before going on to develop attachment theory-proper, Bowlby (1951) proposed the *maternal deprivation hypothesis*. This stated that a child requires the continuous presence of a primary carer throughout a sensitive period lasting at least the first 18 months to 2 years. Bowlby (1951) identified two particularly serious consequences of the failure to form an attachment or serious disruption to the attachment during this sensitive period (for example prolonged separation from the primary carer).

- **Affectionless psychopathy:** This is the inability to experience guilt or deep feelings for others. Naturally this interferes enormously with one's relationships in later life. It is also associated with criminality, as affectionless psychopaths find it difficult to appreciate the feelings of their victims and so lack remorse.

- **Developmental retardation:** Bowlby proposed that there is a critical period for intellectual development and that if children are deprived of a maternal relationship for too long they would suffer retardation, i.e. very low intelligence.

Bowlby provided evidence for the link between affectionless and psychopathic behaviour and early experience in a classic study conducted at the child guidance clinic where he worked.

classic
research

can disruption to attachment cause affectionless psychopathy?

Bowlby, J. (1946) *Forty four juvenile thieves.* London: Balliere, Tindall & Cox.

Aim: Bowlby believed that prolonged separation from the primary carer during the first two or three years of life could cause permanent emotional damage. One way in which this damage manifests itself is affectionless psychopathy. Bowlby aimed in this study to see whether teenage criminals who displayed affectionless psychopathy were more likely to have had an early separation than those who had not.

Method: Forty-four of the teenagers referred to the Child Guidance Clinic where Bowlby worked were selected on the basis that they were involved in criminal activity, and that they were living with their biological parents. Bowlby interviewed them in order to assess whether they exhibited signs of affectionless psychopathy. This was identified by lack of affection to others, lack of guilt or shame at their actions and lack of empathy for their victims. Bowlby also interviewed the families of the adolescents in order to establish whether the children had had prolonged early separations from their primary carers in their first two years. Bowlby then matched up those young people who had been classified as affectionless psychopaths with those who had had prolonged maternal deprivation in the first two years. A control group of non-delinquent young people was established in order to see how commonly maternal deprivation occurred in the non-delinquent population.

Results: The results were striking. Of the 14 children identified as affectionless psychopaths, 12 had experienced prolonged separation from their mothers in the first 2 years. By contrast, only 5 of the 30 delinquent children not classified as affectionless psychopaths had experienced similar separations. Of the 44 people in the non-delinquent control group, only 2 had experienced prolonged separations.

Conclusions: The young criminals who had a prolonged separation in their first 2 years were several times more likely to exhibit affectionless psychopathy than those who had no such separation. This provides strong support for Bowlby's maternal deprivation hypothesis.

Taken at face value, the *Forty four thieves* study provides powerful evidence for a link between early disruption to attachments and later emotional impairment. However, when we look more closely at the study we can see some important design flaws, which detract somewhat from its credibility (Flanagan, 1999). Firstly, information about the early separation was collected *retrospectively* during interviews. This relies on the participants' accuracy of recall, not to mention their honesty, hence it does not carry the same weight as information obtained from an objective source such as medical records. Secondly, Bowlby himself carried out both the interviews and the psychiatric assessments. As he knew what he was expecting to find, he may have been biased in his assessments. It is now standard procedure in this type of study for researchers to assess participants without knowing any details that might predispose them towards bias. This is called a *double blind* procedure.

media
watch

Spain in shock as girls admit murder 'to become famous'

Two teenage girls hacked to death a schoolfriend because they wanted to become famous and enjoy extreme experiences, they confessed to a judge near the southern port of Cadiz. The case has stunned Spain and prompted psychologists to warn that lack of family affection is producing a generation of young psychopaths.

Clara Garcia Casado, 16, was found dead early on Saturday on scrubland in the town of San Fernando, bearing more than 18 knife wounds and with her head almost severed.

Psychologists warned that cold-blooded violence by alienated youngsters was increasingly common. One said abusive family relationships could produce personality defects in adolescents. Such character flaws flourished in a climate that was seen to encourage violence and risk-taking.

Source: The Independent, 31st May 2000

Questions

1 The psychologists quoted in the article appear to have been influenced by Bowlby's ideas. How might have Bowlby explained this case?

2 Reading ahead, how have ideas changed since Bowlby's maternal deprivation hypothesis, and what factors might we now implicate in the behaviour of these two murderers?

Contemporary psychologists generally believe that, while early relations with the primary carer are very important, Bowlby overstated his case in his early work. They believe that children are more resilient to early experiences – for example temporary separation from their primary carer – than he gave them credit for. In fairness to him, Bowlby did later acknowledge this (Bowlby, 1957). Maternal deprivation hypothesis opened up a debate about the possible effects of day care on children that continues today. We shall look at this in detail in Chapter 3.

One way in which our ideas have changed since Bowlby's time is that most psychologists would make a distinction between deprivation and privation. *Privation* occurs when no attachment is formed, whereas *deprivation* takes place when a child is separated from an attachment figure after an attachment has been formed (Rutter, 1981). Bowlby did not distinguish between deprivation and privation, and nowadays psychologists tend to associate the very serious effects of affectionless psychopathy and retardation with *privation* rather than deprivation.

However, a new line of research into overnight visits to absent parents following parental separation has recently revived interest in maternal deprivation. Solomon and George (1999) assessed the security of attachment in 44 infants aged between 12–20 months whose parents were separated and who had overnight visits with the absent father. These infants were significantly less likely to have a secure attachment with the mother than those in a control group whose parents were separated but who did not have overnight visits. You can thus see that although Bowlby's ideas about the effects of maternal deprivation were limited, they remain very important in thinking about attachment. We return to the issue of maternal deprivation in Chapter 3 when we look at research into the effects of short and long-term separation of children from their primary carer.

Bowlby's ideas developed considerably following research in the 1950s and 1960s. What follows is sometimes called *attachment theory-proper* and is considered as a separate theory from maternal deprivation hypothesis.

The evolutionary basis of attachment

Bowlby had an interest in *ethology*, the study of animal behaviour, as well as in child development. He noted that other species apart from humans formed attachments, and suggested (Bowlby, 1957) that there may be evolutionary advantages to the formation of secure attachments. Think back a million or so years ago to more dangerous times. Wolves and other predators posed a serious threat to humans and for obvious reasons children were among the most vulnerable individuals. Children who maintained close proximity to their carers and who returned often to them for comfort were less vulnerable to predation. Attachment, which led to children maintaining proximity, was thus *adaptive*, i.e. it increased the chances of survival.

All evolutionary explanations in psychology present us with something of a problem, and Bowlby's idea of an evolved tendency to form attachments is no exception. While we can make logical links between attachment in different species and speculate about what might have been adaptive for humans a million years ago, there is no *direct* evidence for the evolution of any human behaviour. That said, evolution is generally accepted as an influence on infant behaviour and this aspect of Bowlby's theory is not generally considered controversial.

Social releasers and parenting responses

Bowlby noted that infants are born with a set of instinctive behaviours, including smiling, sucking, gesturing and crying. He proposed that these have evolved in order to maximise the chances of being well looked after and hence surviving. He famously said:

> 'Babies' smiles are powerful things, leaving mothers spellbound and enslaved. Who can doubt that the baby who most readily rewards his mother with a smile is the one who is best loved and best cared for?'
> Bowlby (1957, p.237)

27

Bowlby called these behaviours *social releasers*. Their function is to elicit instinctive parenting responses from adults. The interplay between social releasers and parenting responses is the process that builds the attachment between infant and carer. Failure on the part of the carer to provide the appropriate parenting response to the child's social releasers leads to psychological damage. This is a crucial aspect of Bowlby's theory as it means that the most important factor in a child's development is the effort and skill of their primary carer. We shall revisit this idea (p.40) when we examine the social constructionist critique of attachment theory – that it allows mothers to be blamed for anything that goes wrong in a child's development.

Subsequent researchers have observed the interplay between social releasers and parenting responses proposed by Bowlby. Brazleton *et al.* (1979) systematically observed mothers and babies during their interactions, and noted that both mothers and babies imitated each others' movements and took turns to initiate a new movement. They called this *interactional synchrony*. The researchers also tried asking the mothers to ignore the babies' signals. It was found that the babies quickly became concerned and some curled up and became motionless. Brazleton's findings support Bowlby's ideas about social releasers and the importance of responding to them.

It is important to emphasise that when Bowlby talked of 'parenting' or 'mothering' he did not mean that the carers need to be the biological parents or that the primary carer need be the biological mother. He did, however, believe that it was necessary for there to be a primary carer or carers who would spend a considerable amount of time with the infant during their first two to three years. Bowlby believed that the first two to three years of a child's life are crucial to its social development. These years are thus a *sensitive period*, and if a successful attachment is not formed during this time it will be more difficult to form one later on.

Internal working models

One of the most important aspects of Bowlby's theory was his idea of internal working models (Bowlby, 1969). Bowlby proposed that the developing child formed a mental representation of their first attachment relationship and that this would have profound effects on their later relationships and on their own success as a parent. He called this mental representation an internal working model. If the child internalises a working model of attachment as kind and reliable, they will tend to bring these qualities to their future relationships. If, however, they are neglected or abused, there is a chance that they will reproduce these patterns. Bowlby believed that patterns of behaviour were transmitted down through families through the formation of internal working models.

It is something of a myth that only those who have had model upbringings can be successful parents themselves, and that those who have been

This baby and adult are clearly interacting successfully

abused as children will necessarily go on to become abusers themselves. However, it does seem to be true that, as Bowlby suggested, people's mental representations of their early experiences of being parented affect their own formation of attachments with their children. This was demonstrated in a study by Fonagy *et al.* (1993). They assessed pregnant women's internal working models using a standard interview called the adult attachment interview (AAI). They then measured how securely attached their babies were at 12 and 18 months. It emerged that those mothers who reported insecure attachments with their own parents tended to be those whose babies displayed insecure attachment towards them. This strong association between mothers' reports of their own maternal attachment and their attachment with their own babies is powerful evidence for the importance of internal working models.

for and against

Bowlby's ideas

+ Bowlby appears to be correct in stating that the formation of the child's first attachment(s) is important to its future development.

– It does seem, however, that Bowlby underestimated children's ability to survive delayed attachment and periods of separation from the primary carer (see Chapter 3).

+ There is strong evidence for Bowlby's idea of social releasers, for example from the Brazleton study.

+ There is also strong evidence for the importance of internal working models in affecting people's attachment with their own children.

– Although Bowlby's view of attachment as having evolved because it is adaptive is highly credible, it is very difficult to test, so we have to take it 'on faith'.

where to now?

▶ **The following are good sources of further information about the work of John Bowlby:**

Bowlby, J. (1988) *A Secure Base*. **London: Routledge** – based on a series of introductory lectures by Bowlby on the field of attachment. Less technical than most of Bowlby's writing, so a good starting point for people wishing to read some Bowlby.

▶ **Holmes, J. (1993)** *John Bowlby and Attachment Theory*. **London: Routledge** – a detailed account of the life and works of Bowlby.

Mary Ainsworth's theory: classifying and explaining attachment types

A number of researchers, sometimes called the *NeoBowlbyites* because of their emphasis on the importance of attachment, have researched extensively the factors associated with the development of attachments and the long-term effects of the first attachment. In a naturalistic observation study, based in family homes, Ainsworth (1967) observed children's behaviour with caregivers and strangers, and proposed that different attachment types could be seen, based on the independence shown by playing infants, the anxiety they displayed when left alone or with a stranger and their response to being reunited with the primary carer. Based closely on this observational study, Ainsworth and Wittig (1969) developed a laboratory procedure to classify attachment types. This is called the *Strange Situation*, and it is still the most popular procedure for classifying attachments.

Classifying attachment types – the Strange Situation

This is a laboratory procedure designed to determine how securely attached a child is to the primary carer. The rationale is that infants display different behaviour towards the primary caregiver and towards strangers according to the security of attachment. The *Strange Situation* has eight episodes, lasting three minutes each. These are shown in Table 2.1 and the diagram on p. 32.

1. The caregiver and the child are placed in an observation room.
2. The child is left free to explore.
3. A stranger enters and speaks to mother, then attempts to play with child.
4. The carer leaves the child and stranger alone.
5. The carer re-enters and the stranger leaves.
6. The carer leaves the child alone.
7. The stranger re-enters and tries to play with the child.
8. The stranger leaves and the carer re-enters.

Table 2.1 The Strange Situation

Based on the Strange Situation, Ainsworth *et al.* (1978) proposed three types of attachment:

- *Type A* – **avoidant**; these children play independently and do not show distress when the mother leaves nor make contact when she returns. Between 20 and 25 per cent of British children aged 12 to 18 months are classified as type A (van Ijzendoorn and Kroonenberg, 1988).

- *Type B* – **securely attached**; these children play independently and do not show much distress in episodes 3 and 4. They greet the carer positively when she returns. They are likely to be distressed in episode 6 when left alone. They require and accept comfort from the carer in episode 8. Between 60 and 75 per cent British children aged 12 to 18 months are classified as type B.

- *Type C – resistant (or ambivalent)*; these children explore less in episode 2 than others. They are very distressed on being left with a stranger but, although they rush to the carer on her return, they do not readily accept comforting. Around 3 per cent of British and 15 per cent of American infants are classified as type C.

So how useful is the Strange Situation as a test of attachment? A large number of studies have confirmed that children classified as type B according to the Strange Situation go on to do better in tests of both intellectual and social development than those classified as types A or C (see p.34). The Strange Situation thus has good *predictive validity*, i.e. it can predict how a child will turn out. On the other hand, there is some question as to precisely what the Strange Situation actually measures. How distressed a child becomes in the anxiety-provoking stages 4, 6 and 7 could depend as much on their temperament as their attachment (see p.15 for a discussion of temperament). Temperament does not, however, predict the child's responses to the primary carer's return in stages 5 and 8 (Sroufe, 1985), so it does appear that the test measures something more than temperament.

The origins of attachment type – sensitive responsiveness

Like Bowlby, Ainsworth believed that the major determinant of the quality of a child–parent attachment was the quality of care provided by the primary carer. She saw the crucial ingredient of successful parenting as *sensitive responsiveness*, i.e. how successfully the parent picks up and responds to the child's signals. Tracy and Ainsworth (1981) tested whether there was an association between which mothers displayed low levels of sensitive responsiveness and which babies developed insecure attachments. They observed mothers interacting with their babies in their own homes and rated them on a scale of sensitivity. The babies were meanwhile given an attachment classification based on the Strange Situation. It was found that the mothers of insecurely attached children (types A and C) tended to be less responsive to the child and to cuddle them less than did mothers of the type B children, supporting the idea that responsiveness is important in the development of secure attachments.

Interestingly, it seems that a primary carer's sensitivity is related to her own attachment to her primary carer. In a recent study Levaenan and Silven (2000) assessed the attachment of 49 Finnish mothers to their own mothers by interview and then recorded them interacting with their infants. A strong relationship emerged between the sensitivity of the mothers and their own

1. The caregiver and the child are placed in an observation room.

2. The child is left free to explore.

3. A stranger enters and speaks to mother, then attempts to play with child.

4. The carer leaves the child and stranger alone.

5. The carer re-enters and the stranger leaves.

6. The carer leaves the child alone.

7. The stranger re-enters and tries to play with the child.

8. The stranger leaves and the carer re-enters.

The eight stages of the Strange Situation

reported attachment to their mothers, suggesting that quality of maternal attachment is a major factor in determining mothers' sensitivity. This is not to suggest that a mother's sensitivity is fixed or that a mother with a poor relationship with her own parents cannot be an effective primary carer. Recent studies have tested the idea that primary carers can be trained to be more sensitive. We can look at one such study in detail.

research now

can we improve sensitive responsiveness?

Juffer, F., Hoksbergen, R.A.C., Rene, A.C., Riksen-Walraven, J.M. and Kohnstamm, G.A. (1997) Early intervention in adoptive families: supporting maternal sensitive responsiveness, infant–mother attachment and infant competence. *Journal of Child Psychology & Psychiatry and Allied Disciplines, 38, 1039–50*

Aim: Past research has suggested that adoptive parents sometimes report having a harder time forming an attachment with infants than is typical for biological parents. The aim of this study was to see whether training adoptive parents in sensitive responsiveness improved the quality of attachment in their adoptive children. If there were an improvement in attachment associated with better sensitive responsiveness, this would be further evidence for Ainsworth's view that sensitive responsiveness is the major factor in the development of attachments. This study can therefore be seen as a test of the sensitive responsiveness hypothesis.

Method: Ninety families took part in the study. The adoptive families were from The Netherlands, and the adopted infants were from Sri Lanka (71 participants) and Korea (19 participants). The sample was divided into three groups that underwent different conditions. Thirty families formed a control group who had no intervention. The second group of 30 received training in sensitive responsiveness. This involved being filmed interacting with infants and going through the film being advised on appropriate responses to make in a range of situations. The third group received a self-help manual giving advice on sensitive parenting. Following the three conditions, sensitive responsiveness in the carers and the infants' attachment type were assessed.

Results: The control group who had had no intervention did not differ in either levels of sensitive responsiveness or quality of attachment from the population norms. Neither was there any difference between the responsiveness of the parents in the control group and those who received the self-help book (nor any difference in the attachment type of their infants). However, the adoptive parents who had had three sessions of training in sensitive responsiveness showed significantly higher levels of sensitive responsiveness and their infants were rated as more securely attached.

Conclusion: This study has important practical and theoretical implications. On a practical level it indicates that it is possible to use parenting training to improve the quality of infant attachments. On a theoretical level it is significant that improvements in sensitive responsiveness were associated with improvements in the quality of attachment. This provides strong support for Ainsworth's theory.

A weakness of Ainsworth's approach to explaining the formation of different attachment types seems to be that she did not take account of individual differences in the temperament of children and the contribution this can make to attachment type. Children with type B attachments come from the complete spectrum of temperament types (Sroufe, 1985), but it seems that type A attachments are associated with both controlling and rejecting parenting (Vondra *et al.*, 1995), *and with* a temperament characterised by low sociability and low emotional reactivity (Fox *et al.*, 1991). Similarly, type C attachments are associated with both under-stimulating and unresponsive parenting (Vondra *et al.*, 1995) *and* an irritable temperament (Goldsmith and Alansky, 1987). It thus seems that sensitive responsiveness is one important influence on attachment type but it is not the whole story. This is important because a by-product of research into sensitive responsiveness has been the *blaming* of parents of insecurely attached infants for not being sensitive enough. This is most unhelpful for parents already struggling with a difficult baby.

Training in sensitive responsiveness like that performed by Juffer *et al.* can be particularly useful in supporting parents of children with difficult temperaments. Van den Boom (1994) offered training to 50 mothers of babies aged 6 months assessed as having an irritable temperament. At 12 months they were compared to a control group of 50 irritable babies whose parents had not had the training. It was found that, unlike the control group, the number of securely attached babies in the training condition had increased significantly.

Later consequences of attachment type

The NeoBowlbyites have gathered considerable evidence linking attachment type to both social-emotional and intellectual development. Hazan and Shaver (1987) investigated the relationship between adults' romantic love behaviour and their infant attachment type. They printed a 'love quiz' in a newspaper, which included items related to their parental attachment and to their dating behaviour. It was found that those people classified as securely attached according to their descriptions of their relationship with their parents tended to be those who reported that they believed in long-term relationships, trusted their partners and were not threatened by intimacy. The insecurely attached adults appeared to have much greater difficulty in their relationships. This study tells us not only that the patterns of the first relationship are reflected in adult relationships, but that a secure attachment gives us a head-start when it comes to falling in love.

Of course the Hazan and Shaver study has its limitations. It relied upon respondents to a newspaper quiz, by definition not a representative sample of the population because most of us do not reply to newspaper quizzes. None the less, the principle that a secure attachment to a primary carer is helpful when forming adult relationships is well supported by more rigorous research. We can look in detail at one such study.

research now

do women with insecure attachments have relationship difficulties as adults?

McCarthy, G. (1999) Attachment style and adult love relationships and friendships: a study of a group of women at risk of experiencing relationship difficulties. *British Journal of Medical Psychology 72, 305–21*

Aim: Results of previous studies had suggested a link between attachment type and the type of adult friendships and romantic relations experienced. The aim of this study was to see whether women known to have had poor attachments in their childhood were experiencing difficulties in their adult relationships.

Method: Forty women aged between 25 and 44 years (mean age 36) were identified as being likely to have insecure attachments on the basis that, as children, they had been identified in previous studies as having insecure attachments to their primary carers. They were asked to take part in the study by means of a letter, then interviewed in their own homes. A standard interview called the Adult Personality Functioning Assessment (APFA) was used to find out as much as possible about their friendships and romantic relationships during the previous five years. The participants also completed a questionnaire (from Hazan and Shaver) designed to indicate their attachment type, a test of depression called the Beck Depression Inventory (BDI) and a test of self-esteem.

Results: As expected there was a much higher rate of insecure attachment in this sample than in the population as a whole. Only 43 per cent were classified as securely attached, as opposed to about 65 per cent in the whole population. The women with the secure (type B) attachments were significantly more likely to have successful romantic relationships and friendships. They also tended to have better self-esteem. Participants with avoidant (type A) attachments had the greatest difficulty in romantic relationships, while those with ambivalent (type C) attachments had the poorest friendships. There was no relationship between attachment classification and mood as measured by the BDI. Twenty per cent of the women had abnormal attachments characterised by both avoidant and ambivalent behaviour. Overall these women experienced the greatest relationship difficulties.

Conclusion: Attachment type predicts relationship difficulties in adult women. Type A attachment is particularly associated with problems in romantic relationships, while type C is particularly associated with problems in friendships. Atypical attachments, i.e. those not falling within types A, B or C appear to cause the most problems of all.

Hazan and Shaver (1990) went on to investigate the relationship between attachment and work-related behaviour in adulthood using questionnaires to measure both attachment and behaviour at work. They found that securely attached adults were the best at balancing the demands of work and social lives, and that they had the greatest confidence in their work. A tendency emerged for avoidantly attached adults (type A) to use work as a means of getting away from other people. Type As also tended to stress the importance of career success over relationships. Adults identified as having ambivalent attachments (type C) had the most difficulty in reconciling the demands of work with family and social commitments. They often lacked confidence in their work and feared rejection by colleagues.

There is also a body of research linking attachment type with cognitive development. Frankel and Bates (1990) gave two-year-old children a series of tasks involving practical problems including joining two sticks together to extract a toy from a tube and weighing down one end of a see-saw in order to reach a biscuit on the other end. In all such tasks securely attached children did better than those without a secure attachment.

Meins (1997) performed a series of studies comparing securely and insecurely attached children on a variety of cognitive tasks. In one study mothers of 30 securely attached and 18 insecurely attached infants aged 12 to 13 months were trained to record the children's use of language. At 19 months the records were analysed. Children were classified as 'faster' in language acquisition if they have a vocabulary of 25 words or more at 19 months and 'slower' if their vocabulary is less than 25 words. Seventy-seven per cent of the securely attached group as opposed to only 12 per cent of the insecurely attached group were classified as 'faster' in their development of language.

Culture and attachment

Studies of attachment across different cultures, using the Strange Situation, have revealed wide variations in the proportions of securely attached infants. Ijzendoorn and Kroonenberg (1988) combined results of a large number of studies in a variety of countries and produced percentages of infants classifiable as avoidant, securely attached and resistant in these different cultures. Some of these are shown in Table 2.2.

	Avoidant	Secure	Resistant
Britain	22	75	3
West Germany	35	57	8
USA	21	65	14
China	25	50	25
Japan	5	68	27

Table 2.2 percentages of attachment types in different cultures. From Ijzendoorn and Kroonenberg (1988)

As you can see, it appears at first that there are some differences in the proportions of different attachment types in these cultures, but we cannot accept such a conclusion uncritically. Takahashi (1990) has suggested that the Strange Situation is simply not appropriate for testing different cultures because of differences in maternal behaviour. Thus the Japanese children had no opportunity to show avoidant behaviour in the final stage of the Strange Situation as mothers inevitably went straight to them and picked them up.

An alternative explanation for differences in rates of attachment types across nationalities comes from Grossman and Grossman (1990). They suggest that attachment has different meanings in different cultures. Thus, what we call 'avoidant' in Britain and America might be called 'independent' in Germany. As independence is valued more highly in German than British or American culture, we would expect a higher proportion of type A attachment in Germany. As you can see in Table 2.2 this is in fact the case.

The cross-cultural study of attachment poses an important challenge to the ideas of Bowlby and Ainsworth, who saw attachment as universal. If attachment has different meanings in different cultures, then it may be that the usefulness of attachment theory and research is *culture-bound*, i.e. it is applicable in Anglo-American culture but not world-wide.

for and against

Ainsworth's attachment types

+ The Strange Situation appears to reliably distinguish between securely and insecurely attached infants.

− Temperament as well as attachment affects infant behaviour in the anxiety-provoking parts of the Strange Situation. We therefore need to be cautious about labelling a child insecurely attached based on how much anxiety they show on separation from the primary carer and the presence of a stranger.

+ Many studies have found, in line with Ainsworth's theory, that the style of maternal behaviour (that we could call sensitive responsiveness) towards infants is associated with particular attachment types.

− Contrary to Ainsworth's theory, in which attachment type can be accounted for entirely by sensitivity, it seems that infant temperament is also associated with attachment type.

+ Attachment type does predict later social and intellectual development.

− Attachment type is just one of several influences on development, and Ainsworth, like Bowlby, may have underestimated the impact of other factors.

> --- Although the majority of infants fall into types A, B and C, a small but significant
>   proportion have *atypical* attachments, that are not accounted for by Ainsworth's
>   classification.
>
> --- Ainsworth's classification appears to be culture-bound. It is unclear whether this is due
>   to the different meanings of attachment to different cultures or the difficulties in
>   measuring attachment in different cultures.

where to now?

The following are good sources of further information on the ideas of Mary Ainsworth:

▶ **Ainsworth, M.D.S. (1985) Patterns of infant-mother attachments: antecedents and effects on development.** *Bulletin of the New York Academy of Medicine 61(9), 771–91* – based on a lecture given to non-experts, this is a good, non-technical first step in reading some of Ainsworth's original work. She explores the relationship between her work and that of Bowlby, and outlines the Strange Situation, attachment types and sensitive responsiveness.

▶ **Cowie, H. (1995) Child care and attachment. In Barnes, P. (ed.)** *Personal, Social and Emotional Development of Children.* **Oxford: Blackwell** – a very clear and readable account of attachment issues with a particular focus on Ainsworth's theory.

▶ **Schaffer, H.R. (1996)** *Social Development.* **Oxford: Blackwell** – includes an excellent chapter on the causes and effects of attachment types.

▶ **Gross, R. (1997) Attachment Theory, Extensions and Applications.** *Psychology Review* 4(1), 10–13 – an excellent account of aspects of adult behaviour, including romantic relationships, work and religiosity that are associated with different attachment types.

what's new?

atypical attachments

We can think of Ainsworth's types A, B and C as normal variations in attachment style, and 85–90 per cent of children fall into one of these categories (Main and Solomon, 1986). However, there are a minority of children who have *atypical* attachments that fall outside these classifications. In the Gerard McCarthy study for example (see p.35), women who showed the characteristics of both type A and type C attachments emerged as having the most serious difficulties in their adult relationships. Mary Main and Judith Solomon (1986) have called this category of mixed avoidant and resistant behaviour *type D* attachment (combined avoidant and resistant behaviour is also sometimes known as *type AC*). Type D children placed in the Strange Situation may alternate between avoidant and resistant behaviour, or they may combine them, maintaining proximity but avoiding contact and resisting when cuddled. They may also freeze or move very slowly. Typically they appear afraid of the primary carer and may prefer the company of the stranger.

Type D or *disorganised/disoriented attachment* is associated with a number of situations that interfere with the development of a more typical attachment. For example, Radke-Yarrow *et al.* (1995) found that 23 per cent of infants of depressed mothers and 42 per cent of infants of mothers suffering manic depression (in which periods of depression alternate with periods of euphoria or irritability) had type D attachments. It appears that depression, especially manic depression, can interfere with the capacity of primary carers to respond sensitively and consistently to babies.

Carlson *et al.* (1989) compared the attachments of 22 children identified as needing help from Social Services because they had suffered abuse or neglect with those of a control group of 21 children. The two groups were matched for poverty and other social factors. 81 per cent of the maltreated group had type D attachments as opposed to 19 per cent of the control group. This shows clearly that maltreatment by a carer can have a dramatic effect on attachment, and is presumably linked to the high incidence of psychiatric problems in adults who suffered emotional, physical or sexual abuse in childhood.

The studies of Carlson *et al.* (1989) and Radke-Yarrow *et al.* (1995) tell us that type D attachment is associated with certain situations, but it is only very recently that researchers have begun to link specific patterns of behaviour on the part of the primary carer with the development of type D attachment. Lyons-Ruth *et al.* (1999) assessed the attachment types of 65 infants aged 18 months. Their mothers were videotaped interacting with them at home. Maternal behaviours that were associated with type D attachments included frightened or frightening behaviour and the consistent failure to respond to clear infant signals. The researchers also looked at the possible role of infant behaviours, but the type D infants appeared to have no less skill in communicating their wishes to the carers than those characterised as types A, B or C; they were simply not responded to. This study therefore supports the idea that type D attachment is a product of behaviour on the part of the primary carer.

There is a substantial body of research showing that type D attachment leads to serious disadvantages for children. Whereas having a type A or C attachment influences development consistently but only to a moderate degree, type D attachments can have disastrous consequences. In the McCarthy study the women classifiable as type D had the most serious relationship difficulties, both with regard to friendships and romantic involvement. In the Meins study of language acquisition (p.36), type D children were found to have the smallest vocabulary of the four attachment types.

where to now?

The following is a good source of further information regarding disorganised attachment:

▷ **Vondra, J.I. and Barnett, D. (1999) Atypical attachment in infancy and early childhood among children at developmental risk.** *Monographs of the Society for Research in Child Development*. Oxford, Blackwell.

The social constructionist challenge to attachment theory

We have already looked at the idea that attachment has different meanings in different cultures. The social constructionist perspective (see p.19) is concerned with how the meaning we attribute to attachment in Anglo-American culture may have arisen as a result of social and historical factors. Erica Burman (1994) has identified how a number of such factors might have influenced the development and popularity of attachment theory. For example, much of Bowlby's early work on maternal deprivation took place immediately after the Second World War, a time when soldiers were returning home and seeking to take back the jobs that had been done predominantly (for the first time) by women during the war. This meant that men were set to benefit at the expense of women from a theory that emphasised the importance of women's mothering role. The government also benefited from the social construction of women as mothers rather than workers as it gave them a way to tackle post-war unemployment. It may thus be that the tremendous popularity of attachment theory in the 1950s was due to the fact that it served the needs of the male-dominated society.

Burman (1994) goes on to suggest that the attachment perspective is fundamentally misogynist (anti-women), because it lays the blame for anything that goes wrong in an individual's development firmly at the door of their mother. Women who are not 'model mothers' (this can include those who work or study, who have an active social life or are single parents) tend to be judged to be in some way immoral. This helps secure men's dominant position in society by placing restrictions on the 'acceptable' activities of women. The concept of sensitive responsiveness has caused particular problems, because it suggests that the only 'good' mothers are those who focus exclusively on the needs of their baby. Measures of sensitive responsiveness may also be discriminatory in that they tend to find higher scores in middle-class than working-class primary carers, so helping to reinforce the idea that middle-class norms are somehow the 'correct' ones to which all women should aspire.

The social constructionist approach is helpful in reminding us that there are social inequalities – between men and women and between working and middle classes – and that these can be an important influence on the development of psychological thinking. However, before we become too outraged and throw out the baby with the bath water it is worth considering the social benefits that have come from attachment theory and research. Day care and hospital care have been revolutionised by the principle that children should be allowed as much contact as possible with their primary carer and be provided with a substitute attachment figure when appropriate. This is why nurseries and other childcare settings now often employ a *key-worker* for each child, who builds a relationship with them and takes prime responsibility for their welfare. Prior to Bowlby's time it was customary to *forbid* childcare workers to become attached to children in their care, and this made hospital and nursery care unnecessarily traumatic for children.

A further benefit to women of the attachment approach has been in putting a value on mothers and motherhood. This was certainly Bowlby's aim (Holmes, 1993), as opposed to the oppression of women. Remember that prior to Bowlby's time, women were discriminated against in employment *and* undervalued as mothers, so Bowlby certainly did not make life harder for women in general. A particularly controversial aspect of Bowlby's work was his view that parenting ideally requires two parents (Bowlby, 1988), and that it is extremely unwise for a woman without a partner to deliberately have a child. From a social constructionist perspective, this fosters the view that single parents are immoral and irresponsible, and has legitimised discrimination against single parents. On the other hand, we can also use attachment research to argue that, given the importance of parenting and the isolation and lack of support faced by many single parents, it is especially important that single parents are given every support possible. It is thus perhaps unwise to associate attachment theory with a particular political ideology.

where to now?

The following is a good source of further information about social construction and attachment:

▶ **Burman, E. (1994) *Deconstructing Developmental Psychology*. London: Routledge** – a fascinating book, looking at a number of aspects of child development and exploring their historical and political influences and implications.

Conclusions

Attachment theory, derived from the work of Bowlby and Ainsworth, is a highly influential perspective on child development. Its fundamental principles that the formation of an attachment with a primary carer in infancy is (at least partly) the product of sensitive and responsive parenting, and that a secure attachment greatly advantages the child in its later development, are upheld by contemporary research. However, traditional attachment theory has neglected the importance of infant temperament, which may be as important as sensitive responsiveness in the development of attachment types and the child's personality. Attachment theory is also firmly bound up in Anglo-American culture and has proved difficult to apply to a range of cultures.

Attachment theory has proved invaluable in understanding the relationship between early experience and later development. It has led to vast improvements in childcare facilities in nurseries and hospitals, and helped professionals understand and intervene in families at risk of passing on patterns of abuse and neglect through generations. On the other hand, as the social constructionists have emphasised, attachment theory has been used to discriminate against women and aid attempts to put them 'back in the home' by constructing a view of the 'good mother' as being focused exclusively on childcare.

what do you know?

1. Define social releasers.

2. Outline one study into maternal deprivation.

3. What is sensitive responsiveness? What other factor appears to be important in determining attachment type?

4. Outline one study into the long-term effects of attachment type on future development.

5. Why might attachment be a culture-bound concept?

6. Outline two ways in which social constructionists believe that attachment theory has disadvantaged women.

3

Early experiences: deprivation and privation

In this chapter we will be looking at various experiences that children can have, both typical and atypical, and discussing children's responses to and the possible long-term consequences of these events. There will be a degree of overlap with the subject matter of Chapter 2, because of course one thing that may be affected by childhood experiences is attachment. We will begin by distinguishing between different types of childhood experience, then go on to look at the possible effects of short-term separation from primary carer with a particular focus on day-care, and long-term separation resulting from parental separation or the death of a parent. We shall then look at privation, which occurs when children are orphaned before they have the chance to form an attachment, and in cases of severe neglect and abuse. Adoption often follows privation and we can examine studies into the development of children who have suffered privation, then been adopted. Finally, in *What's new?* we can look at the concept of the *developmental life path* and examine the importance of early experiences for later development.

Classifying different types of early experience

In Chapter 2 we looked at Bowlby's ideas about attachment, including his *maternal deprivation hypothesis* – the idea that failure to form a secure attachment or experiences that disrupt this attachment lead to serious long-term consequences for the child, both in their intellectual and social development. As previously discussed (p.26), Bowlby has been criticised in his early work for not distinguishing between short and long-term separations from carers, and between *deprivation*, i.e. separation after the formation of an attachment and *privation*, the failure to form an attachment (Rutter, 1981). In contemporary research, we tend to classify deprivation experiences into three categories:

- *Short-term separation* – as occurs when working primary carers make use of day-care provision or the infant or carer has a short stay in hospital.

- *Long-term separation* – as occurs when families split up and one parent gets custody of the child, or when one or both parents die.

- *Privation* – as occurs when a child is orphaned very young and receives institutional care, or when a child is severely neglected or abused by carers so that an atypical attachment is formed.

In this chapter we will be examining research under these three headings.

Short-term separation

Hospitalisation

Before Bowlby's work became influential the conventional wisdom surrounding children in hospital was that, provided their physical care was good, they would experience few difficulties. It was thus standard practice for parents to be allowed very little access to their children when they were in hospital. Robertson and Bowlby (1952) created quite a stir when they filmed a two-year-old girl called Laura when she went into hospital for eight days for a minor operation. Laura deteriorated throughout the eight days and by the end of her stay she was severely withdrawn and no longer showed trust or affection towards her visiting mother. Robertson and Bowlby filmed several more children in hospital and, based on their observations, proposed three stages children go through when experiencing this type of separation.

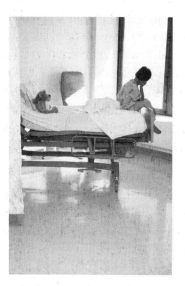

The trauma of surgery can be made worse by being separated from parents

1 *Protest:* children at first were often panic-stricken and upset. They cried frequently and tried to stop their parents leaving.

2 *Despair:* after a time, children cried less frequently, but became apathetic and uninterested.

3 *Detachment:* children eventually began to take an interest in their surroundings. However, if they reached this stage, children frequently rejected their primary carer.

Subsequent research has revealed that not all children go through the stages described by Robertson and Bowlby. There are in fact wide individual differences in children's reactions. Kirkby and Whelan (1996) reviewed research into the effects of hospitalisation on children. They concluded that, although it *can* have negative consequences, there are many variables that impact on the effects. These include the age of the child and the quality of their parental attachments, the seriousness of the condition and the severity of the medical intervention. However, Robertson and Bowlby made a huge contribution to our understanding of the effects of hospitalisation, and as a consequence of their work hospitals now go to great lengths to reduce the trauma of hospitalisation for children, for example encouraging parents to be around as much as possible.

Day-care

Day-care is a routine part of the lives of a huge and steadily growing number of children. Nowadays, economic circumstances mean that it is has become the norm for both parents in two-parent British and American families to work. Given what we have said about the importance of attachment and Bowlby's suggestion that disruption to attachment can result from prolonged separation from the primary carer, the question is begged; does day-care harm children?

Different researchers have found wildly differing results as regards the effects of day-care on children. Andersson (1996) followed up 128 Swedish children who had been in day-care in early childhood, and assessed them on their intellectual and social-emotional development at 13 years. Their development was compared with that of a control group who had had full-time maternal care in their early childhood. It emerged that the children who had spent time in day-care scored higher in both measures of academic achievement and social skills. This study indicates that day-care can have very positive effects.

On the other hand some research has shown that day-care is associated with insecure attachment, behavioural difficulties and intellectual deficits. Baydar and Brooks-Gunn (1991) surveyed over 1,000 families and found that if mothers started work in their first year the children were more likely to be reported to have behavioural difficulties or poor intellectual development. In a *meta-analysis* (combining the results of several past studies weighting the results of each study according to the sample size) of 101 studies of day-care published between 1957 and 1995, involving a total of 32,271 children, Russell (1999) found that, overall, research has shown negative rather than positive effects for day-care. However, the majority of research included in Russell's analysis involved middle and upper-middle class families in which the mother returned to work from choice rather than necessity. While evidence regarding the

effects of day-care is mixed, there is no doubt whatsoever about the effects that *poverty* can have on children's development (Cross *et al.*, 1998). If working and using day-care facilities frees a family from poverty it is likely ultimately be beneficial for the child.

Yet other studies have found mixed results in the relationship between day-care and development. Harr (1999) measured emotional adjustment and academic attainment in 628 children and found very few differences between children of mothers who did not work and those who worked full time. However, once children reached school age, those children whose mothers worked part-time were better adjusted than those of full-time employed mothers. Interestingly, children's emotional adjustment and academic progress were positively associated with mothers' satisfaction with their parent/worker status. This supports the common-sense view, often neglected by psychologists, that it is *happy* mothers rather than working or non-working mothers who are the most successful parents. This study has important implications in terms of informing mothers' decisions as to whether to work – it *is* legitimate for mothers to consider their own wishes.

Why are research findings so inconsistent?

As is often the case in psychology, it seems that the issue is more complex than it first appeared, and just asking whether day-care *per se* is a good or a bad thing is simply the wrong question. The results of different studies conflict because there are several factors that can influence whether day-care has positive, negative or no effects. We have already established that whether the mother wishes to return to work is one important factor. The age at which day-care commences may be another. Most of the research that has found negative effects of day-care has looked at children whose primary carer returned to full-time work in the child's first year. There is almost no evidence that day-care in older children can have any harmful effects.

Another important factor in determining the effects of day-care is the type and quality of day-care provided. It is estimated that unregistered childminders outnumber those registered and inspected by Social Services by two or three to one. Yet research has found that many unregistered childminders provide poor care. Nursery care can run into different problems. While nurseries typically have a stimulating environment and well-trained staff, they also tend to have a lower staff:child ratio and a higher turnover of staff, thus limiting the ability of children to form attachments.

Perhaps the best question to ask is not 'Is day-care good?', but rather 'What factors contribute to good day-care?'. A study by Melhuish *et al.* (1990) may hold many of the answers to this. We can look at this study in detail.

classic
research

what makes good day-care?

Melhuish, E.C., Mooney, A., Martin, S. and Lloyd, E. (1990a) Type of childcare at 18 months I. Differences in interactional experience. *Journal of Child Psychology and Psychiatry 31, 849–59.*

Melhuish, E.C., Lloyd, E., Martin, S. and Mooney, A. (1990b) Type of childcare at 18 months II. Relations with cognitive and language development. *Journal of Child Psychology and Psychiatry 31, 861–70.*

Aim: Researchers were interested in the relative progress – both social-emotional and intellectual – made by children who remained in full-time maternal care and those who experienced different forms of day-care. They were also interested in what factors differed between alternative forms of day-care and may have contributed to any differences in the development of the children.

Method: Two hundred and fifty-five first-born children from two-parent families were followed from birth to 3 years. All the mothers were in full-time work before they had a child and 75 per cent returned to work before the baby was 9 months old. Of the children in day-care, 30 per cent were cared for by a relative, 50 per cent by a childminder and 20 per cent at a nursery. At 18 months and 3 years the four groups of children were all assessed on their social-emotional development (by several measures including an adaptation of the *Strange Situation* – see Chapter 2 for details of this), and on their intellectual and language development, using observation and interviews with the carers. The day-care environments were also assessed for factors that might contribute to the child's level of development, including adult:child ratio, stimulating environment, age, training and experience of the adult carers.

Results: Some measurements did not vary across the different environments. The amount of crying, playing and physical contact with adults was the same for children cared for by their mother, another relative, a childminder or a nursery. However there were some differences in the childrens' behaviour. The amount of vocalisation in 18 month olds was greatest with the mothers, then with a relative, less with a childminder and least of all in nurseries. On measures of aggression children in nurseries came out highest and those with mothers lowest. This was reversed for affection, this being greatest with mothers and least in nurseries. No differences emerged in the proportion of children showing secure attachments to their mothers between the four groups. At 3 years the children with their mothers showed the most affection but those in nurseries the best social skills.

Considerable variations in the quality of care were noted. The nurseries looked at in the study were characterised by low level of responsiveness to children's communications and a low adult:child ratio (mean 4.6:1). The nursery staff were younger than the carers in the other conditions and much less likely to have children of their own. The nurseries also had a high turnover of staff, meaning that children did not have consistent adults with whom they could form an attachment.

Conclusions: On most though not all measures the children in nurseries did less well than the others. Perhaps, however, the real message of this study is not that there is anything wrong with nurseries *per se*, but that good care of young children is associated with good responsiveness to the child, a high staff:child ratio, experienced staff and a low staff turnover, whatever the type of childcare.

Based on the Melhuish study we can begin to get a picture of what makes good day-care. Mothers wishing to return to work after having a baby can take comfort in the fact that in this study children in day-care were no more likely to display an insecure attachment than those of full-time mothers. The key seems to be finding good-quality provision.

This nursery has a high staff–child ratio and a low staff turnover

What the Gurus say

'We know that daycare doesn't do children any harm, especially if it is of good quality'

Tony Munton, London University's Institute for Education

'When a child's mother dies, that is a terrible tragedy. But we impose that tragedy on every child when we leave them to go to work'

Kathy Gyngell, Full Time Mothers Association

'It is best for babies to have something close to full-time mother care for six months at least'

Penelope Leach, childcare author and expert

'The entire debate has been hijacked by a feminist clique. You can always go back to work, but the damage done in the early years can never be rectified'

Patricia Morgan, Institute of Economic Affairs

The Observer, 10 October 1999

Questions

1 From your reading of the research reviewed in this chapter, to what extent would you agree with each of the four statements?

2 What might have influenced each of these 'gurus'? Think about psychological theory and possible political factors.

for and against

day-care

+ Some research has found beneficial effects for good quality day-care.

– A larger body of research has revealed negative effects of day-care.

+ Most of this research showing negative outcomes for day-care has involved very young children and much has involved poor quality day-care.

+ Research has revealed that poverty resulting from not working, and frustration resulting from not working when mothers wish to, have negative consequences for children. Using day-care can help avoid these situations.

where to now?

The following are good sources of further information on the effects of day-care:

▶ **Cowie, H. (1995) Child care and attachment. In Barnes, P. (ed.)** *Personal, Social and Emotional Development of Children*. **Oxford: Blackwell** – very clearly written with a good selection of research.

▶ **Flanagan, C. (1999)** *Early Socialisation*. **London: Routledge** – contains a very clear but detailed and up-to-date account of day-care research.

Long-term separation

This type of separation is associated with parental separation and death of a parent. Although these events are less frequent than short-term separation, a large number of children do experience them. It appears that these events are traumatic for children and can have lasting effects.

Parental separation

Some readers will have parents who are divorced. It is important as we look at the possible consequences of divorce to realise that there are a number of factors that determine the effects divorce has on children. The differences reported between children of divorced and intact couples are typically quite small and do not apply to all children.

Richards *et al* (1995) has identified a number of typical effects of parental separation on children. You should note that these differences are very small, although they occur in many cases:

- Lower levels of academic attainment.

- Higher rate of behavioural problems.

- Earlier average ages for beginning sexual relationships, leaving home, cohabiting and marrying.

- More distant relationships with family as an adult.

- Lower socio-economic status and psychological well-being as an adult.

An important question you might ask is whether children are more affected by parental conflict or *discord* within an intact family or by parental separation/divorce/remarriage, collectively called *family reordering*. This is important to families in discord who have to make a decision whether to reorder or remain intact, based partly on their beliefs about the effects on the children. The results of studies seeking to find out whether reordering or discord is worse for a child are mixed. A classic study by Cockett and Tripp (1994) aimed to compare directly the effects of discord with those of divorce.

research now

how do divorce and separation really affect children?

Cockett, M. and Tripp, J. (1994) Children living in reordered families. *Social Policy Research Findings* 45, Joseph Rowntree Foundation.

Aim: A number of studies have shown that children whose parents have separated are at increased risk from social and educational problems. Cockett and Tripp set out to investigate the effects of family reordering and discord on children, and what factors children reported as particularly difficult during reordering. This was the first major study that involved interviewing children themselves about their responses to family reordering.

Method: One hundred and fifty-two children and their parents were assessed and divided into three groups. One group consisted of reordered families, those who had separated and who may have joined other families. The second group were those who were still in intact families suffering serious discord. The third group consisted of those in intact families suffering no serious discord. The three groups were matched for age, sex, socio-economic status and maternal education. Children in each group were assessed by interviews and questionnaires on their self-image, their social life, their school success, their behaviour and their health. They were also questioned in depth about their experiences of family reordering, for example how their parents had prepared them for separation and what provision was made for keeping in touch with the absent parent.

Results: On all measures of emotional adjustment and academic success the children of reordered families came out worse than the intact groups. Those from intact families experiencing discord followed next, while children from intact families without discord had fewest problems. Children who had three or more successive reorderings generally came off worst on all measures. Only a small minority of children had been prepared for the parental split, and fewer than half had regular contact with the absent parent. Children who had several reorderings tended to have less support from extended families.

Conclusion: The obvious conclusion from these results is that parental separation and divorce are more harmful to children than parental discord, and this study is often reported as showing that family reordering *per se* is harmful to children. However, it is perhaps more interesting to look at how badly most parents appeared to manage their separation as regards the child's welfare. It is likely that the poor outcomes for children in reordered families could be minimised by preparation before the event and by proper contact after the event.

A problem with using this type of study to compare the effects of reordering and discord is that it is impossible to truly match the groups. It is possible that the reordered group's greater incidence of problems was due to some form of greater conflict or lesser reason for staying together that triggered the family split rather than the split itself. Logically, there *must* be something different in the reordered and intact groups because something led one group of families to remain intact while the others separated.

Other studies have suggested that parental discord can cause more problems for children than family reordering. Fergusson *et al.* (1992) used a different approach to try to tease out what factors in family problems affect children most. They examined a group of 1,265 children who had been studied each year, up to the age of 13. The rates of parental separation, reconciliation, arguments, violence and sexual problems were recorded each year. At 13 years the rate of criminal offending was noted and the rates of offending were looked at in relation to each of the above variables. Significant associations with offending were found for all the variables measured, apart from parents' sexual problems. The most significant factor was parental discord, measured by the number of arguments. Another study by Jekielek (1998) supports the idea that family discord is more damaging than reordering. Responses from 1,640 children aged 6 to 14 in the *National Longitudinal Surveys of Youth* were analysed, and indications of anxiety and depression were compared in intact without discord families, intact with discord families and reordered families. Children in both reordered and discordant families showed significantly more signs of anxiety and depression than those in intact families with discord; however children who remained in families suffering high levels of discord displayed the highest levels of anxiety and depression of all.

An important question you might wish to ask, particularly if your own parents are separated and you are beginning to wonder what the effects might have been on you, is why some children are so much more affected than others by family reordering. We have already seen from the Cockett and Tripp study that most parents neither prepare children adequately prior to separation nor make adequate arrangements for children to keep in regular touch with the absent parent. There is also evidence to suggest that the temperament of the child (see p.15 for a discussion of temperament) affects children's responses. Some children have a particularly *resilient* temperament, and are significantly less affected by reordering than more sensitive children (Nair, 1999).

Are the effects of parental death different?

As you might expect, it seems that separation from a parent by death has different psychological effects on children from separation by family reordering. Certainly the circumstances are different. In the case of parental divorce children may blame themselves for the parent leaving. The stress resulting from integrating into a new family as the remaining parent remarries is likely to come sooner. On the other hand it is likely that the absent parent will not be entirely gone from the child's life. Bifulco *et al.* (1991) studied 249 women whose mothers had been lost before they were 17 years old, either through family reordering or death. The whole group suffered more from depression and anxiety disorders than the norm for the population. However, the highest rate of depression occurred in those whose mother had died in the first six years of their life. The same effect did not occur for women whose mother had *left* during the first six years. This implies that parental death at a young age has more serious effects than parental divorce.

where to now?

The following are good sources of further information about the effects of family re-ordering and discord:

▷ **Cockett, M. and Tripp, J. (1994) Children living in reordered families.** *Social Policy Research Findings* **45, Joseph Rowntree Foundation** – a fascinating and fairly non-technical paper intended for a general as well as psychological audience. Very influential, but contains a number of findings not often discussed, therefore well worth reading in full.

▷ **Das Gupta, P. (1995) Growing up in families. In Barnes, P. (ed.)** *Personal, Social and Emotional Development of Children.* **Oxford, Blackwell** – an excellent account of the issues discussed here.

Privation

Privation occurs when children never have the opportunity to form an attachment to a primary carer, or when any attachment they do form is distorted due their treatment by carers. This means that prived children do not experience the close relationship most of us enjoy in childhood, and it seems that this lack of an early close relationship can have serious effects on children.

While we are confident that privation *can* produce serious social-emotional and intellectual problems for children, what remains open to debate however is the extent to which these effects *inevitably* result from privation, and the extent to which they can be *reversed*. As you can imagine, there would be serious ethical problems with any kind of controlled experimental study on privation in humans, as this would mean deliberately inflicting privation on infants knowing that it would harm them! We do, however, have two sources of evidence that help us understand the effects of privation:

● case-studies of severely abused children

● studies of children in institutional care from an early age.

Case-studies of severely abused children

There have been a tragically large number of cases of children who have suffered privation because of the treatment they received at the hands of those responsible for them. If we examine two cases with very different outcomes we may be able to tease out some of the factors that affect how serious and permanent the effects of privation are.

1   Koluchova (1972, 1991) described the case of two identical twin boys (generally known in Britain as the 'Czech twins'). The twins were born in 1960, lost their mother shortly after birth and were cared for in an institution for a year before being fostered by an aunt for a further six months. Their father then remarried and the twins were reared by a cruel stepmother who kept them locked in a dark, cold closet the whole time and regularly beat them severely. When rescued at the age of seven, the boys were severely retarded and had no speech. They were terrified of adults. After two years of intensive institutional care including physiotherapy, speech therapy and psychotherapy, a pair of exceptionally caring and attentive sisters fostered the boys. By the age of 14 they showed no social-emotional or intellectual deficits. By 20 they both showed above average intelligence, and were working and experiencing successful romantic relationships. They both did National Service in their 20s, and later married and had children. Both are reported (Clarke and Clarke, 1998) to have successful relationships and careers.

2   Curtiss (1977) has described the case of Genie. Genie was discovered and rescued at the age of 13 years. She had been kept tied to a potty by day and tied into a sleeping bag at night by her father who believed that she was brain-damaged. Genie was regularly beaten, especially when she tried to communicate verbally, and she received virtually no intellectual stimulation or affection. She had developed little language and she was indifferent to adults. When rescued Genie was fostered for a time by a teacher, then by one of the psychologists studying her. She showed consistent progress and developed limited language and attachments to her carers. However, when funding for the research was withdrawn she was returned to Social Services and cared for by a succession of foster-parents. In one foster-home she was severely beaten for vomiting, and this traumatised her greatly, causing her to lose the language skills and emotional stability she had developed. She was briefly reunited at this point with the psychologists, to whom she expressed considerable anger. Genie was eventually settled with an adult foster-carer, who understandably did not wish her to have anything to do with psychologists again. We thus have no recent information on her condition.

We can see that at the time of their rescue, both the Czech twins and Genie displayed considerable emotional disturbance and intellectual deficits. However they went on to have very different outcomes. By comparing the cases of Genie and the Czech twins we can see three major differences that may have contributed to the difference in outcome:

- Whereas Genie was largely alone throughout her childhood (although her mother claimed to have a relationship with her), the Czech twins were able to form a close attachment to each other. Thus technically they had not suffered *privation* at all, rather very severe *deprivation*.

- The Czech twins were rescued at a much earlier age than Genie. It seems likely that the younger we can intervene in cases of privation the better the chances of success.

- Following their rescue the Czech twins received excellent care from their foster-carers. By contrast, Genie was abused again and this triggered a worsening in her condition.

We should be very cautious in assuming that these differences in circumstances account for the difference in outcome in the two cases. Because the cases were recorded *retrospectively* we cannot be sure about what other factors affected the children prior to their discovery. Furthermore, Genie's father may have been correct in his belief that she had suffered brain damage as well as being appallingly treated. We can see, however, that early intervention and good after-care are helpful when dealing with privation.

Studies of institutionalised children

The study of institutional care is very much tied up with the study of adoption. Adoption gives psychologists the chance to study the extent to which any effects of early institutional care can be reversed later. Perhaps the most influential study of institutional care and adoption was begun by Tizard and Rees (1974) and followed up by Tizard and Hodges (1978), and Hodges and Tizard (1989). We can look at this series of studies in some detail.

classic research

should children taken into care remain there, be restored to their family or be adopted?

Tizard, B. and Rees, J. (1974) A comparison of the effects of adoption, restoration to the natural mother and continued institutionalisation on the cognitive development of four-year-old children. *Child Development 45, 92–9.*

Tizard, B. and Hodges, J. (1978) The effect of early institutional care on eight year old children. *Journal of Psychology and Psychiatry 19, 99–118.*

Hodges, J. and Tizard, B. (1989a) IQ and behavioural adjustment of ex-institutional adolescents. *Journal of Child Psychology and Psychiatry 30, 53–76.*

Hodges, J. and Tizard, B. (1989b) Social and family relationships of ex-institutional adolescents. *Journal of Child Psychology and Psychiatry 30, 77–98.*

Aim: The aim of this series of studies was to compare the development of children who had been taken into institutional care at a very young age under the three possible conditions that could follow, i.e. remaining in an institution, being adopted or being restored to their biological family.

Method: A total of 65 children took part in the study. All had been in institutional care since prior to 4 months of age: 24 had been adopted; 15 had been restored to their biological families; and 26 were still in institutional care. All were about $4^1/2$ years old at the time of the initial study. All the children in a home setting (i.e. not in an institution) had been there at least 6 months when assessments were made. The design was a naturalistic experiment in which development in each of the three conditions of institutional care, restoration and adoption could be compared. Assessment of development was carried out by interviewing carers and teachers, by observation and by IQ tests. Both intellectual and social development were assessed. Assessments were carried out again at 8 years of age (Tizard and Hodges, 1978). By this time 25 children were adopted, and a further 3 were in long-term foster homes. Thirteen were now restored to their original families. The participants were assessed once more at 16 (Hodges and Tizard, 1989).

Results: At $4^1/2$ years, the adopted group had the lowest number of reported behavioural problems. Both adopted and restored children were more visibly affectionate and attention-seeking than is typical of children who have always lived with their family. The restored group differed from the adopted group in displaying more 'clingy' behaviour. Of those still in institutions, the majority showed clingy behaviour and most were said by staff to 'not care deeply about anyone'. At the age of 8, the differences between the groups had increased. The adopted group were now generally reported as having strong attachments to their carers, although they were generally slightly more physically affectionate than is typical of children who have always lived with their biological parents. Only half of the mothers in the restored group felt that their child was attached to them, and these children displayed less than the usual levels of physical affection. At school, all three groups were reported by teachers to be unpopular with peers, restless and aggressive in comparison with other children. At 16, the adoptees had family relationships indistinguishable from those of children who had always lived with biological parents, although they still had some problems getting on with their peers. On all measures of intellectual development and academic attainment the adopted group did far better than the restored or institutional groups.

Conclusion: Spending time in institutions as an infant had some lasting effects, irrespective of whether infants were restored to their families, adopted or remained in institutions. This suggests the effects of privation are only partially reversible. However, the outcomes were considerably better following adoption than either of the alternatives. We need to be clear, though, about what this series of studies does and does not show. There was no attempt to match adoptive carers with the biological parents in the restoration group. The adoptive parents were older, wealthier, better educated and more likely to have stable family lives and previous experience of child rearing than the mothers in the restored group. They were also more motivated than the biological parents, most of whom reported mixed feelings about taking back their children. This is *not* therefore an experiment showing that restoring children to biological parents is harmful. It *does* show that, following a poor start in life, children are more likely to make up lost ground if they have experienced and committed carers.

Following the fall of President Ceaucescu in Romania in 1990, much public attention in Europe and America was focused on the plight of the many children left in crowded and understaffed Romanian orphanages. A large number of these orphans were adopted, including in Britain, and the progress of 111 such orphans was followed up by Michael Rutter and colleagues.

Romanians in orphanages following the fall of Ceaucescu lived in very poor conditions

Rutter *et al.* (1998) aimed to see the extent to which good care could make up for very poor early institutional experiences. A secondary aim was to compare the Romanian adoptees with a group of British adoptees in order to see whether some of the effects often observed in privation are due to maternal deprivation itself, or to the physical hardships associated with privation. Adoptees were followed up to the age of 4 years and measured with developmental tests of physical and intellectual development. On arrival in Britain the Romanian children were developmentally delayed. About half showed signs of mental retardation and they tended to be severely underweight (half were in the bottom 3 per cent of children their age). The British children did not show these delays, showing that factors other than maternal deprivation had contributed to the delays in the development of the Romanian children. At 4 years, the Romanian children had caught up with the British group on both physical and intellectual development. There was a relationship between age at adoption and development at the age of 4. The older the child on adoption, the less ground they had made up.

Given the results of studies like Rutter's and of case-studies such as the Czech twins, we can be reasonably optimistic about the prospects for children who have suffered early privation and who then receive good care. However, high-quality care is absolutely essential, and the earlier it begins, the better the child's chances of healthy development.

what's new?

the life path approach to understanding early experiences

Clarke and Clarke (1992, 1998) have reviewed the evidence for the impact of early experiences on later child development and challenged the popular view that particular experiences *will* lead to particular later effects. They reviewed many of the studies we have looked at in this chapter and noted that in no case do *all* participants in a particular condition go on to develop in the same way. In the series of Tizard studies for example, not all the adopted children developed better socially or intellectually than all the restored or all the institutionalised children, although there were fairly large differences in the average development achieved by the three groups. Similarly, in the studies of attachment we looked at in Chapter 2, not all securely attached children did better than all insecurely attached children, even though overall a secure attachment did seem to give them an advantage.

What this means is that particular experiences have a *probabilistic* effect on development, i.e. they affect the *likelihood* of certain outcomes, not the certainty. However serious an early experience, there is always a next stage of development for the child to enter with new opportunities and pitfalls. Thus children with secure attachments are more likely to do well at school because they are more likely to have good relationships with peers and teachers. However, if they do not develop these relationships (and some will not due to other factors) then their attachment no longer places them in such good stead. The converse is that a child who has suffered early hardship, but who has particularly good care from an adoptive family and/or particularly dedicated and skilled teachers, can overcome completely a poor start. Thus early experience puts us on a particular life path, but later experience, both good and bad, can alter this developmental path. Clarke and Clarke cite the case of the Czech twins as an example of children whose life paths involved multiple experiences, initially negative in the form of their mother's death, their early institutionalisation and their abusive step-parenting. However, they also had a number of positive experiences in the form of their attachment to each other and their excellent care when adopted.

The Clarkes' approach is not to suggest that early experience is not important – it clearly is. However, all children carry on developing along a 'life path' regardless of particular experiences, and no individual experience, however extreme, can *determine* future development; it can only be one of several influences on it. The life path approach is not only helpful in understanding why early experiences do not have identical experiences on all children, it is also highly optimistic, and gives professionals and adoptive families a way of looking beyond experiences that have disadvantaged children.

where to now?

The following are good sources of further information on privation:

▷ Flanagan, C. (1999) Early privation and developmental catch-up. *Psychology Review 6(1), 24–5* – a simple but very up-to-date review of research following the adopted Romanian orphans.

▷ Skuse, D.H. (1993) Extreme deprivation in early childhood. In Messer, D. and Dockerell, J. (1999) (eds) *Developmental Psychology, A Reader*. London: Arnold – an excellent account of case studies of privation and the implications of findings.

▷ Clarke, A.D.B. and Clarke, A.M. (1998) Early experience and the life path. *The Psychologist 11, 433–6* – a fascinating look at how early experience can affect but does not necessarily determine later development.

▷ Hodges, J. (1996) The natural history of non attachment. In Bernstein, B. and Brannen, J. (eds) *Children, Research and Policy*. London: Taylor & Francis.

Conclusions

When talking about the long-term effects of early experience, most psychologists have found it helpful to look at short-term separation, long-term separation and privation separately. Short-term separation takes place most commonly when working mothers make use of day-care. Results concerning the effects of day-care are mixed, with the larger body of evidence showing negative effects. However, most of the research showing negative consequences for children of working mothers has involved very young children and poor day-care. There is also research showing that maternal poverty and frustration can have serious consequences for children, so there remains a strong argument for mothers to work and make use of day-care. The most common cause of long-term separation is family reordering. Findings are clear that children from families with discord or reordering are disadvantaged, but it remains unclear whether discord in intact families or parental separation have the more serious effects. The effects of the death of a parent may be more serious than those of family reordering.

Privation is perhaps the most serious early experience a child can have. By looking at the cases of Genie and the Czech twins we can tease out some of the factors that influence the severity of privation and the prospects for recovery. Studies of prived and later adopted children have yielded mixed results, but we can say that the outlook for prived children is reasonably optimistic provided adoption is early and by committed parents. Clarke and Clarke (1998) have suggested that we can best conceive of the effects of privation and other early experiences as probabilistic influences on the life path of the child. This means that they increase the probability of certain outcomes but do not determine them.

what do you know?

1 Outline one study into the effects of hospital treatment on children.

2 Based on psychological research, outline one argument for and one argument against day-care.

3 What are discord and reordering in families, and how might each affect a child's development?

4 What have adoption studies taught us about the reversibility of privation?

5 What is a life path, and how has the idea affected our understanding of the effects of early experience?

4

Friendship and play

In this chapter we will be looking beyond children's initial relationships with their families to *peer relationships*, i.e. their relationships with other children. We shall look at the typical development of friendships in childhood and adolescence, and what factors might affect individual differences in children's abilities to form friendships and their popularity with other children. It is then interesting to consider children's friendships in cultural context and look at friendships in different cultures. Tied up with peer relationships is play. We can identify several categories of play and examine factors that may affect individual differences in play. In *What's new?* we will look at the study of rough and tumble play. We shall then look at two important theoretical perspectives on play, the cognitive-developmental approach, which emphasises the importance of play in intellectual development, and the psychodynamic approach, which emphasises the emotional significance of play. Based on a psychodynamic understanding of play we shall finish by introducing the therapeutic value of play and the use of play in child psychotherapy.

The development of friendships in children

In early childhood, children's most important relationships are those with their primary carer and other family members. Relationships with peers are initially far less significant than those with family members. However, the importance of peer relationships increases throughout childhood and by mid-adolescence most young people tend to use friends as their primary sources of social and emotional support. So what benefits does friendship have for children? Erwin (1998) has suggested a number of gains that children derive from being in stable friendships. Childhood friendships serve as a training ground for future relationships in which social skills, such as getting one's own way and resolving conflict, can be developed. They also give children experience of intimacy with peers and sensitivity for other people's needs. The experience of friendship can compensate to some extent for earlier poor relationships in giving children valuable experience of intimacy. Friendship also allows children to make *social comparisons* with peers, i.e. they can compare their own behaviour with that of others and modify it where it appears to differ from the norm. A stimulating environment is associated with good intellectual development. Clearly social interaction with peers is one source of such stimulation, so friendship can aid intellectual development. Friendship also provides social and emotional support, particularly important during conflict with family.

Changes in friendships with age

From about six months of age, children can be seen to show interest in their peers. Vandell *et al.* (1980) observed that if two infants are given the opportunity to interact they will typically look at each other, touch, imitate each other's movements, smile and vocalise at each other. However these interactions are not normally sustained longer than a few seconds. In the second year of life, peers become a real focus of attention, and although toddlers generally maintain proximity to their primary carer they will spend considerable time looking at other toddlers if they are present in the room (Lewis *et al.*, 1975). Interestingly, toddlers are more likely to try to interact with another toddler if that toddler is interacting with an adult. In a study by Tremblay-Leveau and Nadel (1996) French infants of 11 and 23 months were placed in pairs in a room with a familiar adult. Some spontaneous interaction took place between the toddlers but this increased dramatically when the adult played with one of them. Toddlers were five times as likely to initiate contact with the other toddler at 11 months and eight times as likely to do so at 23 months when the other was interacting with the adult.

These two children are displaying the signs of friendship

Hinde *et al.* (1985) have defined friends as children who choose to play together more than 33 per cent of the time. According to this criterion Hinde *et al.* observed that 20 per cent of 18 month olds and over 50 per cent of 4 year olds had stable friendships. Newcomb and Bagwell (1995) compared interaction between friend and non-friend peers and described four main differences. Firstly friends played together more frequently. Secondly the type of play was different, being more likely to involve fantasy and extended periods of speech. Thirdly, although friends were involved in just as much conflict as non-friends they were much better at *resolving* conflicts. Finally, friends were much better at helping each other with difficult tasks. At primary school, behaviour between friends and non-friends becomes increasingly different, and friendships increase steadily in complexity and intimacy. Children's beliefs about friendship also change during their school years. O'Brien and Bierman (1988) asked American children and adolescents aged 9, 13 and 16 to describe friendship groups. The younger participants defined friendship groups as those who did things together. By adolescence the criterion for belonging to a friendship group had shifted to sharing values and appearance.

The formation of friendships

We have already looked at how children's friendships change with age. This is sometimes referred to as the *vertical* development of friendship. However friendship also develops *horizontally*, i.e. individual friendships change over time. Levinger and Levinger (1986) have developed a five-stage model to describe the typical course of children's friendships.

1 *Acquaintance* – Relationships begin with casual contact. At this stage it is important that two children come into close contact regularly; thus most friendships form between children who live near one another or go to the same school. Children do not necessarily establish contact with all the peers with whom they come into regular contact, but usually choose to interact with those who are attractive and socially skilled.

2 *Build-up* – After establishing casual contact, children go through a process of getting to know each other. This does not follow a set pattern, but may happen quite gradually – for example when two neigh-bouring children meet up regularly over a period of weeks – or in one go – for example when two families go on holiday together. Common attitudes and interests are established at this stage, as is trust.

3 *Continuation and consolidation* – Friendship is now established, but if it is to be maintained certain conditions must be met. Children expect each other to disclose intimate information and secrets, and may break off friendships if this is not forthcoming. Children also need to demonstrate trust and the ability to share in order to keep relationships going.

4   *Deterioration* – Most friendships decline over time. As in the build-up stage, there is no set pattern to deterioration. Some children simply grow apart due to differing interests. If friends at the same primary school go to different secondary schools they are likely simply not to bother maintaining the friendship. Permanent falling-out following conflict is more common in adolescents than younger children. In very young children, some friendships simply fail because the children do not have the social skills to maintain them.

5   *Ending* – When relationships have deteriorated they typically end altogether. There may be a formal ending where former friends announce that they are no longer so, or they may simply start to avoid contact with one another.

The Levinger and Levinger model is useful in reminding us that relationships are not static but are constantly changing and developing. There are, however, some fairly obvious limitations. Different stages are particularly important for children of different ages; thus the consolidation stage is more significant in older children and adolescents. Of course, not all friendships begun in childhood and adolescence deteriorate or break down. Some are maintained throughout life and others may enter a moratorium, for example when a child moves house or school, only to be picked up later. They may alternatively simply end at this point without a deterioration stage.

Individual differences in children's popularity

You will know from your own experience that some children have more friends than others, and that some children tend to be liked by the majority of peers while others are ignored or even actively disliked. Coie and Dodge (1983) identified five categories of *sociometric status* or popularity type. Children were asked to categorise their peers as 'liked most' or 'liked least' and every child was categorised according to their tendency to be identified as liked most or least.

- *Popular children* were identified as those who tended to be categorised by peers often as 'liked most' and seldom as 'liked least'.

- *Average children* were identified as moderately and equally likely to be categorised by peers as 'liked most' or 'liked least'. Children tended not to have strong opinions for or against them.

- *Controversial children* were identified as being frequently categorised as both 'liked most' and 'liked least'. They were therefore very popular with some peers and very unpopular with others.

- *Neglected children* were identified as those rarely categorised as 'liked most' or 'liked least'. They appeared to be little noticed by their peers.

- *Rejected children* were identified as those frequently categorised as 'liked least' and rarely as 'liked most'. They were thus the most unpopular group.

Factors affecting sociometric status

Physical attractiveness

A number of factors can impact on children's popularity. Physical attractiveness appears to be one factor. Coie *et al.* (1983) rated children for attractiveness, then asked members of peer groups to rate each other as 'most liked' and 'most disliked'. A strong relationship emerged, with the most attractive children being those most likely to be categorised as 'most liked' and the least attractive children as those most likely to be categorised as 'least liked'. Cash (1995) reports that facial disfigurement seriously handicaps children socially, as it interferes with non-verbal communication and so makes the affected child more difficult to interact with. Langlois *et al.* (1995) examined parental attitudes towards physically unattractive children from infancy and discovered that premature and disfigured babies tended to receive less attention and lower expectations from adults. There may thus be a *self-fulfilling prophecy* at work here, in which physically unattractive children are not less popular with peers merely because they are unattractive to *them*, but because their development has already been adversely affected by adult attitudes.

Social skills

While there is no doubt among child psychologists that some children are more socially skilled than others or that highly skilled children are more likely to have successful relationships with their peers, exactly what the essential social skills are has proved much more difficult to pin down. Coie and Dodge (1988) had American boys of 6 to 9 years old rate each other as 'most liked and 'most disliked', then observed classroom behaviour and questioned teachers about the strengths and weaknesses of each child. It emerged that three social factors were associated with high popularity; sporting prowess, skilful use of humour and *pro-social* (generous) behaviour. Asher *et al.* (1990) looked at rejected children and concluded that they were more aggressive and critical than the other sociometric types, and that they were more likely to be hyperactive. Rejected children often play alone, sometimes in games typical of younger children (Rubin *et al.*, 1983).

It is, however, difficult to untangle cause and effect from these findings. Children may make themselves unpopular by being critical, aggressive and immature, *or* it may be that they become critical and aggressive, and regress to immature behaviour *in response* to rejection by their peers. Ladd *et al.* (1988) set out to test whether social incompetence led to unpopularity or whether unpopularity resulted in behaviour normally classified as socially incompetent. Researchers followed children aged 3 to 4 for a year, assessing popularity and social behaviour three times. It was found that early argumentative behaviour predicted later unpopularity. It seems then that rejected children are less socially skilled than others, and that their lack of social skill leads to their being rejected.

Some children lack the social skills to become popular

Attachment

In Chapter 2 we looked at theory and research in the area of attachment, and concluded that the security of a child's attachment to its primary carer was an important factor in its later development. Securely attached children (type Bs) tend to have better peer relationships than insecurely attached children. Remember that type A attachment is characterised by *avoidant*, i.e. distant, unemotional behaviour (see p.30), and type C by *resistant*, i.e. bad-tempered behaviour. If these patterns of relating to others persist through childhood and characterise other relationships apart from that with the primary carer, you can imagine that they would cause problems for children. Research has found that type A children tend to have the lowest social status among peers (LaFreniere and Sroufe, 1985) and are most likely to be bullied (Troy and Sroufe, 1987). A recent study by Myron-Wilson and Smith (1998) confirmed this and further suggested that type C children are the most likely to be bullies.

research now

is bullying behaviour related to attachment?

Myron-Wilson, P. and Smith, P.K. (1998) Attachment relationships and influences on bullying. *Proceedings of the British Psychological Society 6(2), 89–90.*

Aim: Previous research using American child participants had established that type A (avoidantly attached) children are at increased risk of being bullied at school. This study aimed to test this idea and also to test whether there was an association between attachment type and participation in bullying behaviour, either as a bully or victim.

Method: One hundred and ninety-six children aged between 7 and 11 years from a South East London primary school took part in the study. All children were assessed for attachment type and quality of relationship with parents using a test called the *Separation Anxiety Test*, which looks at how distressed a child becomes on being separated from their attachment figures and a *Parenting Styles Questionnaire*, which assesses children's perceptions of their relationship with their parents. Involvement with bullying, both as a perpetrator and victim were examined by a test called the *Participant Roles Scale*, in which each child identifies their peers as either a bully, a victim of bullying or uninvolved in bullying. Children were then divided into types A, B and C attachment, and the number of bullies and victims identified by peers in each category were counted.

Results: Securely attached (type B) children were assessed by their peers as very unlikely to be involved in bullying, either as a perpetrator or victim. Type A (avoidantly attached) children were the most likely to be identified by peers as victims of bullying, while type C (ambivalently or resistantly attached) children were the most likely to be rated by peers as bullies.

Conclusion: Attachment classification is associated with bullying behaviour. Securely attached children are less likely than insecurely attached children to be involved with bullying, either as bully or victim. Taking bullying as a negative social behaviour and the avoidance of bullying as a positive social behaviour, we can say that insecure attachment predicts some of the most negative types of interaction between peers.

Attachment type is not merely associated with popularity and positive patterns of social interaction with peers, but also with the formation of friendships. Kerns (1994) studied interactions between pairs of 4-year-old friends with secure and insecure attachments. It emerged that pairs of securely attached friends had more successful and positive interactions than pairs where one had an insecure attachment. The implication of this is that securely attached children will find it more rewarding to interact with each other, while insecurely attached children, who would benefit most from interacting with securely attached peers, are likely to find themselves isolated (Erwin, 1998). There is some evidence that the relationship between attachment, popularity and friendship is different in adolescents than in younger children. Kerns and Stevens (1996) found that securely attached adolescents had more frequent and successful interactions with peers than insecurely attached individuals, but they were no more likely to have close friendships.

Benefits for children of popularity and friendship

Earlier in this chapter we identified some of the possible benefits of having friends. We can now explore this idea further, and look at the separate question of whether popularity is also of benefit in children's development.

Erwin (1998) has suggested that friendships convey benefits to children, both in terms of their social and intellectual development. We can consider evidence for both of these benefits. In terms of social benefits, having friends is, unsurprisingly, associated with lower levels of loneliness (Jones *et al.*, 1982). In adolescence, when peer relationships become increasingly important and friends replace family as major sources of social support, loneliness for friendless individuals becomes an increasing problem, and loneliness is one of the most frequently reported problems in adolescence (Shultz and Moore, 1989). Friendship is also associated with fantasy play (see p.70 for a discussion), which is in turn associated with the development of social competence. Connolly and Doyle (1984) looked at the time spent and the complexity of pretend play in children and found that both were greater in pairs of children who exhibited signs of friendship. This suggests that friendship advantages children in their social development because it increases the type of play that aids social development.

There is also evidence that friends aid cognitive development. In Chapter 8 we look at Vygotsky's theory of cognitive development and studies showing that children learn quicker if they are in co-operative pairs and groups. In a recent study by Pellegrini and Melhuish (1998), 28 pairs of children were observed in tasks of *literate language*. Literate language can be defined as children's talk about their own mental processes. It was found that pairs of friends were more likely to use literate language than pairs of non-friends. It was also found that the use of literate language predicted good performance in school-based tests. This has an important implication: children who have friends are advantaged in school work, and one thing that may improve the performance of children who are not doing well at school work is friendship.

Having secure friendships thus appears to give children an advantage in social and cognitive development. A separate but related line of research has looked at whether popularity in childhood predicts the course of later social development. Parker and Asher (1987) reviewed studies that looked at whether sociometric status, aggression or shyness predicted early school leaving, criminality or adult mental health problems. It was found that aggression and peer rejection were associated with early school leaving and involvement with crime. Shyness did not predict later school dropout or criminality. None of the measures of popularity showed any consistent relationship to mental health problems.

Children's friendships and culture

Friendships in childhood vary in ways that reflect the culture in which the children are growing up. Whiting (1986) compared social contact in children of 20 communities in various parts of the world and found massive variations in the time children spent with parents, siblings, extended family and friends. At one extreme, the Kung Bushmen of the Kalahari Desert in Botswana live in nomadic extended family groups; thus children tend to have very little contact with peers outside the family. At the other extreme (Tobin *et al.*, 1989) children in the Kibbutzim of Israel live from a very early age with other children and not with their parents at all.

Different cultures have different values, and these will impact on children's friendships. Anglo-American culture is highly *individualistic*, i.e. a strong value is placed on the independence and freedom of the individual. In individualist cultures we place much emphasis on friendships as sources of individual enjoyment and of individual social and intellectual development. We thus encourage children to have friends, both in educational and social situations, for their own benefit. However, in more *collectivist* cultures there is much less emphasis on the importance of the individual and so friendship tends to be seen as less important, and commitment to family and other members of the community are seen as more important (Harrison *et al.*, 1995).

Children's opportunities to make friends and particularly to choose some peers over others as friends are constrained by the practices of their culture, which in turn are influenced by geographical and economic factors. In the education system of Britain and America, most children come into contact with a very large number of peers but are required to spend a great deal of time in the company of children of the same sex and exactly the same age. This cultural norm encourages children to choose their friends among their own age and sex (Montmayor and Van Komen,

1985). Within those limits they can use criteria like physical attractiveness, social competence and sociometric status to make their friendship choices. These bases on which Anglo-American children choose their friends are not universal however. In other societies, for example those which are nomadic or live in small settlements, children are much less likely to be routinely segregated from a young age by age and sex, nor are they likely to have regular contact with such a large number of children in total. This means that children who live in small communities are more likely to have cross-sex friendships and to associate with children of a variety of ages (Whiting and Edwards, 1988).

It is important to remember that most of the research concerned with children's friendships you have encountered in this chapter has been conducted in Britain and America. From looking at this research you might have concluded certain 'facts' about the patterns and effects of friendship and popularity. You should be wary, however, of trying to apply the results of studies conducted in Britain and America to all children.

where to now?

The following are good sources of further information about children's friendships:

 Erwin, P. (1998) *Friendship in Childhood and Adolescence*. **London: Routledge** – a simple and user-friendly overview of research into all aspects of children's friendships.

Smith, P. (1998) Social development. In Eysenck, M. (ed.) *Psychology, An Integrated Approach*. **Harlow: Longman** – includes some good information on sociometrics and the use of social skills training to improve children's popularity.

Play

For the remainder of this chapter we will be looking at children's play. Children spend a great deal of time engaged in play and psychologists have suggested that play is important in intellectual, social and emotional development. The importance of play was recognised in the early 20th century. Educational experts began to champion the role of play in education. Susan Isaacs (1929) described play as 'the child's work' and A.S. Neill, founder of the famous Summerhill School in England, where lessons are voluntary, described childhood as 'playhood'. Play certainly has benefits for children's development, although psychologists are still debating just *how* important it is and in precisely what ways it aids children's development.

Categories and types of play

An early but still very influential system for classifying types of play comes from Mildred Parten (1932). Below, we look at her research in detail.

classic
research

how do children play?

Parten, M. (1932) Social participation among pre-school children. *Journal of Abnormal and Social Psychology 27, 243–69.*

Aim: The aim of the study was to examine the different ways in which children played when adults were not guiding them. More specifically, Parten aimed to classify play activity in terms of the different types of interaction that took place between children. A secondary aim was to look at how the nature of social interaction during play changed with children's age.

Method: Sessions of free play, i.e. play in which adults did not intervene or direct, were observed in an American nursery school. The participants were children aged between 2 and 5 years. Parten classified the children as either occupied or unoccupied. The play activities of the occupied children were carefully noted and later classified according to the social interactions involved.

Results: Children's activities were classified into four types:

- *Solitary play* – children play alone with their own toys and make no effort to get close to other children. Children engaged in solitary play are not influenced in their play by the activities of nearby children.

- *Parallel activity* – the child is still playing independently and does not directly interact with surrounding children, but may be in closer proximity to peers, and is influenced by them in choice of toys. Play is thus *around* but not *with* peers.

- *Associative play* – children play the same game together. The common game is a major topic of conversation, and toys are swapped and borrowed. There is, however, no organisation to the game; thus there is no competition or co-operation.

- *Co-operative play* – children play games that have rules and involve a division of labour. There may be competition, for example in sporting activities, or there may be co-operation to achieve a goal, for example in building a model. There may be role-play in which adult activities are imitated. Typically one or more of the children direct the activity of the others.

The different categories of play were found to be associated with different ages. The younger children spent most of their time in solitary and parallel play, whereas the older children spent more time in associative and co-operative play.

Conclusion: Play can be categorised in terms of the interaction between children into four categories. The time spent in each of these categories varies according to the age of the child. Older children tend to have more complex social interactions than do younger children.

Parten's classification of play is still important in contemporary psychology, and it is accepted as one valid way of classifying children's play. However, the approach only tells us about how children interact while playing. It does not tell us much about what they are *doing* (Faulkner, 1995). We can now look at some of the different activities that fall under the heading of play.

Pretend play

Pretending or *fantasy* is an important part of children's play, and pretence of one sort or another dominates most play activities. Think back for a moment to your own childhood. You probably enjoyed a number of different pretend activities. During solitary play you may have pretended to be in an adult role, for example by doing housework or you may have pretended that your toy soldiers were actually fighting. In co-operative play you may have adopted a role, such as a doctor in a game of 'doctors and nurses'.

The beginnings of pretending in play can be seen as early as 12 to 15 months (Smith *et al.*, 1998). Early pretend play tends to involve real objects or objects that closely resemble the objects they are symbolising. Fein (1975) found that 93 per cent of 2 year olds would imitate an adult making a toy horse drink from a plastic cup. However, only 33 per cent imitated the pretence of the horse drinking when a shell was used instead of a plastic cup. Most studies of this type were conducted in laboratory settings, using artificially created conditions and a limited choice of toys. It was not until recently that psychologists began studying the development of pretend play in natural surroundings. Haight and Miller (1993) conducted a longitudinal study into the development of pretence in play, conducted in children's homes.

research now

how and when do children pretend?

Haight, W.L. and Miller, P.J. (1993) *Pretending at Home: Early Development in a Socio-cultural Context.* **Albany: SUNY Press.**

Aim: Earlier research had shown that children in laboratory situations given particular objects to play with tend to use them for pretend activities. However, relatively few studies had looked at the pretend activities children choose to spend time doing, given a full choice of toys in their home environment. The aim of this study was to observe the development of pretend play in children in their home environment from 1 to 4 years.

Method: The participants were four girls and five boys. They were aged 12 months at the beginning of the study. The study was longitudinal, i.e. the same participants were tracked over a period of time. The participants were followed up from 12 months until 48 months, assessing pretend play every 4 to 6 months (seven times in total). Each child was videofilmed playing at home for 3 to 4 hours at a time. The frequency and type of pretend play and whether pretence was alone or in conjunction with another person was noted in each session.

Results: As expected the sophistication of pretend play increased with age. A more surprising finding that had not been picked up in previous observations of children playing alone in a psychology laboratory was that even in young children most pretend play was with another person rather than alone. Overall, 75 per cent of incidents of pretend play were social rather than solitary. In the younger children the primary carer was the most likely partner in pretend play. By 4 years pretend play was equally likely to be with the primary carer or with a peer. Episodes of pretend play with another person tended to be longer than episodes of solitary pretence.

Conclusion: Most pretend play is social rather than individual. Social pretend play is more complex than individual pretend play. The partner for social pretend play is initially the primary carer, but peers become more important in older children.

Dramatic role-play

Dramatic role-play is the term given to play in which children act out adult roles *together*. This is a particular type of pretend play. By 3 to 5 years children act out quite complex roles, including policeman, fireman and princess, and these regularly form part of children's co-operative play. First (1994) observed the emergence of early dramatic role-play in younger children. Five families with 2-year-old children took part in the study. Parents were taught to record signs of role-play and they were regularly interviewed to keep up to date with developments in their children's play. The first game involving role-play emerged in the three girls at 2 years 4 months. First called this the 'leaving game'. The leaving game involves one partner pretending to leave and the other pretending to cry. One of the participants was recorded to say:

'I'm going. You alone. You cry.' (Jane, 2 years 5 months)

This is typical of the leaving game. Interestingly in this excerpt Jane is taking on the role of leaver. In fact children typically swap roles in the leaving game. In the First study, boys developed dramatic role-play rather later than the girls did – 2 years 7 months and 2 years 10 months respectively. However, with such a small sample we cannot say whether this is representative of all boys.

Factors affecting the content of pretend play

An interesting question concerns what determines the content of pretend play. We can look here briefly at three areas; culture, gender and family factors. Some games such as the leaving game may be universal. Another likely universal is that dramatic role-play involves imitating adult roles, but these roles vary according to the culture of the child. Curry and Arnaud (1984) videofilmed and analysed the play of children in five American cultures: Appalachians from West Virginia; Mexican Americans from Texas; black Americans from Texas; Native Americans from Montana; and a mixed group of City children from Pennsylvania. Several universals emerged across the groups. Dramatic role-play in all cases involved domestic play involving food preparation, family roles such as parent–child and sibling interaction, the use of toys to symbolise objects from the children's experience, medical personnel and patient interaction and finally aggression, including to and from monsters. There were, however, differences in the play of the five groups, reflecting their different cultures. For example, while all the cultures played some games involving medical personnel, the settings varied from a city hospital to a rural surgery.

We can see then that culture is one influence on the specifics of play content, although perhaps not the general themes. There are also differences in the play of boys and girls. Boys spend more time in rough-and-tumble play than girls, and their dramatic role-play reflects adult male roles, whereas girls spend more time in role-playing household tasks (Stone, 1981). Tarullo (1994) asked 7-year-old boys and girls to compose a story and tell it using a selection of toys. This is a task of pretend play. Boys' narratives tended to contain more violence, and to describe events in the third person – he did, she did etc. Girls' narratives also contained conflict but it was less likely to be of a physical nature and they tended to use the first person, i.e. they identified themselves as one of the characters. Girls were more likely to describe how characters in the stories *felt*.

Family factors can also influence the content of children's pretend play. Dunn (1988) reported that children with older siblings who instruct them in play become involved in co-operative pretend play at a younger age than first or only children. Remember that in the First (1994) study (which involved children without siblings) the leaving game did not appear until after 2 years. Dunn reports that among children with siblings 15 per cent were engaged in pretend play at 18 months and 80 per cent by 2 years. The content of play also reflects particular events in the child's home. Dunn *et al.* (1999) compared the pretend play of 40 'hard to manage' children with a control group and found significantly more violent fantasy in the 'hard to manage' group, who were more likely than the control group to have experienced poor parental relationships and an unstable home environment.

what's new?

Rough-and-tumble play

Rough-and-tumble play or play fighting occupies up to 10 per cent of children's time spent in play (Smith, 1998). Until recently however it has attracted relatively little attention from psychologists. Play fighting does not fit neatly into categorisations of play such as that used by Parten, nor is it easily explained by the major theoretical perspectives on play (we shall move on to discuss these shortly on p.74). So what exactly is rough-and-tumble play? It involves grappling and wrestling, chasing and kicking. To adults, this type of behaviour is hard to distinguish from real fighting, and children are often mistakenly disciplined when they play fight. The frequency of rough-and-tumble fighting peaks in middle childhood and is greater in boys than girls (Pellegrini and Smith, 1998).

In spite of its violent appearance, however, play fighting appears to only occasionally lead to real violence, and injuries are rare (Schafer and Smith, 1996). There are unwritten but strict rules governing rough-and-tumble play. Participants laugh frequently in order to signal their friendly intentions and blows either do not land at all or they are 'pulled'. Stronger children frequently take turns to let weaker children win (this is called reversal). Play fights turn into real fights either when one child accidentally hurts another or deliberately breaks the 'rules' and takes advantage of a momentary advantage to hurt the other participant. Pellegrini (1994) investigated individual differences in children's behaviour in rough-and-tumble play and found that rejected children (see p.63 for a discussion) were the most likely to break rules. This appears to show a lack of social skills and may contribute to their rejected status.

Rough-and-tumble play looks violent but relatively rarely leads to real fights

Rough-and-tumble play is apparent in a wide range of human cultures, as well as in many animal species. We may take it then that this type of play has not just resulted from imitation of violent role models, but serves some purpose. The benefits of play fighting include strength and endurance training, learning how to really fight and the establishment of hierarchy of dominant and submissive children. Pellegrini and Smith (1998) reviewed the evidence and concluded that the most important function is probably the latter, and that there is little evidence that rough-and-tumble is important in developing fighting ability. Bjorklund and Brown (1998) have suggested that a further function is to provide a break from the demands of intellectual activity.

where to now?

The following are good sources of further information regarding different types of play:

▶ **Faulkner, D. (1995) Play, self and the social world. In Barnes, P. (ed.)** *Personal, Social and Emotional Development of Children***. Oxford: Blackwell** – a good account of research into a variety of categories of play behaviour.

▶ **Smith, P. (1998) Social development. In Eysenck, M. (ed.)** *Psychology, An Integrated Approach***. Harlow: Longman** – particularly useful account of rough-and-tumble play.

Theories of play

We have already said that some types of play, such as rough-and-tumble play, are not easily explained by major theoretical perspectives. However, bearing that limitation in mind it is still worth looking at two perspectives, each of which probably explains well some of the characteristics and benefits of play. The *cognitive-developmental* perspective sees play as important in facilitating intellectual development, while the emphasis of the *psychodynamic* perspective is on emotional expression in play. You should bear in mind that play is probably important in both these domains and that the two approaches are complementary rather than in competition. It is also worth remembering that there may other functions of play, such as the development of social skills, that are not accounted for by the major theories of play.

The cognitive-developmental perspective on play

The cognitive-developmental perspective on child development is examined more fully in Chapters 6 and 7, and in Jarvis *et al.* (2000) *Angles on psychology*. Briefly though, this approach is concerned with children's intellectual development. The best-known figure in cognitive-developmental psychology is Jean Piaget, and we can begin by looking at his views on play.

Piaget's theory of play

Piaget saw the nature of children's play as developing in line with their general intellectual or cognitive development. He emphasised that children play because they enjoy it rather than in a conscious attempt to promote their intellectual development, but that none the less different forms of play could be linked to the development of cognitive abilities at particular ages. He identified three types of play particularly associated with different ages:

- *Mastery play* (1–2 years) – this is associated with Piaget's sensorimotor stage of development (see p.138 for a discussion), in which the child is beginning to learn about itself and its environment. Mastery play involves imitating, repeating and mastering the actions of other people. The purpose of play at this stage is thus to improve the child's mastery of its own body and behaviour.

- *Play stage* (3–6 years) – this is associated with Piaget's preoperational stage, in which children are developing symbolic thought, i.e. the ability to use symbols such as language to think with, as well as physical actions. At this stage children begin to use objects symbolically, for example toys come to represent other people and objects. Piaget saw this kind of symbolic play as essential for the child to fully develop symbolic thinking.

- *Game stage* (7+) – this is associated with Piaget's concrete and formal operational stages. By the start of the concrete operational stage children have developed intellectually to the point at which they can begin to see things from the perspective of other people. This ability means that they can begin to play successfully together, and co-operative play becomes possible.

Interactive angles

Read at the following examples of play. Which example belongs in which of Piaget's classifications?

1 Having watched a film involving submarines on television, a child takes the cardboard centres of kitchen and toilet rolls and plays with them, pretending they are submarines.

2 A child repeatedly climbs on to a sofa and jumps from it on to the floor (until told off by its exasperated parents).

3 Two children play 'doctors and nurses'. They examine each other using toy stethoscopes.

Piaget's fundamental ideas that the sophistication of play increases with age, and that symbolic play is associated with intellectual development, have largely stood the test of time. Nowak-Fabrykowski (1995) has suggested that playing with letters in the preoperational stage facilitates the development of reading, and that the symbolic use of objects (such as a cardboard box to represent a castle) enhances children's developing creativity. Symbolic play may also be important in helping the child construct their mental representation of the world.

Piaget's idea that co-operative play does not become possible until the child achieves concrete operational thinking does neatly explain why co-operative play is much more common in older children than younger. However, Piaget's ages are probably slightly 'out'. Remember that in Parten's (1932) observation, the majority of children spent most time in co-operative play by the age of 5, well before they reach Piaget's concrete operational stage. Another finding that is rather tricky for Piaget's theory to explain comes from Dunn and Munn (1985), who observed that much younger children (80 per cent of 2 year olds) who received instruction from their older siblings were capable of genuinely co-operative play. This finding is much more easily explained by the approach of another cognitive-developmental psychologist, L.S. Vygotsky.

Vygotsky's theory of play

We shall look in detail at the ideas of Vygotsky in Chapter 7. In brief, however, Vygotsky agreed with Piaget on many points including stages of development. However, he placed a great deal of emphasis on the *zone of proximal development* (ZPD), the gap between what a child can achieve on its own and what it can learn under instruction from an 'expert'. This is rather different from Piaget, who saw children's capabilities as being limited by their developmental stage. Presumably in the Dunn and Munn study, young children who had instruction from older siblings were at the upper end of their ZPD, and so were more advanced than the children observed by Piaget, even though they were at the same stage of development.

Vygotsky saw learning as happening between people rather than taking place in isolation, and that an important part of cognitive development is the taking on board (internalising) of a set of 'tools'. In children's early development the term 'tools' can be taken quite literally. Hayes (1998) gives the example of a child learning that it can make more noise by banging a drum with a spoon than with its hand – the spoon is thus a tool. However, tools also include language, rules and social conventions, which are specific to the culture in which the child grows up. To Vygotsky (1967) play was important because it creates a zone in which children can interact with more expert peers and so internalise these mental tools. Vygotsky (1970) emphasised in particular the importance of rules in play. He suggested that all play has rules, because when a child pretends to be someone else or pretends a toy is something else, then they and their toys have to obey the rules governing those objects or people. Every time the child chooses to restrict its play according to rules, it reinforces its understanding of the rules that govern the world. When an expert peer, such as an older sibling, instructs the child in the rules of a game the child takes on board more rules of its culture.

The influence of Vygotsky's ideas has grown in recent years, and they are widely supported by research. Dunn and Munn's study demonstrates that children who receive expert instruction during their play can advance beyond their stage of cognitive development. This in turn indicates that play is a medium in which children learn from others – the central point of Vygotsky's theory. Vygotsky's ideas are also supported by cross-cultural studies, such as that of Curry and Arnaud (1984), which show that children practise culture-specific roles in their dramatic role-play.

One assumption of Vygotsky's approach (like that of Piaget) that has been challenged, however, is the idea that cognitive development is a generalised phenomenon, and that play assists cognitive development as a whole. Recent research has linked play with specific rather than general aspects of cognitive development, in particular with the development of *theory of mind*.

Play and theory of mind

We shall look in some detail at children's *theory of mind* in Chapters 7 and 11. Despite its slightly confusing name, theory of mind is not a psychological theory. Instead, it refers to the child's individual 'theory' or understanding of other people's minds. The acquisition of a theory of mind is an important part of cognitive development, because it allows the child to understand and so successfully interact with other people. Think back to the Haight and Miller study on p.70. They found that 75 per cent of children's pretend play was with another person. To share a pretend idea requires – and perhaps helps develop – the child's theory of mind. Fonagy *et al.* (1997) have suggested that sharing a pretence during play is a key element in developing an understanding of what others are thinking.

This type of game may help children understand what people are thinking

for and against

cognitive-developmental theories

+ Piaget's theory explains why games become more complex as children get older, and why co-operative play becomes more common than solitary play.

− Piaget's theory does not explain why children with older siblings have more co-operative play than others.

+ Other theories, such as that of Vygotsky, do address the weaknesses of Piaget's explanation.

− Cognitive-developmental theories alone do not explain the emotional significance of play.

The psychodynamic approach to play

In contrast to the cognitive-developmental approach to play, psychodynamic explanations have centred on its emotional significance. From a psychodynamic perspective, play represents conflicts or anxieties that the child is working through. We have already looked at First's (1994) study of the 'leaving game'. In the leaving game children and their primary carers act out a sequence of leaving one another, the left partner pretending to cry. What might be the emotional significance of such a game? Two year olds are firmly attached to their primary carer (although of course they may have other attachments as well), and a feature of attachment is distress at being separated from the attachment figure. Two year olds have virtually all experienced some separation from their primary carer and been distressed by the experience. A psychodynamic explanation of the leaving game might thus be that it represents the child's expression of its distress when left.

Freud's theory of play

The psychodynamic study of play began with an observational study by Freud (1922) of an 18-month-old boy. The boy would throw all his toys as far away as possible while saying 'o-o-o-oh', which according to his mother meant 'go away'. He then threw a wooden reel over the side of the cot by the string, saying again 'o-o-o-oh', then pulled it back into view by the string, expressing great pleasure at its return. This pattern of behaviour was repeated frequently. Freud interpreted this game as representing the departure and return of the child's mother. A year later, at the age of 30 months, the child would say 'go to war' while throwing the reel away. The reel represented the parents, initially the mother and later the father, who could be made in pretend to leave and return *under the control of the child*. Based on this case, Freud proposed that children have a *power instinct*, i.e. a wish to be in control of events, and that play provides this sense of feeling in control. Freud introduced the idea of a *compulsion to repeat* traumatic experiences, in dreams and in play, and so gain mastery over negative events.

Studies of the emotional significance of play

Looking at the classic studies of Freud (1922) and First (1994), we can begin to appreciate both the necessity and the difficulties in adopting a psychodynamic approach to play. It seems extremely likely that, given the emotional nature of children, play does serve some emotional as well as intellectual function. So Freud's explanation seems credible, but it is also highly *speculative*, i.e. the logical link between Freud's observations and his theory are not obvious, and there are numerous other possible explanations for the child's play with the reel of string. Freud himself conceded that looking at 'a single case of this kind yields no sure conclusion' (1922:14). So is there more scientific evidence to support the idea that play can be a way of mastering negative feelings? Experimental studies are limited by ethical considerations – clearly we can't deliberately traumatise children just to see what will happen to their play. However, there have been some ingenious studies in order to get around this problem. Barnett (1984) used a naturally occurring situation of high anxiety – children's first day at nursery school – to test the effects of play on anxiety. Children were individually assessed for their level of anxiety by measuring their galvanic skin response (how sweaty they became). They were then assigned to two groups, one of which listened to stories while the other group had free play. It was found that the anxiety levels of the high- anxiety children declined much more in free play than in listening to stories, and that the high-anxiety children in free play had spent significantly more time in pretend play than low-anxiety children. This study clearly demonstrates that pretend play serves a role in the reduction of anxiety.

In a more recent study by Watson (1994), 18 children aged between 4 and 6 years were told the story of Hansel and Gretel individually in their day-care centres. Recorded sound effects were used to add to the anxiety-inducing effect of the story. Children were rated as low, medium or high anxiety according to their posture, expression and speech. They were then left alone in the room and invited to play with their choice of toys. The toys had been selected so that children had a choice between sets of toys related and unrelated to the Hansel and Gretel story. A strong correlation (0.81) emerged between the anxiety of the child as assessed while listening to the story, and the correspondence between play and the story.

Warren *et al.* (2000) investigated whether the anxieties expressed in the play of 35 children aged 5 corresponded with anxiety-related behaviour. Play was observed and recorded in themes of negative expectations of self, others and experiences. Parents and teachers completed an assessment of the children's behaviour at same the time and again a year later. The themes expressed in play were strongly predictive of children's anxiety at home and school. This study indicates that the systematic analysis of children's play can be a good indicator of likely anxiety-related problems later.

These studies clearly show us that play is of emotional significance to children, as well as being a medium of intellectual development. This is supportive of Freud's approach, fitting in well with both a compulsion to repeat negative experiences and an attempt to gain mastery over negative events. Of course there may be reasons other than those suggested by Freud to explain why play has emotional significance.

A further way of investigating the emotional significance of play comes from studies of play therapy, in which children who have suffered trauma can use play in the presence of a therapist in order to work through the trauma and gain mastery over the event. It is to this area that we now turn.

where to
now?

The following is a good source of further information regarding theories of play:

▷ **Slade, A. and Wolf, D.P. (eds) (1994)** *Children at Play: clinical and developmental approaches to meaning and representation*. **Oxford: Oxford University Press** – reports a selection of studies primarily relevant to understanding the relationship between play and emotional development.

The therapeutic value of play

We have already looked at the way in which children express and master difficult feelings. Play is thus therapeutic in itself. It follows, then, that play can be a useful tool in psychological therapies, predominantly though not exclusively with children. Play can be used in several approaches to psychotherapy, but in this chapter we will concentrate on the psychodynamic approach to child psychotherapy. Central to the psychodynamic treatment of children is the Freudian idea that children play in order to master their negative emotions, such as anxiety or anger. Play can also serve to communicate feelings. Children may lack the ability of older people to talk about the things that are on their minds, but they can express themselves through play, and a therapist can pick up much information about a child's state of mind from the child's play.

A fascinating and touching example of this type of communication comes from Hobson (1985). Hobson was having trouble getting Stephen, a 15-year-old boy, to talk until he began a game called the squiggle. Hobson drew a squiggle and asked Stephen to add to it. Stephen drew a small boat, turning the squiggle into a large wave. Hobson drew a pier and Stephen added a waving figure to the boat. Knowing that Stephen had been traumatised by a separation from his mother Hobson drew a waving woman on the pier. Stephen drew rain across the whole picture, indicating sadness.

Hobson's case example illustrates the usefulness of a play technique in communicating with a reluctant young person. However, you can also see that it is an intensely *subjective* process, i.e. it relies on the individual interpretations of a therapist. This subjectivity raises the hackles of many psychologists who are committed to a more scientific approach.

In adult psychodynamic therapies, patients are encouraged to *free associate*, i.e. to say whatever comes into their minds in the belief that this will lead them to bring up things that are bothering them. In child psychotherapy 'free play' can take the place of free association, as

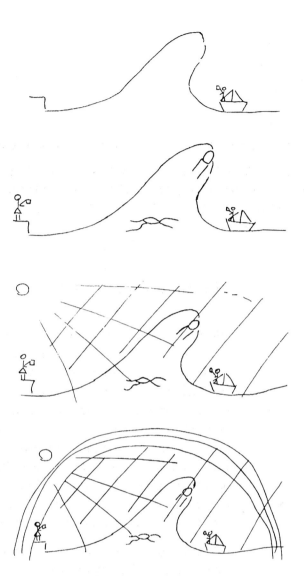

Four scenes from the squiggle
game. From Hobson (1985)

children with a problem who are left to play without direction will tend
to express and explore that problem in their play.

The nature of a child's play can initially be a source of information with
which the therapist can assess the child's psychological state. Parsons
(1999) described the case of Mary, an 8-year-old girl who played with toy
animals in her first therapy session. She began to put up toy fences around
the animals. The therapist commented on the fact that the animals were
fenced in, whereupon Mary enacted a furious fight between lions and
tigers. The therapist judged that Mary was an angry child, but had been
hiding her aggressive feelings. The fences symbolised the way in which
she had been keeping her anger trapped inside herself and the battle
symbolised the hidden feelings.

In another case, Melzak (1999) described the case of Pascal, a refugee
whose father had just died a political prisoner in Zaire. Pascal repeatedly

played out fantasies with dolls, puppets or plasticine figures, all of which ended in death and destruction. Each 'death' was accompanied by a 'shrug of inevitability'. The therapist's interventions involved reminding Pascal that not all stories had to end in death and that real men (like his father) are not superheroes and can be killed. After a year of therapy in which the violent games continued, Pascal accepted what the therapist said and his violent games ceased. Only at that point did he begin to mourn the death of his father. Perhaps the most famous case in child psychotherapy comes from Axline (1947), who described the case of Dibs.

classic research

the case of Dibs

Axline, V.M. (1947) *Dibs in Search of Self.* London: Penguin.

Background: At the age of 5 years Dibs was referred to Axline, a clinical psychologist specialising in play therapy, for very disturbed behaviour. At school Dibs would play alone and bite and scratch other children when they tried to interact with him. He would violently resist any attempt to take him home from school. Dibs's father was a successful scientist and his mother was a surgeon, who had given up her job when Dibs was born. Both parents believed that Dibs was suffering from brain damage or retardation. Adults who worked with him at school, however, suspected that his problems were emotional in origin.

The therapy: In the first session Dibs painted. At this point he revealed for the first time that he could read by reading out the labels of different paints. He was very reluctant to leave the session. The following week Dibs played with a doll's house and closed all the shutters and doors, then drew a lock on the front door. He commented 'A lock that locks tight with a key, and high hard walls. And a door. A locked door' (p.42). Axline noted that Dibs was concerned with locked doors. Dibs then played with finger paint, but commented 'Oh come away Dibs. It is a very silly kind of paint. Come away!' (p.44). In another session shortly after this Dibs commented that he was glad to come to therapy but sad to leave the therapy room. When Axline asked him if he took any of the gladness with him he responded by burying three toy soldiers in sand and saying 'This makes them unhappy. They cannot see. They cannot hear' (p.67). He dug them up but said of one 'this is papa' and punched it to the ground repeatedly.

By now you might have picked up some of what Dibs was feeling. Being locked up seemed to be an issue, and Dibs was clearly very angry with his father. Dibs's father picked him up that day, and was obviously embarrassed by Dibs, saying 'can't you stop that senseless jabber?' when Dibs tried to speak to him. The next day Dibs's mother came to see Axline and told her how, when they got home after the therapy Dibs's father had commented that Dibs was 'babbling like an idiot', whereupon Dibs had attacked him and been locked in his room. Dibs's mother then confessed that Dibs's birth had been accidental and that it had ruined her career and angered her husband. They had both resented Dibs, and found it difficult to relate to him. A week later Dibs took down the locked front door to the doll's house. He sang 'I hate the walls and the doors that lock and the people that shove you in. I hate the tears and the angry words and I'll kill them all with my hatchet and hammer their bones and spit on them' (p.85). Here Dibs appears to be expressing his anger; whether towards just his father or to both parents is unclear. In taking down the front door of the doll's house it seems that he may have been, in Freud's terms, mastering his feelings about being locked up. Note also the clarity of expression from a 5 year old who had been considered brain-damaged or retarded only a few weeks before.

During the period of Dibs's therapy his behaviour at school gradually improved. He would speak to his teachers and he even began to show some interest in other children. However he still had a lot of anger towards his father. In one session Dibs asked to play in Axline's office rather than the play room. He dictated into her tape recorder; 'Once upon a time there was a boy who lived in a big house with his mother and father and sister. And one day the father came home to his study and the boy went in without knocking. "You are mean man" the boy cried "I hate you. I hate you. Do you hear me I hate you." And the father began to cry. "Please" he said, "I'm sorry for everything I did. Please don't hate me!" (p.159). Dibs had feared his father, but it seems that he was now overcoming that fear, using fantasy play. Outside the therapy Dibs's relationship with his father improved. A week after therapy finished Dibs's IQ was tested and he scored 168, in the top 1 per cent of the population. By then he had no emotional difficulties.

Research into play and therapy

We have already looked at the case of Dibs, who showed remarkable improvements in his emotional state following play therapy. However case-studies alone are not enough of a basis on which to judge the effectiveness of play therapy, because we cannot know for certain that Dibs's improvement was a direct result of the therapy, or that he would not have got better over time without intervention. There is, however, a body of more systematic research into the therapeutic value of play that has painted a broadly positive picture. Fonagy and Target (1994) examined the records of approximately 800 children treated psychoanalytically at the Anna Freud centre in London for anxiety and depression. Most treatments lasted between one and two years. Over 80 per cent of the children were completely free of symptoms at the end of the therapy. Of course child psychotherapy consists of more than play, and studies like this do not really demonstrate that play *per se* is therapeutic. However, other studies have looked more specifically at the effects of play therapy. LeBlanc (1999) performed a *meta-analysis* on a large number of studies of different techniques used in therapy with children. Meta-analysis involves combining the results of several past studies weighting the results of each study according to the sample size. He concluded that the use of play was associated with a moderate but consistent improvement in the effectiveness of therapy with children.

Other studies have looked at the impact of therapy based exclusively or almost exclusively on play as opposed to psychotherapy involving play as one of several techniques. Sloan (1999) examined whether play therapy could be used to reduce aggressive behaviour in children. Twenty-two children from New York State referred for aggressive behaviour were allocated to one of two conditions. In one condition, play therapy involving aggressive games was used. In the other condition more usual non-aggressive play therapy was used. After 10 sessions the children in both groups experienced a significant decline in aggressive behaviour. This suggests that play therapy is effective for reducing aggression, irrespective of whether it involves aggressive activities.

for and against

psychodynamic explanations

+ There is ample evidence for the emotional significance of play. Play can be used to predict children's later anxieties.

+ Play can be used therapeutically with great effect.

– Psychodynamic theory alone does not satisfactorily explain the significance of play to cognitive development.

where to now?

The following are good sources of information on the therapeutic value of play:

▶ **Axline, V. M. (1947)** *Dibs in Search of Self*. **London: Penguin** – an absolutely fascinating and touching case study. Don't read it in public if you want to look hard though – it will make you cry!

▶ **Sylva, K. (1994) The therapeutic value of play.** *Psychology Review* **1** – a clear and simple overview of the therapeutic use of play.

▶ **Lanyado, M. and Horne, A. (1999)** *The Handbook of Child and Adolescent Psychotherapy*. **London: Routledge** – contains a number of case studies and a particularly useful chapter on research findings on the effectiveness of psychodynamic interventions with children, including the use of play.

Conclusions

Both friendship and play appear to be important aspects of children's development. Children's popularity is affected by a number of factors including physical attractiveness and social skills. Attachment type is associated with popularity and with bullying behaviour. Both popularity and the successful formation of friendships are associated with benefits in social and cognitive development. Play includes a number of different activities. Different types of play are associated with different ages. There are also some sex differences, with boys spending more time in rough-and-tumble play. There are two particularly important theoretical perspectives on play. The cognitive-developmental approach, particularly associated with the theories of Piaget and Vygotsky, sees play as important in facilitating children's intellectual development. The psychodynamic approach, particularly associated with the work of Freud, places more emphasis on the emotional significance of play. Building upon the work of Freud, therapists successfully use play to help children express and master emotions.

what do you know?

1 What are horizontal and vertical changes in children's friendships? Give examples of each.

2 What is sociometric status? Outline one way in which sociometric status can be classified.

3 Outline one study into the benefits of either popularity or friendship in childhood.

4 Outline one way of classifying children's play.

5 What factors affect the content of children's pretend play?

6 Describe one theory of play.

7 How can play be used in a therapeutic setting?

5

The development of identity: self and gender

A major aspect of our social development in childhood is our perception of ourselves. Individuals' awareness of their unique perspective and characteristics make up their *self-concept*. We all have an intuitive sense of a 'self', but this is hard to describe to others, and it is very difficult to study the self as a psychological entity. In this chapter we will be looking at some major views on the self, and looking closely at the importance of *self-esteem*, i.e. how much we like ourselves. We can look in particular at what factors affect our self-esteem. An important aspect of our self-concept is our gender. The origins of our gender identity are an ongoing controversy in psychology and we can examine four broad theoretical perspectives that have explained how children acquire their gender identity in different ways: biological approaches, cognitive-developmental approach, social learning theory and psychodynamic approaches.

What is the self?

The earliest psychological perspective on the self-concept came from the philosopher and psychologist William James, often called the 'father of modern psychology'. James (1892) distinguished the 'self-as-knower' or 'I' and the 'self-as-known' or 'me'. James wrote thus:

> *Whatever I may be thinking of, I am always at the same time more or less aware of myself, of my personal existence. At the same time it is I*

who am aware; so the total self of me, partly known and partly knower, partly object and partly subject, must have two aspects discriminated in it, of which for shortness we may call one the 'me' and the other 'I'.
(James 1892:176)

James went on to describe the *self as known* or 'me' in detail. This aspect of the self contains the details that are known about the self. This includes the *material self* – comprising knowledge of physique, possessions etc., the *social self* – comprising knowledge of behaviour, reputation etc., and the *spiritual self* – comprising what is now called *metacognition*, knowledge concerning personal knowledge, thinking and memory.

James also attempted to describe the *self as knower* or 'I' (corresponding to Freud's 'I' or ego, see p.2), although he despaired of studying this aspect of the self scientifically. James described four aspects to the *self as knower*:

● awareness of one's power to act in events

● awareness of one's own uniqueness

● awareness of the continuity of one's existence

● awareness of one's own awareness.

Children are fascinated when adults imitate them

Lewis (1990) renamed the two aspects of self-concept identified by James as the *categorical self*, i.e. the self as known and the *existential self*, i.e. the self as knower. While contemporary studies of the categorical self abound, modern psychology still finds the existential self extremely resistant to empirical research. However, Meltzoff (1990) provided evidence that infants enjoy imitating others, and are fascinated at being imitated, implying that they are seeking knowledge of their ability to impact on the world. In Meltzoff's study a 14-month-old child was sat at a table opposite two adults. The child and each adult held an identical toy. One of the adults imitated the child's movements precisely, while the other moved the toy independently of the child's actions. The infant looked more and smiled more at the imitating adult.

Miell (1995) suggests that the first stage of development of the self-concept is establishing that the individual does, in fact, exist. Once this existential self is established the child starts to place itself in categories, e.g. gender, name, size. The number and sophistication of these categories increases with maturity and experience.

Neisser (1988) has produced a new and more sophisticated approach to describing the self, incorporating aspects of the existential and categorical self. According to Neisser we experience the self in five ways:

● the *ecological self* is experienced in relation to the physical environment – 'I am the person in this place, engaged in this particular activity'

- the *interpersonal self* is experienced in relation to others – 'I am the person who is engaged here, in this particular human interchange'

- the *extended self* is experienced as memories of the self in the past and anticipation of the self in the future

- the *private self* is experienced as awareness of one's separateness and uniqueness, appearing in childhood when the individual realises that it is separate and does not share all experience with others

- the *conceptual self* is experienced in relation to cultural beliefs about the individual. Thus the self is experienced in relation to social roles, religious conceptions of a soul, psychological conceptions of a brain, mind and unconscious and in relation to social dimensions, e.g. intelligence, attractiveness and wealth.

The way in which the self is perceived at any moment depends on the situation. When one is socially engaged for example, the interpersonal self is momentarily the dominant experience. We are not aware of the simultaneous existence of multiple selves because all are located in the same place and engaged in the same activities.

Interactive angles

Questions

1 Think of yourself for a moment. What could you say about yourself in each of Neisser's five self experiences?

2 Which of Neisser's five selves fit into James's existential self and which fit more neatly into the categorical self? Are there any which don't seem to fit either self particularly neatly?

The emergence of the existential self

Psychodynamic theorists have addressed the ambitious question of the emergence of the existential self. Psychodynamic writers have theorised on the experience of recognising oneself as a separate individual. Freud (1921) proposed we begin life in a state of *autoeroticism* where there is no differentiation between the self and the outside world. From this we progress to a state of *narcissism*. This is the earliest state of self-awareness, characterised by the perception of the self as omnipotent. The mother is seen as part of the self at this stage. Normally we differentiate ourselves from the mother to develop a full existential self. However a minority remain fixated at this stage – *the narcissistic personality*. This state is characterised by an inability to appreciate others except for what they can do for the individual.

Mahler (1968) has developed the Freudian idea of a shift towards differentiating the self from others. According to Mahler we experience the first month of life in a state of *normal autism*, in which we are shut off from the outside world, engrossed in our own needs and sensations. By the second month the infant recognises the existence of the mother as a separate object, but she is seen initially purely as a means of satisfying needs. Although the mother is now seen as a separate physical object the infant cannot conceive of her having separate thoughts. By the end of the first year the infant is fully aware of its own uniqueness and separateness.

As Damon (1983) says, psychodynamic writings are useful in bringing home to us the formidable task of separating from caregivers. Of course this approach is speculative and we know relatively little about what infants really experience. There is little empirical support for the psychodynamic view of individuation, but this is due to methodological difficulties rather than shortcomings of the theory. In the absence of evidence to the contrary psychodynamic views of individuation remain credible accounts of children's experience of discovering their existential self.

Self-esteem

One of the most important aspects of our developing self-concept is our self-esteem, i.e. the extent to which we (as the existential self) like what we know of our categorical self. A large body of research has revealed that low self-esteem appears to cause difficulties for children. Olmstead (1991) found that low self-esteem is associated with loneliness. Pillow *et al.* (1991) found that those with low self-esteem are more likely to suffer depression. Thus high-esteem individuals are likely to be happy and socially fulfilled.

Rogers's theory of self-esteem

Possibly the most famous and influential theory of self-concept development is that of Carl Rogers (1961). According to Rogers, we hold an image of ourselves as we are and an image of our *ideal-self*, i.e. how we would really like to be. If the two images are *congruent*, i.e. the same, we will develop good self-esteem. The development of this congruence and the resultant self-esteem is dependent on two factors, *unconditional positive regard* from others – in the form of love and affection – and *self-actualisation* – fulfilling our potential and achieving all that we are capable of. These two factors are inter-related. Without a degree of positive regard we cannot self-actualise. However, on some occasions we cannot self-actualise because the achievements necessary for this would endanger our positive regard from others, for example if our ambitions lead us to morally dubious actions.

Some children lack unconditional positive regard from others in childhood due to harsh, inattentive parenting or parenting characterised by conditional love, i.e. love which is only available if the child conforms to certain conditions. Such individuals are likely to have low self-esteem as adults, and are thus vulnerable to mental disorder, especially depression. Rogers developed a form of therapy designed to 'reparent' individuals, giving them unconditional positive regard in order to foster their self-actualisation (see *Angles on Atypical Psychology*, in this series).

There is considerable support for the central ideas of Rogers's theory, i.e. that self-esteem is crucial to our well-being and that unconditional positive regard in parenting is important for the development of high self-esteem. In a classic study Coopersmith (1967) demonstrated both the importance of self-esteem for development and the importance of unconditional positive regard in development of self-esteem.

classic
research

it's important to like ourselves!

Coopersmith, S. (1967) *The Antecedents of Self-esteem*. San Francisco: Freeman.

Aim: Coopersmith was interested in the importance of self-esteem in child development. He aimed to learn about both what effects having high or low self-esteem might have on a child and about what factors might determine a child's individual level of self-esteem.

Method: Coopersmith studied several hundred white, middle-class boys of 9 to 10 years old. He used four measures to establish the self-esteem of each boy. These were a psychometric test called the *Self Esteem Inventory*, teachers' estimates of how well the boys reacted to failure, a test called the *Thematic Apperception Test* (in which pictures are presented and participants say what they think is happening) and assessment of their confidence in an unfamiliar situation. On the basis of these measures, Coopersmith divided the boys into groups of high, middle and low self-esteem. He then looked at the characteristics of the boys in each group, including their confidence, ability to take criticism, popularity and academic success. Coopersmith also went on to investigate the types of upbringing the children had had, using questionnaires and in-depth interviews with both the boys and their mothers.

Results: Distinct differences emerged between the groups. High self-esteem boys were most expressive and active. They were the most successful and confident group, both academically and socially. The middle group were the most conforming. The low self-esteem children were the lowest achievers and tended to under-rate themselves. They were the most socially isolated group, self-conscious and sensitive to criticism. Coopersmith found that parenting style was very significant. High self-esteem children had plenty of positive regard from parents, but they also had firm boundaries on acceptable behaviour. Low self-esteem appeared to follow harsh or unloving parenting or lack of behavioural restrictions. Coopersmith followed up the boys into adulthood and found that the high-esteem group remained more successful in terms of work and relationships.

Conclusion: The Coopersmith study clearly supports Rogers's ideas, both that self-esteem is important for healthy psychological development and that positive regard from parents is a major factor in the development of self-esteem. However, Coopersmith also found that firm boundaries in behaviour laid down by parents predicted high self-esteem and this is perhaps less in keeping with Rogers's ideas.

Although Coopersmith's findings are widely accepted in showing the importance of self-esteem, he has been criticised on the choice of only white, middle-class boys as participants. We cannot assume from Coopersmith's study that different cultures create self-esteem in the same way, that girls develop self-esteem in the same ways as boys or that the same factors are important in different socio-economic groups. Moreover, as Pilgrim (1992) points out Rogers's theory is firmly centred in post-war America, where there was a cultural emphasis on achievement, hence the theoretical emphasis on self-actualisation. Thus, some aspects of Rogers's theory are culture-bound and not readily applied to other societies and historical periods. In addition ideas like 'ideal self' and 'congruence' are vague and difficult to study.

Other factors affecting self-concept

There is little doubt that parenting is a major – possibly the single most important – factor in the development of self-concept in young children. However, children spend an increasing amount of time in the education system, where they have to deal with their peers and other adults. Once in full-time education, children are placed in situations of competition with their peers, and consistent success or failure in this competition can affect self-esteem. In the light of this it is perhaps not surprising that academic and sporting achievement – the two areas in which children are regularly required to compete – have been linked to self-esteem.

Academic achievement

A number of studies have shown that children who do well at school tend to have more positive self-concepts than those who have difficulties in their studies. There is, however, something of a chicken-and-egg problem in deciding whether self-concept affects learning or whether success in academic achievement affects self-concept. Chapman and Tunmer (1997) tested this in a study of 112 5-year-old children starting school. Academic self-concept and reading ability were assessed several times over a 2½-year period and cross-lagged correlations were performed. This means that relationships between early self-concept and later reading ability, and between early reading ability and later self-concept were calculated. The stronger relationship emerged between early reading ability and later self-concept, demonstrating that success at school is an important factor in children's developing self-concept. However, in another cross-lagged study, Coon-Carty (1998) found the opposite effect, that early self-concept has a strong effect on later reading ability. You should note that in both these studies there were relationships in both directions, i.e. self-concept influences reading ability *and* reading ability influences self-concept. Academic achievement is thus both a factor in and a result of self-concept.

An interesting question regarding the relationship between success at school and self-concept is whether children's self-concept becomes healthier if they stand out from their peers, i.e. they are a big fish in a little pond (this is called the big fish little pond effect or BFLPE), or whether they may actually fare better as an average student in an elite group of peers. This is obviously important for parents of gifted children who have to decide whether to put their child in a mainstream school where they will stand out or enrol them in a more academic institution where their peers will be as bright as they are and where teaching can be geared to the high ability of the children. Common sense supports the latter course of action. Zeidner and Schleyer (1999) tested the big fish little pond effect in 1,020 gifted 9 to 12 year olds. Half were enrolled in mixed ability classes and half were in special classes for high ability children. Anxiety before tests, overall achievement and self-concept were compared in the two groups. Self-concept and performance were better and test anxiety lower in the mixed ability classes, supporting the idea that children do better as big fish in small ponds.

Physical development

In Chapter 4 on children's friendships we saw that sporting prowess is one of the most important influences on children's popularity. It is thus perhaps not surprising that children's self-concept can be affected by their perception of their bodies and physical abilities. In a questionnaire study by Guiney and Furlong (1999), for example, a positive correlation emerged between body satisfaction and self-concept in 8- to 13-year-old girls. This has led to attempts to improve children's self-concept by deliberately altering their body type. However, there is considerable doubt as to whether this approach works. Cameron (1999) measured self-esteem before and after a weight-control programme in 49 obese 10 to 15 year olds and found that it declined significantly. In another study Faigenbaum *et al.* (1997) found that, despite significant increases in physical abilities, an 8-week strength-training programme had no effect on the self-concept of 11 boys and 4 girls aged 7 to 12.

Culture

All the views of the self-concept we have looked at so far in this chapter make the assumption that everybody goes through the same experience of recognising their individual and unique existence and compiling information about the self. However, this assumption is *ethnocentric*, i.e. it views the issue from a purely European-American perspective and does not take account of variations between cultures. There appear to be significant cultural variations in the way the 'self' is perceived. Even the European-American assumption that the individual is the basic unit of humanity appears not be universal (Geertz, 1984). Cush (1993) describes the Therevada Buddhist view that there are no individuals and we are all merely parts of the Universe.

An important distinction has been made (Triandis, 1991) between *collectivist* and *individualist* cultures. In high individualist cultures such as Britain and America the basic unit of humanity is seen as the individual person, and accordingly we place great emphasis on ourselves as individuals. Other, more collectivist societies see groups such as the family or community as the basic human unit, and are more reluctant to see themselves primarily as individuals. This phenomenon was discovered accidentally when Greenfield (1966) tested children from the Wolof tribe of Senegal on Piagetian conservation tasks (see p.135 for a discussion of conservation tasks). He found that although they performed well on the tasks, they had difficulty with questions such as 'Which do *you* think is true?'. Greenfield came to believe that the word 'you' said to a single person held no meaning for this close community, and hence that to this highly collectivist community the individual was not the basic unit of humanity.

Mbiti (1970) describes the 'collective self' of African philosophy. The *collective self* does not imply that individuals do not have unique thoughts and feelings, merely that they cannot conceive of the individual without the context of the group (Hayes, 1994). Van den Heuven *et al.* (1992) investigated differences between ethnic groups living in a Western city. They asked Dutch, Turkish and Moroccan children living in Holland for self-descriptions. Although the Moroccan and Turkish children did have an awareness of themselves as individuals, a much higher number of their self-statements focused on their families and communities.

The following are good sources of further information about the development of the self-concept:

▶ **Miell, D. (1995) Developing a sense of self. In Barnes, P. (ed.)** *Personal, Social and Emotional Development of Children*. **Oxford: Blackwell** – an excellent chapter looking in three parts at the development of the existential self, self-esteem and the development of gender identity.

▶ **Schaffer, H.R. (1996)** *Social Development*. **Oxford: Blackwell** – contains a good chapter on the development of self-concept. Has a particularly useful section on self-concept in abused children.

Gender development

If you are reading this chapter in a psychology classroom or lecture theatre, I wouldn't be surprised to find that just reading the title of this section has already sparked off an argument. The issues addressed in this chapter are matters of great public interest and debate – if you could listen in on every conversation in a pub or restaurant simultaneously you would probably find at least one couple or group discussing how different men and women really are, and why these differences exist. These issues have been equally intriguing for psychologists and a number of approaches have been proposed to explain gender differences. Before we look at these, however, it is worth taking some time to look at exactly what we mean when we use terms like *sex*, *gender* and *gender identity*.

Sex and gender

It is important to understand that some writers make a distinction between sex and gender. Most psychologists investigating differences between males and females or seeking to explain how these differences came about have referred to *sex differences*. However, as Brannon (1996) points out, this is somewhat controversial. The term 'sex' normally refers to biologically based characteristics. To use the term 'sex' in psychological research is therefore to support the idea that differences between males and females are biological in origin. Unger (1979) proposed an alternative term *gender*. 'Gender' refers to the socially constructed identity of males and females. Not all writers support Unger's distinction between sex and gender. However, to avoid any possible bias in favour of the idea that differences between males and females are biological in origin, this chapter will use the term 'gender' except where biological differences are the topic of discussion.

The appearance of gender identity

As Miell (1995) has identified, an appreciation of one's own gender forms a major part of one's sense of identity. As children develop a categorical self one of the earliest categories into which they fit themselves is male or female. *Gender identity* thus refers to the individual's personal perception of their gender. Primitive gender awareness is present from a young age. Leinbach and Fagot (1993) found that infants as young as 9 months could distinguish between pictures of males and females. Brannon (1996) suggests that true gender identity involves being able to label the genders. This can be clearly seen by 2 to 3 years. Gottman (1986) observed that by 3 years children could consistently identify peers as male or female and show a preference for same-sex companions. It is generally assumed that *gender identity* as distinct from *gender characteristics* is socially determined. In a study by Dunn and Kendrick (1982) for example, it was found that parents continually emphasise the child's gender during family discussions and games, providing information from which gender identity is constructed.

Differences between males and females

There has been a huge amount of research into psychological differences between males and females – indeed this has been one of the fundamental questions addressed by psychology. Maccoby and Jacklin (1974) carried out one of the largest reviews of studies to see whether gender stereotypes (i.e. popular views of gender characteristics) are borne out by reality. They found that some popular stereotypes hold true but others do not. Their work has been continued and refined over the last 20 years. Gender differences have been examined over three broad areas; cognitive abilities, emotional responses and social behaviour.

Differences in cognitive abilities

A popular stereotype is that boys are better than girls at maths. Hyde *et al.* (1990) conducted a *meta-analysis* of previous studies of gender differences in mathematical abilities. *Meta-analysis* involves combining the results of several past studies weighting the results of each study according to the sample size. Hyde found that overall females came out as slightly better, an exception being that in adolescence boys emerged as superior in problem-solving tasks. Several studies have shown boys to be better at some though not all spatial tasks. Robert (1990) tested boys and girls on Piaget's water conservation task and found that boys emerged slightly but consistently superior. A further popular stereotype concerns linguistic abilities. Some early studies suggested female superiority, although results were mixed. Hyde and Linn (1988) performed a meta-analytic study and found no overall gender difference.

Differences in emotionality

A popular stereotype suggests that females are more 'emotional' than males. This vague notion needs clarifying. Brody (1993) examined the proposal of greater emotional expressiveness in females and found that expressiveness is greater for emotions stereotypically associated with each gender. Thus women show more fear, hurt, warmth and embarrassment, whereas men show more pride and anger. A more fundamental question is whether females *feel* more emotion than males. Zahn-Waxler *et al.* (1994) presented 4-year-old children with hypothetical social conflicts and found that girls became angrier than boys, suggesting greater emotionality. Women are considerably more prone to depression (Nolen-Hoeksema 1990), also suggesting greater emotionality.

Differences in social behaviour

It is generally believed that men are more aggressive than women. Certainly this is true if one takes aggression to mean of the *physical* kind, although differences are smaller than might be imagined. Lauer (1992) found that on average boys showed more aggressive behaviour than did girls although there was greater variance within each gender than between them. In the Zahn-Waxler *et al.* (1994) study (see above), although girls became more angry than boys, they responded less aggressively. Bjorkvist *et al.* (1992) investigated indirect aggression – deliberate exclusion from activities, gossip etc. and found that, based on peer estimates, girls from the age of 11 years onwards were rated higher than boys. It appears then that the nature of aggression is *qualitatively different* in nature between genders as opposed to simply more prevalent in one gender.

The question of bias in research

Gender appears to be one of those areas in psychology – like religion – where researchers tend to be powerfully influenced by their own views. Hyde and Lynn (1988), in their meta-analysis of research into gender differences in linguistic ability, found that all studies showing female superiority were written by female researchers and all those showing no difference or male superiority were written by men. This does not cast doubt on the integrity of the research but it does raise the point that when dealing with emotive issues such as gender differences there are few hard facts.

media watch

Boys will be boys?

Fundamentally, kids do not change from one generation to the next. Boys love football and girls want to be pop stars – so what's new? A recent survey shows that the modern age throws up some interesting differences in the detail.

Fox Kids, a children's cable and satellite channel, commissioned a poll of 1,000 children aged seven to 14 which asked a variety of questions about their loves and hates. Forget the predictable stuff about the Spice Girls, and just look at the boys' interest in clothes!

Boys of seven to 14, says the survey, would prefer Armani to Levis. Furthermore, boys of 13 to 14 know more about Armani and Ralph Lauren than girls of their age. What is going on here?

Completely surprising, given our poor performance in international league tables, was the favourite school subject – mathematics. For girls, mathematics was the overall favourite, followed by English, while for boys it was second – after sport.

But most things do not change. Many more girls wanted to be teachers, nurses and vets than boys. No girls wanted to be car mechanics, in the armed forces, engineers or carpenters. Yet there is progress – equal numbers of girls and boys wanted to be lawyers and doctors

The Guardian, 21 October 1997

Questions

1 What would you conclude about the changes in gender roles in recent generations reported here? How much has really changed?

2 What implications do you see for future changes in society if differences in gender roles do become less?

Theories of gender development

Gender forms one of the major battlegrounds of the *nature–nurture debate* in psychology. Biological (nature) theories explain differences between genders in physical terms, i.e. they propose that gender differences are due to *sex* differences. By contrast cognitive-developmental and social learning theories constitute the nurture side of the argument, proposing that gender characteristics are acquired as a result of the environment. Psychodynamic theories emphasise the importance of both nature and nurture.

Biological theories of gender

Biological theories emphasise the role of genetic and physiological factors on gender development. The psychological environment is seen as playing a minimal role in the development of gender. This approach to gender differentiation focuses on the biological differences between the sexes and proposes that these physiological differences may be the root of gender differences. Whereas we can be reasonably sure that the reasons why men have deeper voices and greater muscle mass than women are biological, the picture becomes much more confused when we look at *psychological* differences between men and women, for example in emotionality or aggression.

Recent technological developments have allowed us directly to compare the operation of the brains of men and women. Shaywitz *et al.* (1995) used a scanning technique called *functional magnetic resonance imaging* (FMRI) to compare activity by different regions of the brain in 19 men and 19 women during a variety of language tasks, which included identifying rhyming words and upper and lower case letters, and understanding word-meanings. No sex differences in brain function emerged when participants were performing word-meaning tasks, nor did any overall sex difference in ability emerge. However, different regions of the brain were activated during the rhyming task. This indicates that in some ways, males and females do deal differently on a physiological level with some aspects of language.

Assuming that there are physiological differences between brain function in males and females, this alone does not tell us the origins of these differences. We know that hormones are involved in organising differentiation between the sexes in the womb, and there is some evidence that hormone levels are associated with differences in cognitive abilities between men and women. Men are traditionally held to be better at spatial tasks. Kimura (1996) looked at the levels of testosterone (a hormone found in higher levels in men than women and associated with sexual development in men) in women and found that women with high levels of testosterone performed better in spatial tasks. This type of study implies that men and women have different abilities as a function of their differing hormone levels.

Animal studies have shown that altering sex-hormone levels in young animals can affect their behaviour. Young *et al.* (1964) injected testosterone into pregnant monkeys. Female offspring displayed male characteristics such as rough-and-tumble play. Follow-ups in which testosterone was added after birth found females who became more assertive and some of which took control of their troop.

Clearly there are ethical constraints that prevent this type of experimentation being carried out on humans. However, there are case studies of children who have been brought up as the opposite gender from their original sex. Money and Erhardt (1972) reported one such case. They

Female monkeys given male hormones before birth engage in more rough-and-tumble play

followed the case of a male child who lost his penis in a circumcision accident, and, at 17 months, was surgically reconstructed and brought up as female. The child had an unaffected identical twin with whom researchers could compare the sex-altered child. This case has implications for telling whether the development of gender identity is a biological inevitability or whether learning is more important. The researchers studied the case by the use of observation of the child, sometimes using the unaffected twin brother as a control condition. Key observations included the child's play and the interaction between the twins. Researchers also interviewed the parents about how well the child had adapted to her new gender role. Observations revealed that the child was robust and 'tomboyish' in her play, but no more than many girls of her age. She was seen to be distinctly feminine as compared to her twin brother. The brother was observed to treat his twin as female, adopting a protective attitude. Interviews revealed that parents considered that the child was generally feminine, and had become daintier and tidier than her brother. For some time the sex-altered child appeared to have adjusted and developed a female gender identity. However, in a follow-up by Diamond (1982), the girl was found to be having an unhappy adolescence with few friends and plagued with worries about her gender identity. As an adult he reassigned his gender and adopted a stable male identity.

for and against

biological approaches

+ There is clear evidence of hormonal and neurological differences between males and females.

− It is not clear to what extent these differences actually affect gender differences.

+ Animal studies have shown that gender-related behaviour can be altered by artificially changing hormone levels.

Cognitive-developmental approaches to gender

Kohlberg (1966) proposed that gender-specific behaviours and the child's concept of its own gender are acquired over time as the child constructs its own mental representation of the world. The complexity of this representation increases in line with cognitive development. Kohlberg proposes three stages through which children pass. At each stage the child has a more sophisticated understanding of gender.

● Gender labelling (2–3¹/₂ years). *During this period the child gradually becomes aware of its own gender. At first this is merely a label. Then children begin to discover which labels can be applied to which people. Children frequently apply sex labels wrongly at this stage and are unaware that gender is permanent. Thus, girls may speak of growing up to be daddies.*

- Gender stability (3$\frac{1}{2}$–4$\frac{1}{2}$ years). At this point children become aware of the stability of gender and can correctly predict their own gender as adults. None the less children's understanding is dependent on physical appearance and they are easily confused by changes in appearance, e.g. in hairstyle or dress – a familiar male appearing in female dress may be perceived to have changed gender.

- Gender consistency (4$\frac{1}{2}$–7 years). By this stage children understand the permanence of gender and the fact that people can change their appearance without changing gender.

Kohlberg regarded environment as important in supplying information about gender characteristics. However, he emphasised the child's tendency to actively explore the environment. As the child's understanding grows so does their motivation to learn more about the expected behaviours and characteristics of their gender.

The central idea that children's understanding of gender becomes increasingly sophisticated with age has been confirmed by much research. Understanding of gender does appear to come in the order predicted by Kohlberg's theory. However, it is not clear whether this increasing understanding is a direct result of cognitive development in stages or merely the result of more learning over time. Moreover, the assumption that gender identity requires gender consistency has been investigated, e.g. by Martin and Little (1990) and has not been substantiated – gender identity appears to come first. Bem (1985) criticises Kohlberg's theory on the basis that it fails to explain why children acquire knowledge of gender earlier than other categories, such as race and religion.

what's new?

gender schema theory

Gender schema theory is a contemporary extension of Kohlberg's ideas. Bem (1985) and Martin (1991) proposed that gender develops as the child realises what gender it is, i.e. it acquires a crude gender identity and seeks out further information to build up its gender schema. A schema is the cognitive structure containing all the individual's knowledge, beliefs, attitudes and feelings about one aspect of the world. Like the traditional cognitive approach of Kohlberg, Martin (1991) saw children as actively seeking out information, but she rejected Kohlberg's idea that learning can only take place in rigid stages.

There is considerable support for the idea that children interpret information in the light of their existing understanding of gender – as we would expect if there is a schema for gender. Martin and Halverson (1983) showed children of 5 and 6 years old pictures of males and females performing gender-stereotypical (e.g. boy with trainset) and gender-atypical activities (e.g. girl sawing wood). A week later memory was tested and it was found that memories had been distorted, such that most pictures were recalled as gender-stereotypical. This suggests that children had had difficulty in incorporating the information into gender schemas. Lavallee and Pelletier (1992) compared the gender-related beliefs of women in traditional and non-traditional jobs. They found quite different beliefs (less gender stereotyped in the non-traditional roles), suggesting that their schemas determined the women's gender identities.

Gender schema theory predicts that children will seek out information about their own sex in preference to that regarding the opposite sex, so as to build up their own gender schema. A study by Luecke-Aleksa et al. (1995) confirmed that children pay more attention to same-sex TV characters. The TV viewing of 24 5-year-old boys was videotaped for 5 days. It emerged that they watched more programmes featuring male main characters. Furthermore, the boys who displayed gender constancy – the understanding that gender is permanent, thus boys grow up to become men and girls to become women – watched significantly more programmes with male main characters than gender-inconstant boys. Presumably the gender-constant boys had more detailed gender schemas and so were more aware of the significance of the gender of the main character.

Also in keeping with gender schema theory is children's tendency to show a preference for other children who are stereotypically of the same sex, and to expect gender-stereotypical behaviour from those conforming to gender-stereotypical appearance. Both these tendencies were demonstrated in a study by Albers (1998).

research now

gender-stereotyping starts early!

Albers, S.M. (1998) The effect of gender-typed clothing on children's social judgements. *Child Study Journal 28, 137–59.*

Aim: The aim of the study was to see whether children would make different judgements about other children based on the gender-stereotypical nature of their dress. Specifically, it was tested whether children would express a preference for children as playmates who were dressed gender-stereotypically over those dressed gender-neutrally or gender-counterstereotypically, for example boys wearing dresses. It was also tested whether children would attribute gender-related behaviours to children in accordance with their dress.

Method: Eighty-one children aged 5 to 10 years were shown pictures of 6 other children dressed in either masculine, neutral or feminine style. Three pictures were of girls and three of boys. For each gender one picture was of a child dressed in a gender-stereotypical way, one in a gender-neutral way and one in a counterstereotypical manner. The children were asked to rate each child according to how much they would like them as a playmate. Participants were also asked questions about what play activities they believed each child would enjoy.

Results: There was no significant difference in the preference expressed for gender-stereotyped children over neutral children; however children expressed a preference for both gender-stereotypical and gender-neutral children over those dressed counterstereotypically. There was also a tendency to attribute play-preferences according to the clothing of the pictured children.

Conclusion: There are important theoretical and practical implications of this study. In practical terms it shows that parents who dress their children in a counterstereotypical way are socially disadvantaging them, i.e. they are likely to be less popular with their peers. On a theoretical level, the study supports gender schema theory in that children appeared to refer to their gender-schemas in order to find information on the likely play preferences of each pictured child.

for and against

cognitive-developmental approaches

➕ There is no doubt that children's understanding becomes more sophisticated with age.

➕ There is ample evidence that children refer to gender schemas when processing gender-related information.

➖ It is not clear whether the cognitive understanding of gender is the major element of gender identity.

Social learning theory of gender

Like other aspects of social development, gender is explained by social learning theorists in terms of learning from other people. Bandura (1986) suggested that although some aspects of gender differentiation may be biological in origin others were clearly not, and were probably socially learned. Social learning theorists reject the idea of stages of cognitive development and explain increases in sophistication of knowledge in terms of a greater number of learning experiences.

Bandura proposed that learning of social behaviours requires four factors, attention, retention, reproduction and motivation (see p.6 for a full explanation of social learning theory). The critical factors are imitation of observed behaviour and the response that imitating the behaviour brings (reinforcement). It is all too easy to imagine a boy who experimented with playing with dolls being greeted with stony silence from parents (non-reinforcement) or maybe even smacked (punishment). On the other hand, that same boy might imitate his father cheering while watching a football match on television and be rewarded with a 'that's my boy', a clap on the shoulder and possibly even his first can of beer (potent positive reinforcers). A girl would be much less likely to receive such reinforcement for imitating this highly gender-specific behaviour. Bandura (1986) did not regard children, however, as merely experimenting randomly with behaviour until it was shaped by reinforcement. He saw children actively seeking same-gender models to imitate.

The effects of the media on gender development

Social learning theory, with its emphasis on learning from observation of adults, would predict that children can acquire gender-specific behaviour and attitudes from the media. Certainly research supports the idea that characters portrayed in the media tend to be gender-stereotyped. Helman and Bookspan (1992) found that soap operas and children's TV feature more characters in gender-stereotypical roles than not. MacArthur and Eisen (1976) found similar effects in children's stories. Gender stereotyping has also been found prevalent in toy catalogues (Schwartz and Markham, 1985) and teen magazines (Pierce, 1993). Some studies, e.g. Levy (1989), have found that the more television is watched the more stereotypical children's gender-role beliefs become, implying that children have learnt by imitating television characters. However, other studies have shown no such effect. Durkin (1995) reviewed studies and concluded that there is little reliable support for the idea that children's gender-role development is significantly affected by the media.

Numerous studies have confirmed the idea that parents reinforce gender-stereotypical behaviour. Idle *et al.* (1993) observed parents both reinforcing and modelling play with gender-stereotypical toys. Lips (1989) found that by adolescence adults were reinforcing ambition more in boys and domesticity more in girls. Furthermore, social learning theory provides an explanation for cultural diversity in gender roles (Durkin, 1995).

However, while it is clear that children do attend to same-gender models, imitate their actions and receive reinforcement, it is less clear whether this is a *complete* explanation for all gender development. Stangor and Ruble (1987) found that children's gender-role beliefs undergo substantial change during childhood – more consistent with a cognitive-developmental approach. There is also surprisingly little evidence that children's gender develops strictly in line with their rearing. Diamond (1997) reviewed three cases in which children had either damaged or ambiguous genitals. The first case was a male raised a female but redefined herself as male at the age of 14. The second case was of a hermaphrodite (i.e. someone with both male and female genitals) who was raised a female but who redefined herself as male as an adult. The third case was also a hermaphrodite who was raised as a girl from 18 months and who maintained a female identity into adulthood. These cases demonstrate that gender identity is not simply a question of rearing, as would be expected were social learning a complete explanation of gender.

for and against

social learning theory

+ There is no doubt that children receive reinforcement for what is seen as 'gender-appropriate' behaviour or that this reinforcement can impact on later behaviour.

+ Social learning theory gives us a way of understanding media effects on gender development.

– Children sometimes assign themselves a gender contrary to that which their models and reinforcement would lead them to.

Psychodynamic approaches to gender development

Psychodynamic theory emphasises the fact that gender development, like other social-developmental phenomena, takes place within the context of a family, and, like other social-developmental phenomena is affected by the nature and quality of family relationships. Parental relationships are seen as being of crucial importance to gender identity development.

Freud's theory

Gender identity is rooted in Freudian theory at the third developmental stage, the phallic stage (see p.3 for an explanation of Freud's view of personality development). During the oral and anal stages gender is not an issue and the sexes develop in parallel. During the phallic stage, however, a crisis emerges as children become fully aware of their biological sex, and the fact that they have parents, one of whom is of the same sex and the other of the opposite sex.

At this point the Oedipus complex arises, whereby the child develops a strong attachment to the opposite-sex parent and sees the same-sex parent as a rival for their affection. As Jacobs (1992) says, Freud's reference to the Oedipus myth, in which a boy, having been separated from his parents at an early age, meets them as an adult and kills his father and marries his mother is 'a metaphor on many levels' and should not be taken too literally. Freud is often portrayed as having said that boys in the phallic stage wish to kill their father and sleep with their mother. It is questionable whether Freud saw children as having an understanding of sex or death in the adult sense, but he did emphasise the importance of what contemporary Freudians such as Brown and Pedder (1991) call the *rivalry stage*. This occurs when the child realises that he is excluded from some parental activities and starts to see the same-sex parent as a rival for the affection and attention of the opposite-sex parent. However, the child is largely helpless in the face of the superior strength of his father. To resolve this difficulty the child identifies with the aggressor – a defence that may be used later to cope with playground bullies by joining their gang. The process of identification involves the child incorporating a mental representation of the same-sex parent into the personality. This process is called *introjection*. Thus the child acquires a gender identity directly from the same-sex parent.

Survey studies, e.g. Jarvis (2000), have confirmed the fact that in many two-parent families a three-way rivalry dynamic does develop in early childhood in which children go through a phase of seeing one parent as a rival for the affection of the other. It seems certain, however, that Freud greatly overstated the significance of Oedipal conflict in the development of gender identity. For one thing children appear to have quite a good awareness of their own gender well before the Freudian phallic stage. Furthermore, Freud's theory would predict that children in single parent or same-sex parent families would have difficulty in acquiring a normal gender identity. There is in fact no evidence for this. Patterson (1997) assessed the social development – including gender identity – of American children both born to and adopted by lesbian mothers and found no difference from children born to and adopted by heterosexual families. Tasker and Golombok (1998) found similar results in Britain. While Tasker and Golombok found that the children of lesbian families were more likely to have considered or tried a same-sex relationship, they were no more likely to settle on a homosexual orientation than children of heterosexual families. In any case, sexual orientation is independent of gender identity and, according to Tasker and Golombok, no study has found a single case of gender identity disorder (in which the child has the gender identity of the opposite sex) in children of gay families.

Object relations perspectives

The most influential branch of psychodynamic psychology in Britain today is not Freudian but the Object relations school. This approach diverges significantly from Freud's notion of gender-identity development. A central feature of Object relations theory is the emphasis in the mother–child relationship. In Object relations theory all children are seen as initially having a female gender identity (called *primary femininity*) due to the close and exclusive relationship with the (usually) female primary caregiver. Dinnerstein (1990) suggests that in late capitalist society, where for most children care is predominantly by the mother, children experience fear of the mother's total power over them. The child, of whichever sex, seeks out the father as an escape from the fearful mother. To Dinnerstein the universally lower status of women in human society is a result of our inability to overcome this fear of our mothers. Chodorow (1994) agrees that mothers are objects of omnipotence to be escaped. She proposes that because of the societal norm that children experience a female primary caregiver, all children initially identify with the mother and begin with a 'female' identity. Boys are then differentiated by different parental treatment. Both boys and girls attempt to identify with the father but because of the different ways fathers treat sons and daughters, the former manage to identify with the father whereas the latter do not.

The object relations approach has several advantages over the traditional Freudian view of gender development. Firstly, the view that gender identity is acquired much earlier than the phallic stage is supported by research. Secondly, unlike the Freudian view, Object relations theory would predict no disruption to the development of gender identity in lesbian and single-parent families. There is also evidence to support Chodorow's central idea that girls have a closer relationship with their mother than do boys. Benenson *et al.* (1998) videotaped 41 mothers playing with children aged 4 to 5 years. They found that girls showed more eye-contact, greater physical proximity and more apparent enjoyment during play with the mother than did boys. These results are the reverse of what we would expect if the Freudian Oedipal conflict were a significant factor in the mother–child relationship.

Another line of research into gender identity disorder has supported the Chodorow–Dinnerstein proposal that gender identity is rooted in the child's first relationship. Zucker and Bradley (1998) examined the incidence of gender identity disorder in boys adopted in the first two years, those adopted later and those not adopted at all. One-and-a-half per cent of non-adopted boys and late-adopted boys suffered gender identity disorder, but the risk increased to about 8 per cent when adoption was in the first two years. This suggests that disruption to the first attachment relationship can affect gender development.

for and against

psychodynamic explanations

- While there is evidence that the Oedipus complex exists, there is little support for its impact on gender development.

- Children of single and lesbian parents develop normal gender identity, contrary to what we would expect from a Freudian perspective.

+ There is much more support, however, for an Object relations view of gender. Gender identity disorder is much more common in children who are separated from their primary carer in the first two years.

where to now?

The following is a good source of further information about the development of gender:

Brannon, L. (1996) *Gender: psychological perspectives.* **Boston: Allyn & Bacon** – an excellent account of numerous gender issues in psychology, including good coverage of the theories discussed here.

Conclusions

In childhood we acquire our sense of identity, an understanding of who we are. James (1892) made the early distinction between the existential self and the categorical self. More recently, Neisser (1988) has distinguished five aspects of the self which we experience in different situations. An important aspect of our self-concept is our self-esteem, i.e. how much we like ourselves. Self-esteem is associated with parenting style, academic success and body satisfaction. There are important cultural differences in self-concept, and it would be a mistake to assume that European-American views of the self can be applied to understanding people world-wide. Gender-identity is another particularly important aspect of our self-concept. We can understand the acquisition of gender in terms of biological, cognitive-developmental, social-learning and psychodynamic perspectives. It seems likely that gender identity is complex and involves all the processes emphasised by these perspectives.

what do you know?

1 Distinguish between the existential and categorical self.

2 Briefly outline Rogers's theory of self-esteem.

3 How is academic achievement related to self-concept?

4 What is gender identity? Distinguish between sex and gender.

5 Outline one psychological difference between males and females.

6 Describe one study into a biological factor implicated in gender development.

7 What is gender schema theory?

8 Outline one psychodynamic explanation of gender development.

6

Adolescence

what's
ahead?

In this chapter we look at adolescence, the period between true childhood and true adulthood. We shall first consider whether adolescence is a fixed stage of human development or whether it is merely a social construct, and look at cultural variations in dealing with youth. We will then look briefly at the types of change we undergo in adolescence and look in detail at how our identity changes as we leave childhood behind. Three theories are of particular importance here, namely those of Erikson, Blos and Marcia. With reference to these we can consider the extent to which adolescence is really a time of identity crisis. In *What's new?* we can look at the importance of adolescence for developing our adult ethnic identity. Finally we look at the importance of relationships with peers.

Cultural variations in adolescence – is it a universal stage?

Clearly the young people we normally think of as adolescents really exist! However, there are good reasons for questioning whether adolescence truly exists as a fixed stage of human development, or whether in fact we would be wiser to think of it as a social construct. One reason for questioning the existence of adolescence is the difficulty in pinning down just precisely when it happens. Although we typically think of adolescence as beginning with puberty and ending at the end of full-time education this laypersons' model has its problems. Puberty can begin at any time from 8 to 16. Does this mean that some 8 year olds are adolescents while other 15 year olds are not? Education is no more reliable an indicator than puberty. Are 18 year olds in full-time education still adolescents while those who are married with children at the same age adults?

Although references to 'youth' can be found as far back as ancient Greece, adolescence as a stage of development has only been acknowledged in the last hundred years. G. Stanley Hall (1904) is often credited with 'discovering' adolescence. The term itself comes from the Latin *adolescere*, meaning 'to grow to adulthood' (LaFreniere, 2000). Hall spoke of the stage as one of '*sturm* and *drang*' (translated as 'storm and stress'), a time of powerful, unstable emotions and passionate political idealism. As Modell and Goodman (1990) have pointed out, Hall's approach has helped us view adolescence as a vulnerable period and adolescents as in need of help. Prior to Hall's time the dominant view of 'youths' was of troublesome upstarts who needed to be kept in their place.

We can look back through history and speculate on why adolescence has not always been acknowledged. In British rural societies of the 16th and 17th centuries there was no real period of 'youth' or 'adolescence' because children worked in agriculture alongside their parents, and so they were treated as small adults from an early age (Barnes, 1995). Throughout the 20th century children have received education then gone on to go to work as adults, so there has been a real transition in their social role, most commonly in the teens. Elder *et al.* (1993) have suggested that as an adolescent you would have experienced variations in a number of experiences, according to the historical period in which you grew up. These are shown in Box 6.1.

- **The family**; divorce, single parenthood, working parents, fathers absent due to war.
- **Education**; level of education available, career choice, availability of training.
- **Employment**; availability and variety of work, benefits for the unemployed.
- **Attitudes to sex**; birth control, frequency of sexually transmitted disease, attitudes to homosexuality and premarital sex.
- **Religion**; how seriously religion is taken, religious choice and freedom.
- **Dominant social issues**; war, politics, the environment.

Box 6.1 Variations in the experience of adolescents. After Elder *et al.* (1993)

Another more sinister development is the commercialisation of adolescence, so that industries such as fashion and music have a huge vested interest in socially constructing adolescence as a time associated with particular sounds and images. It is possible (Rutter, 1979) that one reason why we think of adolescence as such an important stage is because so much money is spent promoting it.

A further reason for questioning the existence of adolescence as a fixed stage of human development is that the nature of transition from childhood to adulthood varies considerably in different human societies. In some cultures puberty is marked by *rites of passage*. According to Gennep (1960) rites of passage typically have three stages, an initial stage of isolation, a stage in which the resistance of the adolescent is broken down by some hardship and finally a stage of reinstatement where the adolescent is brought back into the community as an adult. Kenyatta (1965) has described one such rite of passage (see Box 6.2).

The traditional rite of passage practised by the African Gikuyu people until the 1930s involved circumcision of both boys and girls. The youngsters are brought to one homestead and introduced. At this stage they are all ceremonially adopted by that settlement. Three to four days before the initiation ceremony there is an all-night dance, seen as a communion with the ancestral God, who will then protect the initiates. The day before the initiation boys and girls are separated and the girls move to a sacred tree. The boys race there and the first to get to the sacred tree and throw his spear over it is elected leader and spokesman of the age group. The next day the ritual-proper takes place, and both boys and girls are circumcised. The rest of the settlement sing praise songs and the initiates are taken to a quiet hut to recuperate for around a week.

Box 6.2 The traditional rite of passage of the Gikuyu people from Kenyatta (1965)

Not all cultures involve such elaborate rituals, but there are many parallels. Graduation ceremonies such as those that take place at the end of American high school and British university courses are highly ritualised passages into adulthood. Aside from the obvious difference in the nature of the ritual one interesting difference between the old Gikuyu ceremony and the modern graduation is its timing. The Gikuyu used to have their rite of passage shortly after puberty, and afterwards the 'graduates' were seen as adults, without any extended period that we might call adolescence without adult responsibilities. By contrast high school and university graduation marks the end of a long period of education in which young people are largely free from the responsibility to earn a living and support a family. It is this extended period of preparation for adulthood that marks adolescence as a social construct of modern European and American society.

One of the saddest responsibilities a young person might have to take on at an early age is going to war. War is a reality for children in many societies and it is not unknown for children much younger than those we normally think of as adolescents to be involved in fighting. Cultural attitudes to the role of young people tend to be quite different in societies involved in prolonged war. Peters and Richards (1998) have investigated

This teenage soldier is not experiencing what we think of as adolescence

the role of young people involved in the military conflicts of Sierra Leone. An interview (cited in Valsiner, 2000) with a young woman who had been in the army from the age of 16 revealed that she had killed numerous rebels, both in battle and as captives. Her belief was that she had been defending her country and therefore had done nothing wrong by killing numerous people. While she had been raped by her fellow soldiers, she believed that the rebels raped any women they captured and were 'less careful' when doing so than the government forces. This interview reveals a set of cultural beliefs and attitudes that might seem quite alien to us in Britain. The point of looking at this study, however, is not to think how civilised we are in Britain as opposed to people in other parts of the world, but to show how an event such as war can lead to hardened attitudes, and to demonstrate how young people can take on vastly different roles according to the demands of their society.

An important part of adolescence is the gaining of sexual maturity. While puberty is universal, different cultures respond to it quite differently. Remember here that a culture does not mean a nationality or an ethnic group. It is a set of shared beliefs, practices and values that characterise a group. We can thus look at different historical periods in the same society for cultural differences as well as across different societies. In America prior to the 1920s heterosexual interaction came in the form of 'courting'. The aim of courting was not to have a steady or casual relationship but to secure a marriage partner. Much of the process of courting (at least in the middle classes) was done in the presence of a chaperone who prevented any kind of sexual activity.

When dance halls (the original nightclubs) opened in the early 1900s they were met by a wave of public outrage at the lack of sexual supervision involved and the likelihood of 'vice'. By the 1920s courtship had been firmly replaced by dating as the dominant form of heterosexual interaction (Spurlock and Magistro, 1998). Nowadays dating remains the norm, and marriage, although still common, tends to take place rather later than in past generations, typically following a number of sexual relationships.

where to now?

The following are good sources of further information about cultural variations in adolescence:

Valsiner, J. (2000) *Culture and Human Development*. **London: Sage** – a very advanced book, but Chapter 13, which deals with adolescence, is very readable. Lots of up-to-date research.

Physical change in adolescence and its consequences

Puberty brings with it dramatic physical changes. Growth speeds up and height, weight and strength rapidly increase. Primary sexual characteristics, i.e. the male and female reproductive organs, assume adult functioning. Secondary sexual characteristics, e.g. breasts in girls and body hair and deepening voice in boys, also appear. Tanner (1989) studied a large sample of adolescents in Britain and charted male and female physical development. Results in the form of mean ages are shown in Table 6.1.

	girls	boys
height spurt	10.5yrs	12.5yrs
pubic hair	11yrs	12yrs
breast/penis growth	11yrs	12.5yrs

Table 6.1 Physical changes in adolescence. Adapted from Tanner (1989)

You can see from Tanner's findings that on average girls begin puberty earlier than boys. However, the variance within each sex is greater than the variance between sexes. The physical changes that take place at puberty and throughout adolescence have profound psychological consequences for individuals.

Adolescents tend to be sensitive to their changing physique and often compare themselves unfavourably to media images of physically 'perfect' models. In a study of body type and body satisfaction Richards *et al.* (1990) measured the satisfaction with their weight and related findings to actual weight of boys and girls of 11 to 13 years. Satisfaction was lowest in overweight adolescents. Worryingly, underweight girls expressed the highest levels of satisfaction. This type of finding is perhaps not surprising in societies like Western Europe and America that often portray the pre-pubescent body shape as the physical ideal for women, for example in fashion. In extreme cases this phenomenon may lead to eating disorders, most commonly bulimia – characterised by binge-eating followed by vomiting and purging, and the less common but more deadly anorexia – characterised by refusal to eat and other behaviour directed towards weight-loss (see *Angles on Atypical Psychology* in this series for information on eating disorders).

About 90 per cent of adolescents diagnosed as having eating disorders are female. However, Lemma (1996) has pointed out that, although male eating disorders are undoubtedly less common, the low rates of diagnosis may be in part due to the fact that adolescent males tend to speak of getting fit and maintaining their health rather than losing weight for vanity. Males also tend to exercise rather than diet – attracting less attention.

The timing of physical changes also appears to have psychological consequences for adolescents. Brooks-Gunn and Reiter (1990) reviewed past studies and concluded that timing of physical change has rather different effects on males and females. Boys who mature early appear to have an advantage over their late-developing peers in terms of popularity and self-esteem. By contrast early-maturing girls appear disadvantaged, showing more negative body image and depression, and higher incidence of conflict with family and school (Magnusson *et al.*, 1985). It appears likely that the root of these timing-effects lies in society's beliefs about what is the 'normal' or 'right' age for physical maturation.

Identity change in adolescence

Most people's image of adolescence is as a time of identity crisis, where young people struggle with existential questions such as who they are and who they want to become. Because these are emotional questions and demand an in-depth understanding of individual experience, theories of adolescence have been predominantly psychodynamic in origin (see p.2 for a discussion of psychodynamic approaches to child development). We can look here at two psychodynamic theories of adolescence, those of Erik Erikson and Peter Blos.

Erikson's theory

Erikson (1959) saw each stage of lifespan development in terms of developmental stages, each of which is characterised by a task, which needs to be accomplished before the person can move on to the next stage (see *Angles on Psychology*, p.148). The developmental task of adolescence is to establish *identity* and prevent *identity diffusion*. Erikson (1968) has defined identity as a subjective sense of sameness and continuity. Throughout our lives we tend to have a fairly stable identity, but this is threatened in adolescence. Because of the rapid physical changes of puberty and the rapidly changing social demands associated with the period, the self-concept loses its stability, as the childish identity no longer suffices for the adolescent. This leads to a temporary state of confusion where the adolescent perceives the adult roles they must choose – occupational, sexual, political etc., but does not yet have the answers to these role-choices. Thus the child identity has failed and the adult identity is not yet formed.

The failure to maintain a stable identity through adolescence – identity diffusion – is associated with a number of consequences. Rather than forming a stable sexual orientation the diffused adolescent is likely to be bisexual. They are also likely to be delinquent, have very difficult relationships with authority, and to fail to settle into employment or further education. Erikson believed that parents are critical at this stage, and the only thing that can save a diffused adolescent from a lifetime of identity confusion is the refusal of adults, particularly parents, to classify the youth as delinquent. The clichéd phrase 'it's just a stage he's going through' is, according to Erikson's approach, a very healthy attitude for dealing with an adolescent identity crisis.

As well as parents, Erikson placed a lot of emphasis on peer relations in adolescence. According to Erikson adolescents tend to overidentify with *cliques* – small groups of friends. This is a psychological defence against identity diffusion, but it has a negative consequence, namely intolerance of those not part of the clique. This may lead to racial conflict and exclusion of peers, including former friends who might be no longer 'appropriately' dressed, or who may not meet the demands of the clique in other ways. Erikson saw the appeal of extreme political movements and youth subcultures to adolescents as being due to the fact that they provide a temporary comfort against the insecurity of not having a stable identity.

Research findings

Because of its emphasis on individual experience rather than observable behaviour, Erikson's theory has proved quite tricky to test in a scientific manner. However, there is support for some of his ideas. Research has supported the idea that identity is weaker in adolescence than in early adulthood, and that adolescents have less intimate relationships. Whitbourne *et al.* (1992) followed up late adolescents (aged 20) and followed them up through early and middle adulthood, assessing intimacy and identity with a battery of psychological tests. They found that scores of both intimacy and identity increased sharply after adolescence. There is also a strong body of support for the idea that accepting parents benefit adolescent development and can even prevent long-term delinquency. We now look at one such recent study by Carlo *et al.* (1998) in detail.

research now

how important is parental support to troubled adolescents?

Carlo, G., Roesch, S.C. and Meltby, J. (1998) The multiplicative relations of parenting and temperament to prosocial and antisocial behaviours in adolescence. *Journal of Early Adolescence 18, 266–90.*

Aim: Erikson (1959) proposed that supportive and accepting parenting is essential in adolescence, especially for adolescents who have begun to go 'off the rails'. The aim of this study was to examine the extent to which pro and anti-social adolescent behaviour can be related to the degree of support and acceptance provided by parents.

Method: Eighty adolescents, both males and females (mean age 14.2 years) and their parents took part in the study. The study involved psychometric testing of both the young people and their parents. A number of self-report questionnaires were given to the adolescents designed to assess their aggression, anti-social behaviour, sympathy and pro-social behaviour. Parents also completed measures of their perceptions of their child's sociability and anger, and on the level of support they provided. Complex statistical analysis of the responses to both adolescent and adult questionnaires was carried out in order to see whether there was a relationship between parental support and the behaviour of the adolescent.

Results: There were indeed quite strong relationships between parental support and adolescent behaviour. High levels of aggression and anti-social behaviour on the part of the adolescents were associated with low levels of parental support and vice versa. They were also associated with high levels of parental anger. Adolescent anger (as rated by parents) was negatively correlated with pro-social behaviour and positively related to anti-social behaviour.

Conclusions: Results firmly support the idea that parental support is associated with adolescent anger, aggression and anti-social behaviour. Highly supportive parents had adolescent children with fewer emotional and behavioural problems. Less supportive parents tended to have more angry, aggressive and anti-social adolescents. This finding is in line with Erikson's theory.

A more recent study by Vitaro *et al.* (2000) provides further support for the idea that the quality of parental relationships can prevent delinquency. The relationship between delinquency of adolescents' best friends and their own delinquent behaviour was assessed, and found to be significant, i.e. if your best friend is a delinquent your own chances of delinquency are increased. However, this is mediated by the quality of relationships with parents. Thus, if your best friend is a delinquent but you have a good relationship with your parents you are less likely to be influenced by your friend to join in their delinquent behaviour.

Of course there are some elements of Erikson's theory with which we would not tend to agree nowadays. Erikson's idea that bisexuality is a negative outcome on a par with delinquency and inability to settle in study or employment is perhaps best seen as just a product of the attitudes of his time. Feminist writers have also commented that Erikson's views may describe male development in adolescence rather better than female development. For example, Schiedel and Marcia

(1985) have proposed that, while adolescent boys might have to establish a stable, adult identity before they can have intimate relationships, for girls identity and intimacy are tied together and develop together.

media watch

Where lost kids find they have a future

Suzanne knows exactly what Keeping Kids Company has meant to her young life.

'This place makes me free. Without it I think I would be dead,' the quiet 15-year-old said as she picked at the chipped silver varnish on her fingernails.

She is not exaggerating. Suzanne's life has been an unrelenting litany of suffering as she grew up on one of Peckham's toughest estates amid the drugs and the violence that blight so many lives in this deprived area of south London.

Both her parents are heroin addicts, and by the age of 12 Suzanne had already dropped out of school to look after her three siblings, sometimes being forced to scavenge for food in bins. Her father is in jail and her mother is still on drugs. Suzanne lives in a care home but now knows what it means to have a future.

Kids Co provided her with education courses, people to talk to and a job. She works as a classroom assistant in a local primary school and wants to become a teacher. 'I love it here. I come every day,' she said. At first glance the row of converted railway arches tucked under a busy commuter line seem an unlikely beacon of hope. Though the murder of Damilola Taylor just a mile away threw a media spotlight on the area's problems, Kids Co had already been here for years, battling with the conditions that bred such an awful crime.

The Observer, 17 December 2000

Questions

1 Erikson emphasised the importance of adults as stabilising influences in adolescence. Why might Suzanne have come through her ordeal in spite of her parents' difficulties?

Blos's theory

Erikson's friend and colleague Peter Blos (1967) proposed an alternative view of the development of adolescent identity. You will be familiar, from Chapter 1, with Freud's view of the anal stage, from 1 to 3 years, in which children are faced with their first conflict with authority, and seek to establish their own identity. This process is called *separation-individuation*, 'separation' because it involves a distancing from the parents and 'individuation' because it is important in forming the individual's identity as a person in their own right. Blos's great contribution to our understanding of adolescence was to suggest that adolescence is effectively a repetition of this separation-individuation process. Blos (1968) suggested that individuation is the most critical task that needs to be accomplished in the mind of the individual before they can function as an autonomous (independent) adult.

Individuation

In childhood a major part of our identity is composed of the mental representations of our parents. Before we can replace these with our own set of mental representations of our adult relationships and hence form an adult identity, we need to *disengage* from the family unit. Failure to gain autonomy in adolescence and hence failure of disengagement can result in a distortion of adult relationships, so that we simply replace members of our family with new adults who adopt the same roles. An important part of the mental representation of parents is our *superego*, the image of the parent in an authority role that (according to psychodynamic theory) forms our conscience. While this does not disappear in adolescence its power over us tends to lessen as we separate ourselves from the influence of our parents. One way in which this separation takes place is in replacing parents with other, younger idols such as pop stars (Kroger, 1996). Another aspect of separation is the rejection of the political and social views of the previous generation, replacing them with a different set of views.

Other tasks of adolescence

Blos (1962) proposed that adolescence is an important time for reducing the impact of earlier negative events. Trauma in Blos's theory does not mean merely extreme events, but any event that has left an impact on the child. Self-esteem in adulthood is, to Blos, largely a result of the individual's success in mastering childhood traumas as they recur in adolescence. For example, Oedipal conflict is likely to recur and be resolved as children come into conflict with same-sex parents. Success in managing parent–child conflict is thus important in overcoming any residual difficulties left over from the first Oedipal conflict, including difficulty in gender or moral development, and in managing relationships with members of the same and opposite sex. In this sense, adolescence is a *second chance* to establish a healthy identity.

While we have established a stable *gender identity* in early childhood, Blos saw adolescence as important in establishing a *sexual identity*, a different concept. Our sexual identity comprises our perceptions of our sexual orientation, preferences and competence. Our sexual identity can only be formed following successful resolution of the Oedipus complex in adolescence. Blos suggested that unusual sexual behaviour in adolescence, such as promiscuity, is the result of difficulty in coping with relations with the same-sex parent.

Research findings

As with Erikson's closely related theory, Blos's ideas are very tricky to test because they are centred on the experience of the individual. Some of his ideas, such as that adolescents idealise pop stars in order to replace their mental representations of their parents with self-chosen adults, are enormously appealing, but not directly testable. Some findings back up Blos's idea that adolescence involves breaking away from parents. The time spent with parents certainly decreases in adolescence. In one study by Larson *et al.* (1996) it was found that the percentage of waking time spent with parents declines from 35 per cent in childhood to 14 per cent in adolescence. Honess and Charman (1998) questioned 300 11 to 15 year olds and found that the young people reported a steady decline in levels of support from parents, in line with Blos's theory of disengagement. The frequency of conflict with parents is greatest in early adolescence and declines steadily through later adolescence (Laursen and Collins, 1994), further supporting the idea that conflict is part of the process of separation. However, conflict in adolescence is not necessarily associated with a weakening of family relationships, as we would expect if Blos were correct (LaFreniere, 2000).

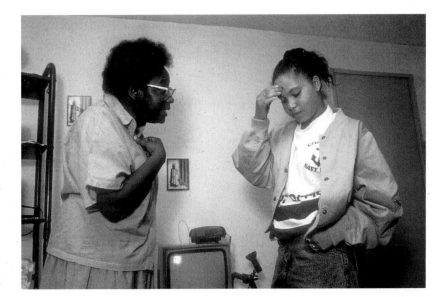

Families do argue, but arguments are not necessarily associated with weakened bonds

Blos's views on the development of sexual identity in adolescence have partial support. Anxiety over heterosexual relationships peaks at around 11 years in boys (Coleman and Hendry, 1999) and declines throughout adolescence, suggesting that a stable sexual identity is formed during this period. However, there is little support for the idea that Oedipal conflict is played out in adolescence. Both boys and girls report seeing mothers as the major confidant (Hendry *et al.*, 1993), and both boys and girls have more conflict with mothers than fathers, suggesting that the importance of mothers and fathers to adolescents is not gender-specific. Moreover, if Oedipal conflict were an essential part of adolescence, we would expect adolescents without two resident parents to be psychologically disadvantaged. In a recent study by Salem *et al.* (1998), in which the development of adolescents aged 14 to 17 years from two-parent families were compared with those from one-parent, mother and step-father, and extended families, no difference in outcome emerged from these different family structures. This suggests that Oedipal conflict is not necessary for adolescent development.

Marcia's theory of identity statuses

Marcia (1980, 1993) has built on Erikson's ideas, remaining very much within his conceptual framework. In an effort to develop Erikson's clinically derived ideas by more systematic research, Marcia interviewed adolescents in an attempt to uncover two dimensions of identity-related behaviour. *Exploration* refers to the extent to which the adolescent seeks information before making identity choices. *Commitment* refers to the extent to which the adolescent makes a genuine investment in the choice. By relating these two dimensions Marcia identifies four types of identity status in adolescents:

- *identity diffusion* – characterised by little or no exploration or commitment

- *foreclosure* – characterised by commitment with little evidence of preliminary exploration

- *moratorium* – characterised by exploration but failure to commit. This is a crisis state

- *identity achievement* – characterised by commitment following exploration.

	commitment	
	yes	no
exploration yes	identity achievement	moratorium
exploration no	foreclosure	identity diffusion

Table 6.2 Marcia's adolescent types

These four states represent four possible results as adolescents work through their identity crises. Marcia proposed that identity diffusion should be most common in early adolescence before an identity crisis takes place and identity achievement should be most common in late adolescence when many individuals would have resolved their conflict. The theory also predicted that those identified as in a state of identity achievement should have higher self-esteem and mental health than others, while those in a state of identity diffusion should come off worst in self-esteem and frequency of psychological problems.

Research has supported many of Marcia's ideas. Coleman and Hendry (1999) have reviewed research comparing adolescents assessed as falling within the four categories, and concluded that identity achievers generally report the fewest psychological problems, while those assessed as having a diffused identity tend to be the most withdrawn and have poorest social skills. These findings support Marcia's position. Coleman and Hendry have also reviewed evidence for associations between age and classification. As predicted by Marcia, identity diffusion was found to be most common in early adolescence and identity achievement was most common in older adolescents.

Marcia's theory has also given us a useful way of reconciling the stereotype of troubled adolescence as described by Erikson and Blos, with research findings showing that the majority of adolescents come through the period without serious conflict or psychological problems. In Marcia's terms, while all adolescents go through some form of identity crisis, it is those who struggle with a diffused identity or moratorium state (particularly the former) who are likely to appear disturbed.

How stressful is adolescence really?

A frequent criticism of both Blos's and Erikson's ideas is that they seem to have over-emphasised the degree of conflict and identity crisis experienced by most adolescents. This is a tricky issue; we may hold a stereotype of adolescence as a time of angst and crisis, but (you may be comforted to know) the vast majority of young people do negotiate it successfully. This is not to say that it is always easy to be adolescent, rather that being moody and angst-ridden does not in itself mean that there is anything seriously wrong with you. The frequency of mental health problems does increase in adolescence, but only mildly (Rutter, 1979) – see Table 6.3.

	10 years	15 years	adults
Girls	12.7%	13.2%	7.6%
Boys	10.9%	12.5%	11.9%

Table 6.3 Percentages of children, adolescents and adults suffering mental health problems. From Rutter (1979)

Although most of us do negotiate adolescence successfully, there is no getting away from the fact that it brings with it significant stress – see *Interactive angles* below.

Interactive
angles

Read the following letter from a 14 year old to a magazine.

My life seems okay to other people as I've grown used to putting on a brave face but in truth I'm a mental wreck. I'm 14 and all sorts of things are wrong. I get stressed out about everything, including homework, school and what people think and I've slowly slipped into a depression. My self-confidence is non-existent. I used to think about suicide a bit but now it's getting more serious. I've thought about going to a counsellor but would I be wasting their time? Also I'd rather talk to someone face-to-face than over the phone. How can I find someone? My mum is the best, most understanding person in the whole world and I've already told her some of my problems but not the worst bits. I need someone who will listen to everything without getting upset.

Desperately needing help.

Mizz Magazine

Questions

1 What sources of stress is this young person facing?

2 Based on your own experience of adolescence, how common are these feelings

The case described in *Interactive angles* is probably far from unusual. A classic study by Csikszentmihalyi and Larson (1984) provides more solid empirical evidence that emotional instability in the teen years is real.

classic
research

how moody are adolescents?

Csikszentmihalyi, M. and Larson, R. (1984) Being Adolescent: conflict and growth in the teenage years. New York: Basic Books.

Aim: Classic theories of adolescence, such as those of Erikson and Blos, emphasise the stressful nature of adolescence and focus on conflict with parents and a crisis in identity. However, only a fairly small minority of adolescents suffer real mental health problems. This leaves us with the question, how stressful is adolescence? One way of investigating this is to record the emotional states of adolescents over a period and see just how unstable they are.

Method: Seventy-five adolescents from Chicago took part in an *experience sampling method* (ESM). Participants comprised young people of both sexes from a range of ages, socio-economic backgrounds and ethnic groups. ESM involves participants carrying a pager and a journal. When the pager bleeps the participants have to make a note of what they are doing and how they are feeling in their journal. In this study the pagers bleeped every two hours of waking activity. Participants were also required to reflect on their feelings at the end of a week by completing a questionnaire.

Results: Data were available for both the adolescents' activities and their moods. In terms of their activities about 40 per cent of the time was spent in leisure while 30 per cent was spent in studying or working, while the remainder was spent in essential activities such as eating and travelling. In terms of the major aim of the study, to see how emotional state varied, the major finding was that adolescents had extreme emotions and frequent and fairly dramatic mood swings. They typically moved from deep unhappiness to extreme happiness in less than one hour. Neutral moods were rarely reported, while embarrassment and awkwardness were reported quite frequently.

Conclusion: Adolescents emerged as quite emotionally unstable, suffering extremes of emotion and dramatic mood swings. This is in keeping with the psychodynamic view of adolescence as a stressful and turbulent period.

Coleman's focal model

Coleman (1974, 1990) has proposed a theory, which aims to explain why a minority of adolescents suffer serious problems while the majority seem to negotiate their development of an adult identity relatively smoothly. Coleman (1974) surveyed adolescents at 11, 13, 15 and 17 years about their main sources of anxiety. Three main anxieties emerged: conflict with parents, rejection from peer group and the threat of imminent sexual relationships. It was found that these anxieties tend to peak at different ages. Results are shown in Table 6.4.

main anxiety	sexual relationships	peer conflict	parental conflict
boys	11	15	17
girls	11 and 17	15	15

Table 6.4 Peak ages for major anxieties in adolescence

Coleman suggested that because of this pattern of anxieties across adolescence, under normal circumstances only one issue reaches a crisis point at any one time. Thus adolescent stress is spread out over a period and maintained at a manageable level. For example, sexual anxiety peaks at around puberty. For late developers this sexual anxiety might coincide with the peaking of anxieties around conflict with peers or parents. Coleman suggests that it is this type of coincidence that leads to serious adolescent crises.

Recent studies have strongly supported the idea that different sources of crisis for adolescents tend to peak at different ages. Goossens and Marcoen (1999) studied the peak-timing of anxieties regarding parental relationships, sexual relationships and peer rejection, and found that in the majority of adolescents the anxieties did not peak at the same time. A similar study on Norwegian young people by Kloep (1999) found similar results. Common sense tells us that the adolescent who does have to face more than one crisis at once will have a harder time than many of their peers. There is not, however, currently a substantial body of research to suggest that these are the adolescents who experience mental health or other serious problems.

where to now?

The following are good sources of further information regarding identity development in adolescence:

▶ **Kroger, J. (1996)** *Identity in Adolescence.* **London: Routledge** – contains detailed information on the theories of Erikson and Blos.

▶ **Heaven, P.C.L. (1994)** *Contemporary Adolescence.* **Basingstoke: Macmillan** – a generally very clear and user-friendly book, covering many aspects of adolescence. Chapter 2 deals with identity issues.

what's new?

the development of ethnic identity in adolescence

While this has actually been an area of interest to psychologists for some time, the last few years have seen some particularly interesting studies, and we are only now in a position to draw some conclusions about the development of ethnic identities (Coleman and Hendry,

1999). Our developing identity will inevitably include a sense of our race or *ethnicity*, given the importance we put on race as a social construct. There seems to be a difference, however, between the importance of racial identity according to whether we are part of a majority or a minority ethnic group. Verkuyten (1995) compared self-esteem and ethnic identity in young people from four groups living in Holland; mainstream Dutch, Moroccan, Surinamese and Turkish. It was found that while self-esteem did not vary significantly between the four groups, ethnic identity was a much more important part of the personal identity of the young people in the three minority groups. This is important in reminding those those who grow up largely oblivious to race because they are in the majority ethnic group that race is likely to be much more of an issue among minority groups. An American study by Martinez and Dukes (1997) found a similar trend in US minority groups, with white Americans seeing their ethnicity as considerably less important than did a range of minority ethnic groups.

A study by Phinney and Devitch-Navarro (1997) is particularly interesting in looking at how black-American and Mexican-American adolescents coped with living within two cultures, mainstream-American and that of their own ethnic group. This is called *biculturalism*. Researchers interviewed young people about their bicultural identity, and found that people could be divided into six distinct patterns of identity. These are shown below.

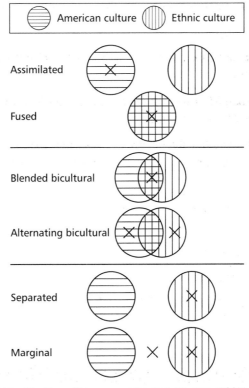

Patterns of cultural identity. From Phinney and Devitch-Navarro (1997)

Coleman and Hendry, 1999

Assimilated adolescents saw their ethnic culture and mainstream American culture as essentially separate, with themselves firmly located in American culture. *Fused* individuals saw their ethnic culture as entirely integrated into American culture and so did not perceive themselves as having a separate identity other than American. Two patterns of truly bicultural identity emerged, in which there is an overlap between the two cultural identities. The *blended bicultural* person locates themselves in the overlap between American and their ethnic culture, feeling equally part of each. The *alternating bicultural* person, on the other hand, sees himself or herself as existing some of the time in mainstream culture and part of the time in their ethnic culture. The *separated* person identifies only with their ethnic culture and sees himself and herself as outside mainstream culture altogether, while the *marginal* person does not feel part of any culture.

Mixed-race adolescents face a particular set of problems. Tizard and Phoenix (1993) investigated identity in British mixed-race adolescents, and found a range of identities. Sixty per cent of the sample were classified as having a positive ethnic identity, while 40 per cent had either a poor identity or mixed attitudes. Those with positive identities tended to be those who attended schools with a good ethnic mix, whereas those with the most negative attitudes tended to be those who were strongly affiliated to white adults.

where to now?

The following is a good source of further information regarding ethnic identity:

▶ **Coleman, J.C. and Hendry, L.B. (1999)** *The Nature of Adolescence*. **London: Routledge** – has an excellent chapter on identity development, including a substantial section on the development of ethnic identity.

Peer relations in adolescence

Many studies (e.g. Adams *et al.*, 1994) have found that adolescents report an increase in the importance of peers in adolescence. The proportion of time spent with peers correspondingly increases. Peer relationships also become more intimate than those of preadolescence, with a new focus on sharing secrets and disclosing feelings. *Peer groups* assume particular importance. Brown (1990) identifies three levels of peer group:

- *dyads* – pairings, most importantly with best friends or lovers

- *cliques* – groups of friends

- *crowds* – wider 'reputation-sharing' groups with shared images and interests but not necessarily friendship.

Adolescents have been found to place considerable value on peer groups. In one large-scale survey of 600 adolescents aged 16 to 18 years, Palmonari *et al.* (1989) found that 90 per cent of those surveyed considered themselves to be part of a peer group. Most opted for informal groups rather than groups associated with formal activities such as sport, music or religion. Almost all the adolescents surveyed identified affiliation to a peer group as an important aspect of their lives. Although adolescent peer groups are frequently a source of anxiety to adults (getting in with a 'bad crowd'), evidence in general seems to support the idea of peer groups as beneficial. Kirchler *et al.* (1991) identified those adolescents unable to affiliate to a group as particularly prone to social difficulties in adulthood.

Peer pressure and conformity in adolescence

Adult stereotypes suggest that adolescents conform very closely to their own *dress codes*. As Durkin (1995) says 'if being a gothic is in, everyone gets sun-shy, wears black garments and dyes their hair'. While this is an easily observable phenomenon there is no evidence that adolescents conform to dress codes any more than those of any other age – as adults we tend to conform to fashion although we might not be so aware of it as an issue.

Berndt (1979) investigated conformity to pro-social and anti-social behaviour throughout adolescence. Adolescents were presented with scenarios in which they were encouraged by peers to steal (anti-social) or help someone with a difficult homework (pro-social). It was found that conformity to peer demands for pro-social behaviour peaked at 11 to 12, while conformity to anti-social behaviour peaked at 14 to 15.

Punks tend to see goths as lacking in culture

Recent surveys of adolescents regarding their perception of *peer pressure* have yielded results that challenge the adult stereotype of teenagers at the mercy of pressure to conform from peers. Lightfoot (1992) found that participants reported an interest in peers' ways of doing things, but little perceived pressure from others. What may be a more significant factor in adolescent conformity may be a wish for *identification* with a group rather than pressure from other members of the group. Some adolescent groups are so homogenous, distinctive and biased against non-members that they constitute *sub-cultures*. Contemporary British sub-cultures – whose members usually affiliate during adolescence, although membership may continue into adulthood – include skinheads, punks, hippies and goths. It is methodologically very difficult to study such sub-cultures from a psychological perspective – they are unlikely to enter a psychology laboratory *en masse* to be experimented upon! However, Widdicombe and Wooffitt (1990) achieved some interesting results by interviewing members of sub-cultures in their natural environments such as at festivals. For example, punks were found to see goths as lacking in culture.

Experienced goths tended to look down upon newer members of the group. In all groups commitment was a major criterion for respect. Thus, full-time new age travellers particularly despise 'weekenders'.

Conclusions

The idea of adolescence has not existed throughout human history, and there are wide variations between current human societies in how teenagers leave childhood behind and enter adult society. There is thus good reason to question whether adolescence is really an essential stage of human development, as we normally think of it. However, it seems that within teenagers of many societies there are common and important themes, including a crisis of identity, extremes of mood, establishment of sexual identity and a growing importance of peers. The theories of Erikson, Blos and Marcia have proved useful in understanding the nature of adolescent identity crises, although Erikson and Blos have probably overstated the degree of crisis experienced by most adolescents. Research has confirmed that adolescents suffer from extreme mood swings, but that these are usually quickly restored, and that there is a moderate increase in the frequency of mental health problems in adolescence. Coleman has suggested that adolescents who suffer serious disturbance are those for whom normal anxieties have peaked together, instead of one at a time as is more usual. The development of ethnic identity is a further dimension of adolescence that seems particularly important for young people living in minority ethnic groups. A number of distinct patterns of identity have been identified among young people who live both within the mainstream culture of their country and the culture of their ethnic group.

what do you know?

1 Outline one example of cultural variation in adolescence. You may wish to consider a difference between two human societies or between two historical periods in the same society.

2 How might physical development affect the development of identity in adolescence?

3 Outline in detail one study that supports an aspect of Erikson's theory of adolescent identity development.

4 Outline one difficulty with Blos's theory of adolescent identity development.

5 Describe Coleman's focal model of adolescent crisis.

6 Outline one study of biculturalism in adolescence.

7

Piaget's theory of cognitive development

what's
ahead?

In this chapter and the next (*Alternative theories of cognitive development*) we will be looking at the normal processes by which children develop intellectually. The best-known and most influential theory of cognitive development is that of the Swiss biologist and psychologist, Jean Piaget. Piaget researched and wrote on the subject of children's cognitive development from the 1920s until the 1980s. Piaget's great contribution to psychology was his belief that the ways in which children think are not less sophisticated than those of adults simply because they have less knowledge, but that they think in an entirely different way. Piaget was interested in both how children learnt and how they thought. From this starting point Piaget went on to contribute three main areas of theory: how children acquire knowledge, how their thinking differs from that of adults and how we can classify children's cognitive development into stages.

Jean Piaget

The acquisition of knowledge

Piaget saw intellectual development as a process in which we actively explore the world and construct a mental representation of reality based on what we discover in our explorations. Piaget noted that even very young children are very inquisitive about their own abilities and about the details of the world. He proposed that the mind contains two types of structure, *schemas* and *operations*.

Schemas

Schemas are mental structures, each of which contains all the information the individual has relating to one aspect of the world. We have schemas for people, objects, actions and more abstract concepts. Piaget believed that we are born with a few innate schemas, which enable us to interact with others (very similar to Bowlby's idea of social releasers – see Chapter 2). During the first year of life we construct other schemas. An important early schema is the 'mum-schema' that develops as the child realises that its primary carer is a separate (and extremely important!) person.

Equilibration

When we can comprehend everything around us, we are said to be in a state of equilibrium. Look around the room for a moment and consider whether you understand as much as you need to about the contents of the room. The chances are that you do and hence you are in a state of equilibrium. However, whenever we meet a new situation that cannot be explained by our existing schemas, we experience the unpleasant sensation of disequilibrium. It may be that at this moment you are in a mild state of disequilibrium as you try to grasp the details of Piagetian theory! According to Piaget we are instinctively driven to gain an understanding of the world and so escape disequilibrium. He identified two processes by which equilibration takes place, namely *assimilation* and *accommodation*.

Assimilation takes place when a new experience can be understood by altering an existing schema. For example, when an infant who has a 'bird' schema based on the family canary first encounters sparrows in the garden it will assimilate sparrows into the 'bird' schema.

Accommodation takes place when a new experience is so radically different that it cannot be assimilated into existing schemas and so a new schema is formed. An example of accommodation occurs when the infant in the above example first encounters an aeroplane, and this new object is just too distinctive to incorporate into the 'bird' schema, and so an aeroplane schema is formed.

Operations

As well as knowledge of things we will encounter in the world, we also need to understand the rules by which the world operates. Piaget called these rules *operations* and, very importantly, he suggested that the reason that children think in different ways at different stages of their development is because the operations of which we are capable change with age. Piaget believed that, while schemas develop with experience, operations develop as the child's brain matures. The very young child does not have operations at all, and they are thus said to be *pre-operational*. The first operations to appear are *concrete*. This means that children can understand the rules governing something, provided they can see it. Later, rules governing abstract concepts are understood. The rest of Piaget's theory is largely dependent on this idea of operations. The errors of logic that Piaget identified in children's thinking take place because of the limited operations available to them. Piaget's *stage theory of development* is based around the maturing of operations.

for and against

Piaget's view of knowledge acquisition

- Children are certainly curious from a very young age. This fits in well with Piaget's theory.

- The concept of the schemas as the basic unit of knowledge is widely accepted by psychologists.

- We can tolerate rather more inconsistencies and gaps in our knowledge of the world than we might expect if we suffer disequilibrium whenever we are unable to explain something.

- Piaget was largely describing the way that highly intelligent individuals such as himself operated. By definition, researchers in psychology are largely motivated by intellectual curiosity, and it is possible that Piaget overestimated the importance of such curiosity in the rest of us.

Logical flaws in children's thinking

Piaget conducted a number of studies of children's ability to carry out tasks of logic. His earliest studies were observations of children playing. Piaget noted that different children of the same age tended to make the same mistakes, and he suggested that this was because children of the same age tended to commit the same errors in logic. From these observations was born the idea that children do not just know less but think *differently* from adults. Piaget went on to conduct experimental studies, initially on his own children but later on large numbers of children at a psychology laboratory. He also interviewed children (at least those who were old enough) to try to get an idea of how they were thinking when they committed errors in logic. We will look now at some of Piaget's major areas of research into children's thinking.

Object permanence

Piaget was interested in children's intellectual development from birth until adolescence. His best-known work on very young children concerned their understanding of *object permanence*. 'Object permanence' refers to the understanding that objects exist permanently even when they are no longer visible. Piaget observed the behaviour of infants who were looking at an attractive object when it was removed from their sight. Until about 8 months, children would immediately switch their attention away from the object once it was out of sight. From about 8 months, however, they would actively look for the object. If, for example, it were pushed behind a screen within their reach they would simply push the screen aside. Piaget concluded from this that, prior to about 8 months of age, children do not understand that objects continue to exist once they are out of sight. Support for Piaget's idea comes from a variation in his procedure in which the hidden object is covered by a sheet, such that the object's shape is clearly visible to the child. Children still did not respond to the object, suggesting they really did not understand that the object continued to exist.

This 9 month old has no difficulty in locating his teddy bear behind a screen!

It seems that even when young children have grasped the fact that objects still exist after they cannot be seen, they continue for a time to have difficulty with locating hidden objects. In a variation on his object permanence procedure, Piaget noted that when children get used to looking behind a particular screen for the concealed object, they will sometimes continue to look behind the *same* screen even when they have seen the experimenter hide the object elsewhere. This showed that, although grasping object permanence was a significant milestone in the child's development, there are further steps to be taken in the child's understanding of the properties of objects.

Some later researchers have questioned the reliability of Piaget's research on object permanence and his assertion that children do not begin to understand object permanence until the age of 8 months. Freeman *et al.* (1980) replicated Piaget's studies showing that children will look for objects in the place they were previously found, rather than where they were seen to be concealed, and found similar results. However, when they used screens featuring pictures of upside-down faces, the number of children looking in the wrong place rose from 6 to 13 out of the 21. This shows that the environment in which this type of study is carried out causes wild variations in the results and casts doubt on the validity of Piaget's approach. Other research has shown that children may have an understanding of object permanence at an earlier age than was suggested by Piaget. One such study was by Baillargeon and DeVos (1991).

research now

when do babies really acquire an understanding of object permanence?

Baillargeon, R. and DeVos, J. (1991) Object permanence in young infants: further evidence. *Child Development 62, 1227–46.*

Aim: Piaget believed that because infants below about 8 months did not actively pursue an object once it was out of sight, this meant that they did not have an understanding of object permanence. However, there are other possible explanations for Piaget's findings. Younger children might simply not have the co-ordination or the ability to maintain their attention on an object without its being in view. This study aimed to test infants' understanding of object permanence by an alternative method.

Method: We know that infants focus their attention for longer periods on *discrepant events*, i.e. unusual or seemingly impossible events (Kagan, 1977). The researchers aimed to set up an object permanence task in which infants witnessed an 'impossible' condition. A screen was set up with a window in the top half in front of 3-month-old babies. Long and short carrots were passed behind the screen held vertically. This meant that the 'possible' or control condition, long carrots could be seen passing by the window and the short carrots could not be seen until they emerged at the edge of the screen. In the 'impossible' condition the long and short carrots were passed behind the screen, but neither were visible in the window, although they emerged as expected at the edge of the screen. The time the infants spent looking at the carrots in each condition was measured. The idea behind the study was that, if children looked for longer at the long carrots in the impossible condition, they must have identified a discrepant event and must therefore have an understanding of object permanence.

Results: The infants looked for significantly longer at the long carrots, which had not appeared in the window during the 'impossible' condition once they had reappeared at the edge of the screen.

Conclusion: Children had presumably spotted the fact that the non-appearance of the long carrots at the window was a discrepant event, because they looked at these carrots for a longer period once they had reappeared. This suggests that they knew that the carrots were still there when they were out of sight, and hence that they had some understanding of object permanence.

Newer and more sophisticated studies like that of Baillargeon and DeVos appear to show that babies develop some concept of object permanence at a rather earlier age than was suggested by Piaget.

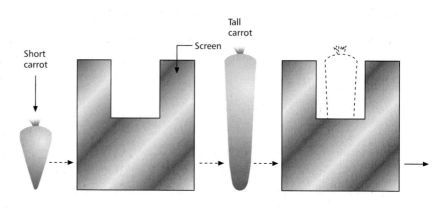

The apparatus used by Baillargeon and DeVos (1991)

Egocentrism

Egocentrism is the tendency to see the world entirely from our own perspective, and to have great difficulty in seeing the world from the viewpoint of others. Unlike difficulty with object impermanence, which is associated with specific ages, egocentrism declines gradually throughout childhood. Piaget saw egocentrism as applying to both abstract and concrete concepts. A classic study by Piaget and Inhelder (1956) illustrated egocentrism in the physical environment.

Piaget and Inhelder's three mountains experiment

In Piaget and Inhelder's famous 'three mountains experiment', each model mountain had a different marker on the top, a cross, a house or a covering of snow. A doll was positioned to the side of the three mountains. Children were sat in front of the scene and shown pictures of the scene from different viewpoints. Their task was to select the picture that best matched what the doll could 'see'. Piaget and Inhelder noted that children aged below 7 years old had difficulty with this task, and tended to choose the picture of the scene from their own point of view. You can demonstrate egocentrism for yourself by watching the television news with a young child, and asking them what the newsreader can see. Young children will often find this concept difficult and believe that the newsreader can see *them*.

Related to egocentrism is the phenomenon of *animism*. Piaget (1973) reported that children aged 2 to 4 years typically attribute lifelike characteristics to inanimate objects. They may, for example, worry about hurting or offending their toys, or indeed they may punish their toys when they are 'naughty'. By about 4 years children have a clear understanding of which objects around them are alive and which are not. Related to animism is *artificialism*, whereby children tend to believe that natural phenomena have been created by people. If you have ever tried to convince a child that the television weather presenter is just reporting the weather and has not in fact created it you will understand artificialism!

Conservation

Conservation refers to the understanding that objects remain the same in quantity even when their appearance changes. Piaget (1952) reported that young children had difficulty with tasks of conservation. He demonstrated this in a number of situations, two of which are particularly well known.

Number conservation

Piaget found that if two rows of counters are laid out side by side, with the same number of counters spaced apart at the same distance, children correctly spotted that there were the same number of counters in each row. If you want to try this at home Smarties make ideal counters (but as the child will probably eat them, check with the parents first!). If, however, the counters in one of the rows were pushed closer together, young children typically thought that there were now fewer counters in that row.

Liquid conservation

Piaget found that if children see two glasses together with liquid coming up to the same height in each they can correctly spot the fact that they contain the same amount of liquid. If however liquid was poured from a

Children at the pre-operational stage say that the two rows contain the same number of pennies...

...but also that there are more pennies in the more spread-out, second row.

Piaget's demonstration of number conservation

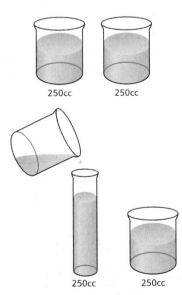

250cc   250cc

250cc   250cc

Children at the pre-operational stage believe that the volume of water is greater after it has been transferred to the taller glass.

Piaget's demonstration of liquid conservation

short, wide glass to a taller, thinner container, young children typically believe there was now more liquid in the taller container.

There have been challenges to Piaget's ideas about conservation. In a classic study, McGarrigle and Donaldson (1974) demonstrated that children's answers in conservation tasks are strongly affected by the circumstances in which the transformation of the material takes place.

classic research

when do children really understand conservation?

McGarrigle, J. and Donaldson, M. (1974) Conservation accidents. *Cognition 3, 341–50.*

Aim: In his research on number conservation Piaget had shown that when he pushed counters closer together so that the row was shorter, children typically responded by saying that there were now fewer counters in the row. From this he had concluded that young children do not have a good understanding of number conservation. However, McGarrigle and Donaldson suggested that actually the children did understand that there were still the same number of counters, but that they had assumed that Piaget had *wanted them to say* that there were now fewer counters, otherwise why would he ask the question? They tested this idea by creating a condition in which the length of the row appeared to change accidentally rather than deliberately.

Method: There were 80 participants aged 4 to 6 years. All took part in both conditions. In the control condition, they were subjected to the standard Piagetian task, in which the experimenter presented them with the two rows of counters, asked them whether there were the same number in each row, then pushed the counters in one row closer and asked them again. In the experimental condition, once the children had been asked whether there were the same number in each row, a 'naughty teddy' ran across the table and, apparently accidentally, pushed the counters in one row closer together. The children were then asked whether there were the same number of counters in each row. The idea was that in this condition the children should not be influenced by the fact that the experimenter moved the counters then asked about them.

Results: The difference between children's apparent ability to conserve in the two conditions was dramatic. In the Piaget condition only 13 of the 80 children (16 per cent) correctly said that there were the same number of counters in the two rows. However, in the experimental condition, 50 of the children (62 per cent) answered correctly.

Conclusion: The results suggest that McGarrigle and Donaldson were correct to suggest that children acquire their understanding of number conservation at an earlier age than was believed by Piaget. They also suggest that Piaget's methods of researching conservation were flawed, because children were responding to what they thought the adult wanted to hear them say rather than what they believed.

It is worth noting that numerous researchers have attempted to replicate this study, and that not all have confirmed the results of McGarrigle and Donaldson. We are thus not really sure exactly when children begin to conserve successfully. However, we can learn much about the difficulties of conducting research with children from looking at the contrasting results obtained by Piaget, and by McGarrigle and Donaldson. It seems that the ways in which adults behave when interacting with children have a profound effect on the behaviour of the children, and that children can respond to adult researchers in quite subtle and unpredictable ways. It is well worth remembering that children are usually more interested in the researcher than whatever task the researcher has for them!

Formal reasoning

Piaget believed that from about 11 years of age, children became capable of abstract or formal reasoning. The term *formal* indicates that children capable of this type of reasoning can focus on the *form* of an argument and not be distracted by its content. For example, if a child capable of formal reasoning is presented with the following syllogism – 'All green birds have two heads. I have a green bird called Charlie. How many heads does Charlie have?' – they should be able to answer 'two' (Smith *et al.*, 1998). Before a child becomes capable of this type of reasoning they would be more likely to become distracted by the content and suggest that birds do not really have two heads.

Inhelder and Piaget (1958) gave Swiss schoolchildren some science questions and gave them the task of devising hypotheses and carrying out experiments to test these. One such task was to investigate the pendulum problem. Children were given pendulums of different weights and string of different lengths. Their task was to determine whether the speed of the pendulum depends on its weight or the length of the string. It was found that most 11 to 15 year olds were capable of setting up and carrying out this and similar tasks.

Piaget believed that we all achieve formal reasoning eventually, although there is some variation in age and some only achieve formal thinking by the age of 20. However, a number of studies have concluded that many people are not capable of formal thinking. In a longitudinal study (one in which participants are followed up over a long period), Bradmetz (1999) studied the cognitive development of 62 children until they were 15 years old. When they were 15 years old he gave them a battery of tests, including the Inhelder and Piaget science task, designed to measure formal thinking. Only one of the 62 young people proved capable of formal thinking, less than 2 per cent. Of course, if they were tested again at the age of 20 many more may demonstrate formal operational thinking, but Bradmetz's results do at least show that formal thinking tends to develop later than Piaget believed.

for and
against

Piaget's research

+ From his early observational studies Piaget developed highly original and effective experimental procedures such as the three mountains experiment and the conservation tasks.

− Later research has uncovered limitations with some of Piaget's procedures. In particular he did not adequately take into account the impact of the social aspects of the experimental procedures on children's behaviour.

+ Piaget's fundamental belief that the sophistication of children's reasoning increases with age is generally supported by later research.

− There have been challenges, however, to Piaget's ideas about the ages at which children develop different abilities. Most contemporary psychologists believe that children achieve object permanence and conservation at an earlier age than was suggested by Piaget, but that abstract reasoning is achieved later, if at all.

Piaget's stage theory

Based on the types of logical error Piaget identified as typical of children of different ages, he proposed a stage theory of development. Piaget identified four stages of development:

- *sensorimotor* stage – 0 to 2 years
- *preoperational* stage – 2 to 7 years
- *concrete operational* stage – 7 to 11 years
- *formal operational* stage – 11 years+.

Piaget believed that we all pass through all four stages in the same order, hence he referred to them as *invariant*. However, we vary considerably in the age at which we arrive at each stage, and the ages given above for each stage are intended only as broad averages. We reach each stage when our brain is mature enough to permit the use of new types of logic or *operations*. Let us look briefly at the type of thinking that takes place at each stage.

The sensorimotor stage

This lasts approximately the first two years of life. Piaget believed that our main focus at this point is on physical sensation and on learning to co-ordinate our bodies. We learn by trial and error that certain actions have certain effects. Infants are fascinated when they realise that they can move parts of their body and eventually other objects. By the second year of life infants are quite mobile, and so are well equipped actively to explore their environment. They are extremely curious and often experiment with actions to discover their effects. By the end of the sensori-motor stage infants are aware of themselves as separate from the rest of the world and have begun to develop language.

The preoperational stage

By the end of the second year, the child has sufficient grasp of language for its thinking to be based around symbolic thought rather than physical sensation. However, the child has not developed sufficiently to grasp logical rules or operations (hence the term *preoperational*) and it deals with the world very much as it appears rather than as it is. Preoperational children are thus highly egocentric, have difficulty in conservation, and tend to believe in animism and artificialism.

The concrete operational stage

The child's mind is now mature enough to use logical thought or operations, but children can only apply logic to objects and situations that are present and physical (hence *concrete* operational). Thus children now lose their tendency for animism and artificialism. They become less egocentric and better at conservation tasks. However, concrete operational children have great difficulty in carrying out logical tasks without the physical objects in front of them. Think back for a moment to the tasks we looked at when we examined formal reasoning earlier in this chapter, such as syllogisms. Children in the concrete operational stage find syllogisms very difficult.

Formal operational stage

In the formal operational stage children become capable of formal reasoning (see earlier in this chapter). Formal operational thinkers can respond to the form of syllogisms and devise and test hypotheses. Piaget took this to mean that children had entered a new stage of adult logic, where abstract reasoning was possible. As well as systematic abstract reasoning, formal operations permits the development of a system of values and ideals, and an appreciation of philosophical issues.

Discussion of Piaget's stages

Piaget's stages have proved extremely useful for anyone who has to explain ideas to children of different ages. One area where this is clearly important is education, and we will spend some time later in this chapter looking at how Piaget's ideas, and those of other cognitive-developmental theorists, have been applied to teaching and designing programmes of study. Another important, though less well-known application of Piaget's stages is in paediatric medicine and nursing. Hurley and Whelan (1988) noted the behaviour and comments of children of different ages in severe pain, and concluded that their understanding of their pain corresponded closely to their Piagetian stage. Hurley and Whelan's findings are summarised in Table 7.1.

How children perceive the cause and effect of pain (Hurley and Whelan, 1988)	
Piagetian stage	**Perception of pain**
Pre-operational	Pain is primarily a physical experience. Children think about the magical disappearance of pain. Not able to distinguish between cause and effect of pain. Pain is often perceived as a punishment for a wrongdoing or bad thought (Gildea and Quirk, 1977), particularly if the child did something he or she was told not to immediately before the pain started. Children's egocentricity means that they hold someone else responsible for their pain and, therefore, are likely to strike out verbally or physically when they have pain. Children may tell a nurse who gave them an injection 'You are mean' (McCaffery, 1972).
Concrete operational	Relate to pain physically. Able to specify location in terms of body parts. Increased awareness of the body and internal organs means that fear of bodily harm is a strong influence in their perceptions of painful events. Fear of total annihilation (bodily destruction and death) enters their thinking (Alex and Ritchie, 1992; Schultz, 1971).
Transitional; formal	Have a perception of pain that is not quite as sophisticated as formal-operational children. Their perception of pain is not as literal as would be expected in children who are in the concrete-operational stage of development. Children in the transitional stage are beginning to understand the concept of 'if …then' propositions.
Formal operational	Begin to solve problems. Do not always have required coping mechanisms to facilitate consistent mature responses. Imagine the sinister implications of pain (Muller *et al.*, 1986).

Table 7.1 Children's perceptions of pain according to their Piagetian stage. From Twycross (1998)

Twycross (1998) has proposed that Piaget's stages form a good basis with which nurses can understand children's perception of pain and to inform them on how to communicate with children of different ages on the subject of pain. She goes on to suggest that current nursing procedures to assess pain in children are flawed because they do not take account of the child's developmental stage.

for and against

Piaget's stages

+ The idea that children become capable of more advanced logic as they get older is generally accepted.

− However, the Piagetian idea of *stages* is controversial. It may be that children gradually learn to tackle more complex logical tasks with greater experience and continual brain maturation.

+ Smith *et al.* (1998) reviewed studies of the concrete operational stage and concluded that there is strong support for the idea of concrete operational logic.

− More controversial is the preoperational stage. Much post-Piagetian research, e.g. McGarrigle and Donaldson (1974), has cast doubt on Piaget's findings concerning children's inability to conserve.

− Numerous studies, for example that of Bradmetz (1999), have found that most teenagers do not reach Piaget's formal operational stage.

where to now?

The following are further sources of good information regarding Piaget's work:

▷ **Phillips, J.L. (1975)** *The Origins of Intellect: Piaget's theory.* **San Francisco: Freeman** − quite old, but still perhaps the best review of Piaget's work. In-depth coverage of the issues we have discussed here, though of course without the newer research findings.

▷ **Smith, P.K., Cowie, H. and Blades, M. (1998)** *Understanding Children's Development.* **Oxford: Blackwell** − an excellent general child development text with a large chunk devoted to the work of Piaget.

▷ **Lee, V. and Das Gupta, P. (1995)** *Children's Cognitive and Language Development.* **Oxford: Blackwell** − the first chapter gives a good, detailed but quite easy to follow account of Piaget's major contributions.

Applying Piaget's ideas to education

Think back to the ways in which you have been taught at school, college and perhaps university. You will by now have experienced a variety of teaching styles, and it might have occurred to you to wonder how teachers decide to teach. You may at times have also wondered who decides what is taught and how they choose what you have to study. In fact, both teaching methods and the curriculum (the content of what you learn) have been powerfully influenced by cognitive-developmental theories. In this chapter we will consider both teaching style and curriculum development. Briefly though, let us look first at the Plowden Report, which began the move towards cognitive-developmental models of teaching and learning.

The Plowden report

You may have heard about or seen film of the ways in which people used to be taught in primary schools. Pupils typically sat in rows and learnt material by rote, i.e. they repeated it in unison until they knew it by heart. Children who were not able to keep up with the pace at which the majority learnt were often punished. In the 1960s, however, the Plowden committee was set up in order to examine ways of improving primary education, and they investigated the work of Piaget and incorporated his ideas into their report. The final report, published in 1967, recommended a shift away from traditional teaching towards *child-centred teaching*, i.e. teaching based on the abilities and wishes of children. We can pick out three main messages from the Plowden report:

- Children need to be given individual attention and cannot all be treated in the same way.

- Children should not be taught things until they are developed enough intellectually to cope with them.

- Children mature intellectually, physically and emotionally at different rates. Teachers should be aware of the stage of development each child has reached, and should treat them accordingly.

Piaget's research was generally not aimed at education. However, following the Plowden report, teachers began to put Piaget's ideas into practice in the classroom. The following are some of the main implications of Piagetian theory for classroom practice and curriculum development (adapted from Smith *et al.*, 1998, Child, 1997 and Faulkner, 1995).

Classroom practice

- As children think in quite different and less logical ways than do adults, teachers should adapt to the ways in which children think rather than expect children to adapt to them. One way in which this can be achieved is for the teacher to create situations where children can learn for themselves rather than simply telling them facts. It is also important to create situations that are appropriate for children of the particular age. We would not, for example, give children still in the concrete-operational stage tasks that require skills of abstract reasoning. Such tasks would become appropriate only after the children had achieved formal operations.

- Children learn best by *discovery*. The role of the teacher is thus to facilitate learning situations in which children can find things out for themselves. This does not, of course, mean simply leaving children to their own devices. In effective child-centred learning the teacher presents children with tasks specifically designed to lead them to discover things for themselves. A wide variety of such tasks needs to be given, in order for the child to construct their knowledge of all necessary aspects of the world. In nursery and primary school, materials like water, sand, bricks and crayons all help children build physical and hence mental constructions. Later, projects and science practicals help children explore the nature of their world.

- The aim of education is to develop children's thinking rather than just to increase their level of knowledge. This means that, when children try to work things out, what is important is their *reasoning* rather than the answer. It is therefore important that teachers encourage children for producing answers that are wrong but well thought-out.

A classroom set up for discovery learning

Curriculum development

- Clearly, if children are capable of understanding different concepts at different stages of development, then the curriculum should be tailored so that children encounter new ideas when they can cope with them. This was one of the aims of the *National Curriculum*, which governs what children are taught in both primary and secondary school in England and Wales. The curriculum also needs to be flexible enough to allow for the fact that different children do not reach the same stage of development at the same age.

- In the primary curriculum, it is important to allow for the transition from preoperational thinking to concrete-operational thinking. Concepts should be included that allow children to test and develop their logical abilities. In practice this means that the curriculum must permit some discovery learning.

- In the secondary curriculum, the concepts that children encounter should reflect children's predominantly concrete thinking. Introducing tasks involving abstract reasoning should be done with caution.

Interactive
angles

Think back to your own schooling. If you attended school since the 1960s the chances are that the way you were taught was influenced to some extent by Piagetian theory. Consider the following points:

Questions

1 Did you spend a lot of time at school listening to your teacher tell you about what you were studying, or did you tend to spend more time working on tasks on your own?

2 Were the tasks you were given at school generally suitable for your abilities? In other words, was there a lot that you simply didn't understand, or that was so easy that you didn't have to think about it? According to Piaget the aim should have been to give you tasks that stretched your abilities and made you think, but were also within your capabilities.

for and against

applying Piagetian principles to education

+ The principle that children are not passive receivers of knowledge but need somehow to construct their own knowledge is generally accepted in educational circles.

− There is, however, considerable disagreement over whether child-centred learning best does this. Modern 'chalk and talk' teaching is much more interactive than the pre-Piaget 'traditional' styles and may be at least as effective as child-centred learning.

− Whereas Piaget believed that children could learn in isolation and this is encouraged in some schools, modern research shows clearly that children learn faster when working in groups and with the intervention of adults. We will look at such research in Chapter 8.

+ Piaget has given us a good base for developing the curriculum, although modern curricula take account of the current belief that Piaget tended to underestimate the abilities of younger children and overestimate the abilities of older children.

what's new?

Case's neo-Piagetian approach

Case (1985) has produced a theory of cognitive development based on information processing theory. The information processing approach to cognitive development is 'the study of cognitive processes by analogy with the computer' (Jarvis, 1994). Case saw children as developing intellectually by solving problems. Like a computer, the child is limited in what problems it can solve by its information-processing capacity. Whereas Piaget saw the *types of thinking* changing during childhood, Case saw cognitive development as depending on the growing capacity of the child's information processing systems. More advanced logical tasks cannot be performed by young children because they would require more information processing capacity than the child has in its early years.

The basis of cognitive development

Like Piaget, Case saw cognitive development as dependent on the development of the brain. However, Case has gone further than Piaget and proposed certain cognitive and neural changes that lead to greater ability to process information:

- *Myelinisation* of brain cells; brain cells develop sheaths of a protein called myelin which insulates the cells. This allows faster transmission of nerve impulses.
- Growth of *mental space*; this is essentially the working memory. The capacity of working memory determines how much material can be thought about at once. As the brain matures the capacity of the child's mental space increases.
- *Automaticity*; with practice some problem-solving strategies become automatic, thus freeing up mental space for other cognitive tasks.

Whereas Piaget saw children as instinctively motivated to explore and understand their environment, Case saw children as having four instincts which together produced cognitive development:

- instinct to explore
- instinct to solve problems
- instinct to imitate others
- instinct to understand and co-operate with others.

The most important of these is the instinct to solve problems. In the last two instincts, to imitate others, and to understand and co-operate with them, you may recognise Vygotsky's ideas of the social basis of cognitive development (Meadows, 1993). Unlike Vygotsky, who conceived of the child as dependent on the attention of others for cognitive development, Case proposed that children instinctively seek out others and interact with them. This fits in well with our current ideas of children's social instincts.

Stages of development

Case identifies four stages that correspond approximately to Piaget's stages. Case's stages are as follows:

- sensorimotor stage
- representational stage (corresponding roughly to Piaget's preoperational stage)
- logical stage (corresponding roughly to Piaget's concrete operational stage)
- formal operational stage.

Case saw the transition between these stages as occurring when the mental space of the child reached a certain level. We achieve adult reasoning at around puberty when our brain has matured sufficiently for us to have our full quota of mental space.

Case has successfully taken aspects of Piaget's theory and rewritten them using the language of modern cognitive psychology. For this reason Case is sometimes called a 'neo-Piagetian'. There is empirical support for the idea that the children's information processing speed and capacity increases with age. For example, Kail (1991) measured the response times of children of different ages on a wide variety of tasks and across different cultures. He found that, with age, processing time speeds up irrespective of culture or the nature of the task.

Case's stages attract the same criticism as Piaget's – namely that not all research has confirmed that children's thinking undergoes the radical changes at certain ages as assumed by a stage-model. Furthermore Case does not place much emphasis on aspects of cognitive development like social interaction, modes of representation and language development that many people, particularly those from the social constructivist school (see Chapter 8), believe to be absolutely central to understanding cognitive development.

Conclusions

Piaget was interested in how children acquired knowledge of the world. He believed that knowledge was acquired as children developed two mental structures, schemas and operations. Schemas develop through experience and each contains our knowledge of one aspect of the world. Operations, which are the rules of how the world works, develop with brain maturity. Piaget was also interested in how children's thinking differs from that of adults. He identified a number of flaws in children's logic, including object impermanence, animism and artificialism, egocentrism, failure to conserve and inability in abstract reasoning. Each of these flaws is associated with particular ages, and from this idea Piaget developed his four-stage theory of development. Piaget's ideas have been applied in education both in terms of classroom practice and in designing the National Curriculum.

what do you know?

1 Distinguish between schemas and operations.

2 Outline one study into object permanence.

3 What is egocentrism? Give an example.

4 What is conservation?

5 Describe one longitudinal study into the development of formal reasoning. What implications does this study have for Piaget's theories?

6 What logical errors would you expect children to make in the preoperational stage?

7 Outline two ways in which Piaget's theory can be applied to education.

8

Alternative theories of cognitive development

Although Piaget's theory is unquestionably the most famous approach to cognitive development and it has been hugely influential in child psychology and education, there are alternative ideas, which have grown in influence in recent years. In Chapter 7 we have already looked at the neo-Piagetian approach of Robbie Case. In this chapter we shall look at the *social constructive* theories of Vygotsky and Bruner, who differed from Piaget in their emphasis on culture, social interaction and language on cognitive development. We then look at how the ideas of Vygotsky and Bruner have been applied to education. In *What's new?* we can see how the ideas of Vygotsky and Bruner can help us understand the use of computers in the classroom. Finally we move on to look at an exciting contemporary area of cognitive-developmental research, the development of children's *theory of mind*.

Vygotsky's theory of cognitive development

Vygotsky was a contemporary of Piaget in Piaget's early days, though Vygotsky died young in 1934. His work was first published in the West in the 1960s, since which time it has grown hugely in influence, especially in the last ten years (Wertsch and Tulviste, 1996). Vygotsky agreed with Piaget on many key points, for example that cognitive development takes place in stages characterised by different styles of thinking. He disagreed, however, with Piaget's view of the child as exploring the world independently, and instead placed a strong emphasis on social interaction during learning and the culture in which the child grows up. Where Piaget's approach is sometimes known as *constructivist* because of the child's construction of its mental representation of the world, Vygotsky's is referred to as a *social constructivist* theory because of this emphasis on social interaction.

The importance of culture and social interaction

Vygotsky placed far more emphasis than did Piaget on the role played by culture in the child's development. Vygotsky saw children as being born with basic mental functions such as the ability to perceive the outside world and to focus attention on particular objects. However, children lack higher mental functions such as thinking and problem-solving. These higher mental functions are seen as 'tools' of the culture in which the individual lives, and are cultural in origin. Tools are transmitted to children by older members of the culture in guided learning experiences (such as lessons in school), and include the ability to use language, art and mathematics. Experiences with other people gradually become internalised and form the child's internal representation of the world. Thus, the way each child thinks and sees the world is shared with other members of its culture.

What this means is that people in different cultures will have quite different sets of tools, hence different ways of thinking. Luria, a colleague of Vygotsky (Luria and Yudovich, 1971), compared styles of thinking in traditional Uzbecki people of Central Asia, some of which maintained their traditional culture while others had adopted a more modern lifestyle. Luria found that traditional Uzbecki tended to respond to reasoning tasks by the use of concrete examples from their own experience. By contrast the educated Uzbecki used abstract reasoning. Luria's study demonstrated that when a culture changes, a different set of tools are transmitted to the next generation and the thinking of the culture changes.

The zone of proximal development

In contrast to Piaget, who emphasised how much a child can learn by exploring its environment, Vygotsky believed that children can develop far more quickly during interaction with others. Children, according to

Vygotsky, could never develop formal operational thinking without the help of others. The difference between what a child can learn on its own and what it can potentially learn through interaction with others is called the *zone of proximal development* (ZPD). Whereas Piaget believed that the limiting factor in what a child could learn at any time was its stage of development, Vygotsky believed that the crucial factor was the availability of other 'experts' who could instruct the child. Unlike Piaget, Vygotsky emphasised instruction from others about how to do things in order for the child to achieve its potential. As the child progresses through a zone of proximal development or *learning cycle*, the amount of instruction from experts will reduce. At first, explicit and detailed instructions are needed but later on, prompts are sufficient to help the child progress.

The role of language

Vygotsky placed far more emphasis on the importance of language in cognitive development than did Piaget. For Piaget, language simply appeared when the child had reached a sufficiently advanced stage of development. The child's grasp of language depended on its current level of cognitive development. For Vygotsky, however, language developed from social interactions with others and was a very important cultural tool. At first the sole function of language is communication, and language and thought develop separately. Later, the child internalises language and learns to use it as a tool of thinking. In the preoperational stage, as children learn to use language to help with tricky cognitive tasks, they speak aloud while solving problems (you can often hear children doing this). Once in the concrete operational stage this inner speech becomes silent.

Vygotsky was probably correct in saying that Piaget underestimated the importance of social interaction with more experienced people during learning. Later in this chapter, when we go on to look at the ways in which the ideas of Vygotsky and Bruner have been applied to education, we will see that children learn more quickly working together than they do alone. A more controversial aspect of Vygotsky's theory was the idea that, because tools are specific to different cultures, cultures that do not have formal schooling do not develop the ability for abstract thinking. Effectively this is saying that some cultures are better at thinking than others; an assumption that we would now criticise for being highly *ethnocentric*, i.e. from the perspective of a single culture. Contemporary psychologists influenced by Vygotsky see different cultures as having different 'toolkits' (Wertsch, 1991), i.e. qualitatively different sets of tools, rather than having more or fewer tools than one another.

for and against

Vygotsky

- **+** Vygotsky was probably correct in criticising Piaget for understimating the importance of social interaction in learning.

- **−** However, Vygotsky may have exaggerated the importance of culture. If all higher mental processes are cultural in origin we would expect different cultures to vary far more than they do in their thinking.

- **+** There is considerable support for the idea that children develop quicker with some instruction. This demonstrates the existence of the ZPD.

- **−** Vygotsky's view of cultural differences in thinking is, by modern standards, ethnocentric because he believed that cultures that use formal schooling to transmit the tools of the culture – as happens in Europe – produce children capable of more advanced thinking than cultures that do not have formal schooling.

- **+** Modern Vygotskians have eliminated this flaw by seeing the tools of different cultures as qualitatively different rather than superior or inferior to one another.

where to now?

The following are good sources of information on the work of Vygotsky:

▷ **Faulkner, D., Littleton, K. and Woodhead, M. (1998)** *Learning Relationships in the Classroom*. **London: Routledge** – a collection of papers from some contemporary researchers that focus on Vygotsky's view of learning.

▷ **Lee, V. and Das Gupta, P. (1995)** *Children's Cognitive and Language Development*. **Oxford: Blackwell** – the first chapter gives a good, detailed but quite easy-to-follow account of Vygotsky's major contributions.

Bruner's theory of cognitive development

Bruner has written more recently than Piaget or Vygotsky, and he has applied and adapted aspects of both theories. Bruner rejected the idea of developmental stages as used by both Piaget and Vygotsky. Instead he preferred to look at cognitive development in terms of the way information is represented in the mind at different ages.

Modes of representation

Bruner (1966) placed much emphasis on *modes of representation*. A mode of representation is the *form* in which information is kept in the mind. When we think, we mentally manipulate information. As a child's mind develops it becomes capable of manipulating information in different forms, and this affects the type of reasoning of which they are capable. Bruner identified three modes of representation, each of which appears at a specific age.

Enactive representation

This is the first type of representation to appear in children's minds and corresponds to the type of representation that Piaget believed to be present in children at the early sensorimotor stage. Thinking in the first year is based entirely on physical actions. What knowledge we have during our first year is entirely dependent on what we can do with our bodies. We thus experience thinking as motor actions. This type of thinking does not disappear once other modes of representation develop, but is present in adults as what we sometimes call 'muscle memory'. Thus when we think of performing a physical task such as tying a shoelace we may think in terms of the necessary hand movements.

Iconic representation

This is the representation of information in the mind in the form of pictures or *mental images*. According to Bruner this appears at about one year of age. Piaget described this type of representation in the second half of his sensorimotor stage. As children the development of iconic representation allows us to reproduce images; thus drawing becomes possible. However, holding images in the mind does not help us solve problems. Bruner and Kenney (1966) demonstrated that children relying on iconic representation could not perform a *transposition task*. We look at this in the *Classic research* section below.

Symbolic representation

Whereas Piaget saw the transition in children's thinking that takes place at around 7 years as a result of the development of concrete operations, Bruner saw it as dependent on the development of *symbolic thinking*. Symbolic thinking means that language (and other symbolic forms such as numbers and music) can now be used for thinking. This use of symbols allows the child to categorise things and start to think logically. Bruner believed that symbolic thought became possible when the child had achieved a certain level of mastery of language. Language was thus very important to Bruner, as it was to Vygotsky.

classic
research

what can children do once they develop symbolic thought?

Bruner, J.S. and Kenney, H. (1966) *The Development of the Concepts of Order and Proportion in Children*. New York: Wiley.

Aim: Bruner and Kenney (1966) set out to demonstrate the differences in the abilities of children who were dependent on iconic thought and those who had achieved the more advanced symbolic thought. The experiment also demonstrated the age at which children achieved symbolic thinking.

Method: Three groups of children, one group aged 5, the second aged 6 and the third aged 7 years, were presented with a grid of nine squares and nine glasses. There were three each of three sizes of glass, arranged with one row of each sized glass. Children all took part in two conditions. In the first condition they performed a *reproduction* task. The glasses were scrambled and children had to put them back in the positions they were in originally. In the second condition, the glasses were removed from the grid and children were instructed to put them back on the grid *back-to-front*, i.e. with the three tallest glasses in the squares previously occupied by the three shortest glasses and vice versa. This is called a *transposition* task. The idea behind the study was that the reproduction task involved iconic thinking, whereas the transposition task required symbolic thinking.

Results: Children tended to succeed on the reproduction task at an earlier age than the transposition task. Of the 5 year olds 60 per cent succeeded in the reproduction task and none succeeded in the transposition task. Of the 6 year olds 72 per cent succeeded in the reproduction task and 27 per cent in the transposition task. By the age of 7 years it seemed that children's thinking had taken a leap forward and 80 per cent succeeded in *both* the tasks. They no longer found the transposition task any harder than the reproduction task.

Conclusion: By 7 years, the children could perform both the tasks, but although most 5 year olds could perform the reproduction task, none of them could perform the transformation task successfully. Bruner and Kenney took this to mean that symbolic thought, which was necessary for the type of mental manipulation required to swap the position of the glasses around, appeared at around 6 to 7 years. The younger children could not perform the transformation task because they were dependent on iconic thought.

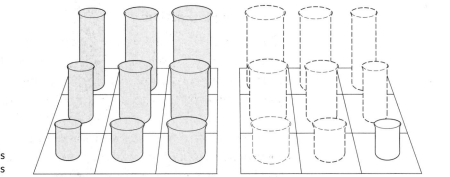

Bruner and Kenney's apparatus

Scaffolding

Bruner built on Vygotsky's idea of the ZPD, introducing the concept of *scaffolding*. Scaffolding has been defined as 'the wide range of activities through which the adult, or more experienced peer, assists the learner to achieve goals that would otherwise be beyond them' (Smith *et al.*, 1998). Scaffolding thus describes the ways in which adults help the child through the zone of proximal development. We will return to the concept of scaffolding in more detail later in this chapter when we look at the ways in which Vygotsky's and Bruner's theories of cognitive development can be applied to education.

Bruner's main influence is in education, and when we revisit his work later in the chapter you should get more of a flavour of how useful his ideas have been. On a theoretical level, Bruner's idea that mode of representation changes with age seems credible and is supported by research. It does seem, however, that logic gets more advanced with age for quite a time after children have mastered language. If Bruner's ideas were the whole story we would expect children to be capable of more advanced logic as soon as they can use language effectively. In fact, abstract reasoning tasks only become possible much later in children's development. One way in which Bruner has undoubtedly contributed to our understanding of cognitive development is in his idea of scaffolding. This plugs a gap in the work of Vygotsky, who emphasised a role for adults but did not explain well how adults go about guiding children through the ZPD.

for and against

Bruner

+ Bruner's ideas have been extremely useful in education.

+ Bruner is probably correct that as children mature they become capable of different types of mental representation, and that this affects their ability to reason.

− It seems likely, however, that other factors apart from mode of representation influence the type of reasoning of which a child is capable. We know that some cognitive abilities like abstract reasoning appear a long time after the appearance of symbolic functioning.

where to now?

The following are good sources of further information on the work of Bruner:

▶ **Bruner, J. (1971) The course of cognitive growth. In Richardson, K. and Sheldon, S. (ed.)** *Cognitive Development to Adolescence.* **Hove: LEA** – a set of readings, including one by Bruner himself, in which he summarises some of his major points.

▶ **Smith, P.K., Cowie, H. and Blades, M. (1998)** *Understanding Children's Development.* **Oxford: Blackwell** – a generally excellent book on child development with a good section on Bruner.

Implications of Vygotsky's and Bruner's theories for education

Unlike Piaget, both Vygotsky and Bruner were interested in applying their ideas to education. We can consider them together here as their ideas are closely related. The following are some of the major implications of Vygotsky and Bruner's work for teaching.

Classroom practice

Vygotsky and Bruner have proposed a more important role for adults in children's learning than did Piaget. Like Piaget however they proposed that children should be actively involved in their learning rather than behaving as passive receivers of knowledge. What this means in practice is that teachers should assist children who are actively engaged in learning tasks. In theoretical terms this means that children are working within their *zone of proximal development* and teachers provide the *scaffolding* to enable children to move through the ZPD.

From a Bruner–Vygotsky perspective, peers as well as teachers can be important influences on children's cognitive development. *Co-operative groupwork* as opposed to individual discovery learning appears to speed up children's development. An extension of the idea of co-operative groupwork is peer tutoring, where one child instructs another who is slightly less advanced. Foot *et al.* (1990) has explained the success of peer tutoring using Vygotsky's theory. One child can be effective in guiding another through the ZPD because, having only recently made that advance themselves, they are in a good position to see the difficulties faced by the other child and provide appropriate scaffolding. Below we look at a study by Nichols (1996), which examined the success of co-operative groupwork.

155

Computer-assisted learning can be used to provide scaffolding, both from the use of the computer itself and the social interaction stimulated by computers. When children use educational software the computer provides detailed help or prompts as required, according to the child's position in the ZPD. Certain children in the class are inevitably more skilled in the use of computers and so take on the role of peer tutors. With pupils working on computers, the teacher is free to target individuals who require help and target appropriate scaffolding to each child. We return to look in more detail at the effectiveness of computer-assisted learning later in this chapter.

Curriculum development

Vygotsky has emphasised that rather than waiting for children to reach a level of cognitive development where they can cope with concepts and tasks on their own, we can be more ambitious in what we expect of children, as long as teachers provide scaffolding. This means that a Vygotskian curriculum would introduce children to new concepts at an earlier age than would a Piagetian curriculum.

Bruner (1963) emphasised that *how* something is taught is more important than *when* it is taught. This means that provided children are presented with concepts in a way that they can understand them we need not worry too much about when to place concepts on the curriculum. Bruner and Kenney (1966) have proposed the idea of the *spiral curriculum*, in which ideas are revisited throughout a child's schooling. Each time an idea is revisited, children encounter it in a more sophisticated form, deepening their understanding.

research now

does co-operative groupwork improve motivation?

Nichols, J.D. (1996) Co-operative learning: A motivational tool to enhance student persistence, self-regulation, and efforts to please teachers and parents. *Educational Research and Evaluation 2(3), 246–60.*

Aim: Previous research has shown that children generally learn faster and achieve more when they work in co-operative groups rather than alone by discovery learning. More controversial is whether children learn better in child-centred classrooms or in traditional 'chalk and talk' lessons. What we do know is that the motivation of learners is enormously important. This study aimed to test whether adolescents of secondary school age were more motivated to learn in traditional lessons or lessons based on co-operative groupwork.

Method: Eighty-one students from an American high school participated in the study. They were randomly assigned to one of three groups. Each group made up one of the three geometry classes. The study was run across 18 weeks (one semester or American term). One group of 27 students had 9 weeks of co-operative group learning followed by 9 weeks of traditional teaching. A second group had 9 weeks of traditional teaching followed by 9 weeks of co-operative group learning. This meant that if motivation changed when the teaching method changed, the researchers would know that results were not affected by the order in which the two styles of teaching were used. The co-operative group activity involved students being divided into small groups and given problems to solve together. The control group had 18 weeks of traditional teaching. The motivation of each group was measured at the start, after 9 weeks and after 18 weeks. Motivation was judged by measuring the students' persistence, self-regulation and effort to please teachers and parents.

Results: The two groups who had experienced co-operative group learning scored significantly higher at the end of the semester on all measures of motivation. Within the two groups that had experienced 9 weeks of co-operative groupwork, it could be seen that the greatest increases in motivation took place during the 9-week period when they were working in groups rather than the 9 weeks when they were having traditional lessons.

Conclusion: The results clearly showed that co-operative groupwork led to improved motivation in the high school students. In theoretical terms, the study supports the effectiveness of student-centred learning, and in particular the approach of Vygotsky and Bruner who emphasised how much children can learn from one another.

for and against

applying the Vygotsky–Bruner approach to education

+ Research has shown clearly that children learn more effectively in groups, and that adults and peers can effectively provide scaffolding.

+ The idea of scaffolding has provided teachers with a way of intervening actively in children's learning without resorting to traditional teaching.

+ The effectiveness of co-operative group work and computer-aided learning have generally been supported by research findings.

– There are practical problems with the use of co-operative groupwork. There are more opportunities for children to be off-task in groupwork, and there are 'free-riders' who do not contribute to the work of the group.

where to now?

We recommend the following as good sources of information about cognitive development and education:

▶ **Child, D. (1997)** *Psychology and the Teacher*. **London: Cassell** – a book intended to give teachers a grounding in general psychology. It is particularly useful for relating psychological theory, including the cognitive-developmental approach to education.

▶ **Hartley, J. (1998)** *Learning and Studying*. **London: Routledge** – this is not focused particularly on a cognitive-developmental approach to education, but is useful in drawing together different psychological approaches and showing how each have influenced educational practice.

▶ **Borich, G.D. and Tombari, M.L. (1997)** *Educational Psychology, a contemporary approach*. **New York: Longman** – a detailed and up-to-date text covering many aspects of psychology and education. Particularly good information on applying Piaget, Bruner and Vygotsky to teaching.

what's new?

computer-assisted learning

If you are or have recently been a student, the chances are that you have encountered computers at some point in your education. *Computer-assisted learning* is a tremendous growth area at the turn of the 21st century, and a large body of research is currently being generated about its effectiveness. Think for a moment about the variety of ways in which you have used computers in the course of your studies. You have probably word-processed assignments. You may have used statistical programs to analyse the results of research. You may also have taken part in or administered studies that present tasks to participants by computer. Packages are available that guide students through sequences of tasks that allow you to master a skill or a topic. Revision tests are also available via computer, and there are now even computer packages available that will mark your essays! You may have had the opportunity to program computers in the course of your study. The usefulness of computers in teaching and learning is interesting in its own right. In this chapter, however, we are interested specifically in understanding the processes of computer-aided learning using ideas from cognitive-developmental psychology.

Theoretical background

Vygotsky died before the use of computers in education became an issue, so we cannot say what he would have thought. However, contemporary psychologists have applied the Vygotsky–Bruner model to understanding the processes of computer-assisted learning. From a Vygotsky–Bruner perspective, computers provide opportunities for co-operative learning. Both teacher intervention and on-screen instructions also provide scaffolding. We can look here at studies of both scaffolding and co-operative learning based on computers.

On-screen scaffolding

Whenever we use educational software, there are a series of on-screen prompts, which help us progress through the task at hand. Crook (1994) has suggested that these prompts constitute a form of scaffolding, which serve to move learners through a zone of proximal development. There are normally choices that the learner can make as to how much detail they require from prompts. This means that, just as a teacher will reduce the amount of help they give as the learner moves through the ZPD, the computer-aided learner can select a declining level of detail in their on-screen prompts.

Grammar checkers, a feature of most modern word-processing systems, are a familiar example of on-screen scaffolding (Hartley, 1998). If, for example, you use *Microsoft Word* you will be familiar with a green underlining function, which identifies possibly suspect grammar in your writing. According to your level of expertise, you can respond to this by ignoring it, selecting the text and considering the options suggested by the computer, or simply going with the computer's advice. From a Brunerian perspective, which option you take will depend on where you are in your word-processing or prose-writing ZPD. If you are new to word-processing or writing extended prose, you will probably just take the computer's advice. As you progress, however, you will probably require less and less scaffolding and use the prompts less often.

Co-operative learning with computers

Another way in which computer-aided learning can be beneficial is in fostering social interaction. According to the Vygotsky–Bruner model, co-operative learning in pairs or groups will achieve greater gains than solo study. Mevarech *et al.* (1991) tested this idea by seeing whether students working together sharing a computer do better than students working alone. Twelve year olds worked on computer-based arithmetic tasks for 5 months. Half the students had their own computer and the other half shared a computer and worked in pairs. The latter group did significantly better when tested later on their arithmetic ability. This finding runs counter to common sense which would suggest that the students who had their own computer would do better than those who had to share. Mevarech's study is also significant in that it lends support to the Vygotsky–Bruner model of education as opposed to the Piaget model.

Students who share computers may do better than those who work alone

for and against

computer-aided learning

+ Computers can provide opportunities for both discovery learning and co-operative learning. They also provide opportunities for both developing individual thinking skills and scaffolding the development of skills. This means that computer-assisted learning is compatible with both the Piagetian view of education and the Vygotsky–Bruner model.

– It has been suggested that the excessive use of computers in the classroom may lead to social isolation and the breakdown of the essential teacher–learner relationship.

+ However, if the majority of learners are receiving on-screen scaffolding this frees the teacher to spend more time with each learner. Provided computer-assisted learning does not lead to the phasing out of teachers, it appears that it will probably not lead to social problems.

where to now?

The following are good sources of further information about computer-aided learning:

▷ **Bancroft, D. and Carr, R. (ed.) (1995)** *Influencing Children's Development*. **Milton Keynes: Open University** – contains an excellent chapter by Karen Littleton on various aspects of computer-assisted learning.

▷ **Messer, D. and Millar, S. (ed.) (1999)** *Exploring Developmental Psychology*. **Arnold: London** – contains a great chapter by Charles Crook, one of the leading researchers in the area of computer-aided learning.

The development of children's theory of mind

One thing the theories of Piaget, Vygotsky and Bruner have in common is that they are *domain general*. This means that they see all the changes in mental abilities that take place during a child's cognitive development as happening because of the same underlying developmental process. Thus, for Piaget, the child's increasing ability to conserve, their declining egocentrism and their loss of artificialism are all results of a general increase in cognitive ability that comes with the maturation of the brain. Similarly, to Bruner, all the mental abilities in which the child achieves mastery after the age of 7 can be explained by the transition to symbolic thinking.

In recent years, however, another approach to explaining cognitive development has been growing in popularity. This is the *domain-specific* approach, which sees different mental abilities as developing independently of one another. One cognitive ability that has attracted particular attention because it does appear to develop independently of general cognitive functioning is the child's *theory of mind*. Children are said to have a theory of mind once they have an understanding of what other people believe, think and know. In other words they develop their own concept (or theory) of the minds of other people.

A classic demonstration of the sudden development of theory of mind comes from Wimmer and Perner (1983). They presented children with a story in which a boy called Maxi had left his chocolate in a green container in the kitchen. Maxi's mother had taken some of the chocolate for cooking and put the rest in a blue container. The child's task was to say which container Maxi would look in when he returned. Of course the correct answer is the green container, because Maxi wouldn't know his mother had moved it. However, this task requires an understanding of the concept of other people's minds, and Wimmer and Perner found that very few 3 year olds gave the correct answer, although the majority of 4 year olds did so. Avis and Harris (1991) replicated the study with children of the Baka people, who live in a remote part of the Cameroon, suggesting that the sudden appearance of theory of mind at 4 years old is universal.

Leslie (1994) has suggested that the sudden appearance of theory of mind in 4 year olds occurs because a particular *module* of the brain suddenly becomes active at that age. Much of the research on theory of mind takes place with *autistic* children. Autism is currently believed to be a genetic condition that appears in early childhood, and is characterised by difficulty in communication, repetitive movements and lack of interest and skill in social interaction and emotional attachment. Baron-Cohen *et al.* (1985) has suggested that autism is associated with impaired theory of mind. Certainly autistic children generally fail the Wimmer and Perner test. The study of autistic children who never develop a theory of mind, although they may go on to develop some mental abilities to very high levels, is important because it provides powerful evidence of *domain-specific* cognitive development (see Chapter 11 for a detailed discussion of autism, including theory of mind). In Piaget's terms, Wimmer and Perner's results could be explained by a decline in egocentrism (see p.134). However, we would not expect autistic children, who do not develop a theory of mind, to go on to develop other mental abilities to a high level, unless theory of mind develops independently of other mental abilities.

Although Leslie's modular approach to theory of mind remains popular, it has the weakness that it does not explain how aspects of the child's social environment can have profound effects on the development of theory of mind. From a Vygotskian perspective, Astington (1998) has suggested that children internalise a theory of mind during their early interactions. This idea is supported by studies that have shown that theory of mind is superior in children who have secure attachments and whose primary carers display high levels of sensitivity. For example, Symons and Clark (2000) measured both maternal sensitivity and security of attachment in 2-year-old children (see p.31 for a discussion of maternal sensitivity), and followed them up to 5 years when they were tested on false belief tasks like that used by Wimmer and Perner (1983). It was found that the children assessed as securely attached and those whose mothers were rated as the most sensitive at 2 years (these were usually but not always the same children) generally had a superior theory of mind at 5 years.

An important application of theory of mind research is in understanding the development of autism (see p.211). It is useful, however, in understanding the development of all children. Recent studies have shown that children with poor theory of mind can be hard for adults to manage because they tend not to have a good understanding of what adults expect from them (Hughes and Dunn, 2000), and are rated by peers and teachers as lacking in social skills (Bosacki and Astington, 1999). It also seems likely that children with poor theory of mind are disadvantaged in the classroom because they have a poor understanding of the expectations teachers have when they set a task.

where to now?

The following are good sources of further information about theory of mind:

▶ **Bryant, P. (1998) Cognitive development. In Eysenck, M. (ed.) (1998)** *Psychology, an integrated approach*. **Harlow: Longman** – contains an excellent chapter on cognitive development, including a detailed but very clear account of theory of mind research.

▶ **Frith, U. and Happé, F. (1994) Autism: beyond theory of mind. In Messer, D. and Dockrell, J. (1999)** *Developmental Psychology, a reader*. **London: Arnold** – an interesting paper concerning research on theory of mind and autism.

▶ **Baron-Cohen, S., Tager-Flusberg, H. and Cohen, D.J. (2000)** *Understanding Other Minds*. **Oxford: Oxford University Press** – contains chapters by some of the leading theory of mind researchers and covers many of the issues raised here.

Conclusions

The major alternative to Piagetian ideas of cognitive development is the social constructivist approach of Vygotsky and Bruner. Vygotsky emphasised the importance of culture and social interaction with a more expert peer or adult in the development of cognitive abilities. He identified the zone of proximal development (ZPD) as the gap between what a child can learn on its own and what it can learn in the presence of an expert. Bruner built on the idea of the ZPD by describing scaffolding, the processes by which experts instruct children in the acquisition of cognitive skills. Bruner diverged from the stage approach of Piaget and Vygotsky, and instead described the development of cognitive abilities in terms of the appearance of different modes of representation of knowledge at different ages. The social constructivist approach has been applied to education, where an emphasis is placed on the use of teacher scaffolding, peer tutoring and computer-assisted learning. Another approach to studying cognitive development is to reject the idea of domain-general theories like those of Piaget and Vygotsky, and look instead at specific aspects of development. An area that has attracted particular attention is the development of children's theory of mind, their ability to understand the emotions and intentions of others. The development of theory of mind now forms part of the nature–nurture debate in psychology. According to Leslie, theory of mind appears when a particular brain module matures at around 5 years. However, Astington has argued that theory of mind is gradually acquired though social interaction.

what do you know?

1 What does Vygotsky mean by intermental and intramental planes?

2 Define the zone of proximal development and scaffolding.

3 What is symbolic representation and why is it important?

4 Outline one way in which the ideas of Vygotsky and/or Bruner have been applied to education.

5 What is meant by the term 'theory of mind'?

9

The development of intelligence and abilities

In the last two chapters we have looked at theories of the ways in which all children develop cognitive abilities. The aim of this chapter is to explain individual differences in children's cognitive abilities; what we might call their *intelligence*. First, though, we need to explore in some detail what we mean by 'intelligence'. We begin by looking at whether intelligence is 'real' or merely a social construct, and then go on to question whether it is better to think of a single intelligence or a range of mental abilities. We then look at IQ (intelligence quotient), the measurement of intelligence, and discuss whether a person's IQ really says much about that person. The major debate in intelligence research has concerned the relative importance of genes and environment in affecting individual intelligence. We shall look in some detail at the evidence for genetic influences in the form of twin and adoption studies. In *What's new?* we look at the rapidly developing field of molecular genetics, which aims to isolate the specific genes associated with particular characteristics like intelligence. We will also look here at the influence of environmental factors such as parenting and the impact of institutional care, and the ways in which our understanding of environmental factors can be applied to boosting intelligence in children. Finally we take a look at the issues faced by gifted children and their families.

What is intelligence?

Before we move on to the major debate of this chapter, the extent to which genes and environment influence individual differences in intelligence, it is perhaps worth looking a bit more closely at what we mean by 'intelligence' and to what extent it is a useful concept. We can do this by examining two questions:

1 Does intelligence really exist or is it merely a convenient social construct?

2 Is there a single intelligence or should we just talk about different mental abilities?

Is there really such a thing?

The most fundamental question we have to address in a discussion of intelligence is whether it really exists as a psychological entity or whether it is just a *social construct* (see p.19 for a discussion of social constructionism). If intelligence is a social construct it must have been constructed for a reason. Cernovsky (1997) suggests that intelligence research is just one way in which psychologists have helped maintain the status quo in society, and hence to maintain social inequalities. For example, an intelligence test called Raven's Progressive Matrices has been used to compare the intelligence of black Africans from poor ghettos with that of highly educated white Europeans (e.g. Rushton, 1988), despite the fact that it contains mathematics which the white Europeans but not the black Africans had learnt at school. Rushton's results showing that the Europeans do better on this test have been used to claim genetic superiority for white people, thus justifying racism.

In their highly controversial book, *The Bell Curve*, Herrnstein and Murray (1994) went further and proposed that all inequalities between racial and socio-economic groups were due to genetic differences in their intelligence, and that as intelligence is innate and unchangeable there is little point in spending public money on trying to reduce inequality. Most psychologists have condemned *The Bell Curve*, but you can see how the concept of intelligence *could* be used to justify an ultra right wing and sinister political agenda. However, most psychologists would say that, although the concept of intelligence can be misused for political ends, this is not in itself sufficient reason to dismiss the whole idea.

There are, however, other reasons for suggesting that intelligence is a social construct rather than a real entity. One particularly tricky issue concerns the ways in which different cultures think of intelligence, and the differing performance of people from different cultures on tests of intelligence. While a wide variety of cultures acknowledge the idea of intelligence, there are wide variations in cultural beliefs about intelligence. In one study Hsueh (1998) used a questionnaire to compare the beliefs of American and Taiwanese children about intelligence. It emerged strongly that the American children (especially the girls) had a greater tendency to see intelligence as fixed and unchangeable, whereas the Taiwanese children tended to see intelligence as malleable. Interestingly the Taiwanese children were more motivated than the Americans to take on challenging puzzles and mathematics than the Americans – presumably the American children did not see the point of stretching themselves when they saw their intelligence as unchangeable.

People from different societies typically do more or less well than one another when different ways are used to assess intelligence. For example, the most commonly used test of intelligence, the Wechsler Intelligence Scale for Children, contains a number of measures, including verbal ability and visuo-spatial ability (for example negotiating a maze). In a comparison of American and Native American children's performance on the Wechsler test, Salois (1999) found that the Native American children came out worse in verbal ability but better in visuo-spatial ability. Clearly the two cultures displayed different strengths and it would be quite meaningless to say that one group is more intelligent than the other. However, if different cultures have such different mental abilities, there is an argument for saying that the general term *intelligence* is redundant. This brings us to the next fundamental question about intelligence, namely, should we think in terms of a single intelligence or rather of a range of different mental abilities?

Children from different cultures have such different mental abilities that we cannot compare their intelligence

Intelligence or abilities?

Clearly, when we talk about or measure intelligence we need to think about quite a wide range of different mental abilities. This raises the question of whether there is any point in speaking of a single 'intelligence'. Gardner (1993) has proposed a theory of *multiple intelligences*, which include linguistic (verbal ability), logical (including mathematical ability), musical, spatial (including artistic ability), bodily (including grace and sporting ability), interpersonal (social) and intrapersonal (i.e. self-awareness). However, broadly speaking (although there are exceptions) people who do well in tests of one mental ability tend to do well in others also. We can therefore speak of *general cognitive ability* (intelligence) or *g* as well as specific abilities. There is an ongoing debate in psychology about the relative importance of general cognitive ability and specific abilities, but that need not concern us here. In this chapter we look at research into the development of both general cognitive ability and specific abilities.

Intelligence and IQ

A fundamental principle of intelligence – if we accept that it exists at all – is that it can be measured. Psychologists measure intelligence using a variety of tests called *intelligence quotient* or *IQ* tests. These measure a variety of mental abilities and give a total score or IQ. IQ can be calculated in two ways. Stern (1911) developed the idea of IQ, the relationship between mental age and actual age:

$$IQ = \frac{\text{mental age}}{\text{actual age}} \times 100$$

For example, if a 10-year-old child gained the score that represented the average score for 9 year olds their IQ would be:

$$\frac{9}{10} \times 100 = 90$$

Binet's intelligence test was developed further at Stanford University in America by Terman (1916), who produced the first true IQ test, the Stanford-Binet test. However, the system developed by Stern and used in the Stanford-Binet test for calculating IQ can only be used for children – clearly a 31 year old is not expected to score more highly than a 30 year old in the same way as a 10 year old is expected to score more highly than a 9 year old.

Wechsler (1939) produced an alternative IQ test, which had two major advantages over the Stanford-Binet test. Firstly it tested a wider variety of cognitive abilities. Secondly it employed a different method for calculating IQ, which could then be used for adults. This approach depends on the fact that intelligence, like all human abilities, is normally distributed throughout the population – see the graph below.

Using this system we call whatever is the mean test score from a large and varied population an IQ of 100. IQ scores of individuals can then be calculated according to where they fall on the normal distribution curve. For example, we know from looking at the normal distribution curve that

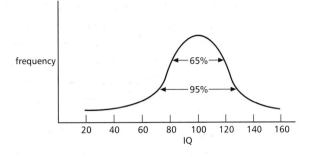

Distribution of IQ across the population

97.5 per cent of the population score over 70 and that 2.5 per cent score below 70. Therefore, a score that appeared 2.5 per cent of the way up from the lowest score in the population would be given an IQ score of 70. This is the method now generally used to calculate IQ, including the modern version of the Stanford-Binet test. Each generation does better on tests of IQ than the last, so psychologists have regularly to test large groups of people and work out the average score, which is then set at 100. Similar systems can be used to assess specific mental abilities. For example, later in this chapter we will look at research into language development that uses the Griffith language test, which yields a *language quotient* (LQ) for each child.

So how good a measure of what we call intelligence in everyday life is IQ? One of the problems of IQ testing is that while we can now measure very accurately a person's cognitive abilities in an artificial test situation this does not necessarily allow us to predict how well that person will function in real-life situations. In a recent study of 85 Canadian university students, Cote and Levine (2000) found that IQ did not predict academic success and that motivation was the most important factor influencing how well the students did in their degrees. Typical correlations between IQ and job performance are around 0.5 for new employees (Cooper, 1999), but these decline with experience (Kamin, 1995). It seems that in most real-life situations motivation and expertise are more important than IQ in affecting performance, so we would be unwise to take our IQ scores too much to heart.

The nature–nurture debate and intelligence

Historically, intelligence and abilities have been major battlegrounds of the *nature–nurture debate* in psychology. On the 'nature' side were those who believed (like the American children in Tsueh's study) that intelligence is determined by our genes and therefore is largely unchangeable. On the 'nurture' side were those who believed instead that our intelligence was determined by environment, and can therefore be altered by changing the nature of our environment. Before we go on to look at the evidence for the roles of genes and environment in developing intelligence it is useful to dispel a couple of myths.

- It is currently believed that neither genes nor environment *determine* intelligence. There are multiple influences on the development of mental abilities and intelligence, probably including a number of genes and a number of environmental factors.

- There is not necessarily a close link between the influence of genes on intelligence and abilities and the extent to which these are changeable. Genes appear to influence people's starting point in developing their intelligence. This does not mean that they are not then affected by their environment.

The role of genes in intelligence and abilities

One of the most important developments in psychology in the last 20 years has been the recognition of the importance of genetic influences on individual differences between people (Plomin *et al.*, 1997). You may have noticed that, just as some families have a number of very tall or redheaded members, some psychological characteristics also appear to run in families. There are thus families in which there are an unusually large number of highly intelligent individuals. One way in which characteristics can pass from one generation to the next is through genes. *Genes* are units of DNA, which contain the information required to build biological structures. The reason that as humans we share so many characteristics is that we share 99.9 per cent of our genes. It is relatively simple to understand how a characteristic like eye-colour can be under the control of genes because eye-colour is obviously physical in nature. The question of how genes might affect psychological characteristics is a more complex one. It appears that genetic differences between individuals produce biological differences between people (sometimes very subtle) that, in combination with their environment, lead them to develop into unique individuals.

Twin studies of intelligence and abilities

We know that identical twins (properly called monozygotic twins or MZs) share 100 per cent of their genes. We also know that fraternal twins (properly called dizygotic twins or DZs) only share an average of 50 per cent of their genetic material. Thus, if identical twins are more similar in their intelligence than fraternal twins, or if separated twins remain similar in intelligence despite having grown up in different environments, this provides evidence that genes play a role in development. The results of early studies appeared to show that separated identical twins were remarkably similar in their intelligence – see Table 9.1.

Study	Correlations between MZs reared together	Correlations between MZs reared apart
Newman *et al.* (1937)	0.91	0.67
Shields (1962)	0.76	0.77

Table 9.1 Results of early studies comparing IQ of separated and non-separated identical twins

There are, however, serious weaknesses with early studies of separated identical twins (based on Howe, 1997). Many twins were not separated immediately after birth and so they shared an early environment for some time. Some so-called separated twins actually lived in very similar environments – frequently remaining in the family and seeing the co-twin every day. We cannot really say that these twins had different environments and so we cannot be sure that genes rather than environment produced the similarity in IQ.

There has been great difficulty in gathering new data on separated identical twins as adoption practices have changed and far fewer twins are now separated as young children. An exception comes from Bouchard (1993, 1995) who has been gathering data on volunteer pairs of separated twins for a number of years. Bouchard's figures show that separated identical twins are very similar in IQ, with correlations of about 0.7. This suggests that genes play a greater role than environment in the development of intelligence. In these studies Bouchard has got around one of the major weaknesses of early twin studies by only including twins who were separated in the first six months. However, there are other methodological problems with this type of research. Many of the participating twins were reunited for some time before testing, sharing an environment and perhaps influencing one another as adults. Many of Bouchard's separated twins also grew up in quite similar environments. Perhaps the most significant flaw in Bouchard's studies is that his twins are a self-selecting sample, recruited by response to advertisements. It is quite possible, then, that many of his participants are not typical separated twins but have volunteered because they are fascinated by their unusual similarity.

Most contemporary twin studies involve comparing the similarity of IQ in pairs of identical and fraternal twins. A study by Grigorenko and Carter (1996) compared IQ in 60 pairs of identical twins and 63 pairs of fraternal twins of Russian adolescents. It was found that the identical twins were significantly more similar in IQ, but also that IQ was associated with parenting style, level of the mother's education and the socio-economic status of the family. These results demonstrate the importance of both genes and environment.

Other twin studies have shown that genes may be more important in the development of some abilities than others. In a large-scale study Reznick *et al.* (1997) compared general intelligence, verbal ability and non-verbal abilities in 408 pairs of identical and fraternal twins. General intelligence was somewhat more similar in the identical twins, suggesting both genetic and environmental influences. There was very little difference between identical and fraternal twins as regards verbal ability but a dramatic difference in non-verbal ability. This suggests that verbal ability is primarily environmental in origin whereas other abilities are strongly influenced by genes.

A possible limitation with studies that compare the similarity of identical and fraternal twins is that, despite living in apparently equally similar environments as fraternal twins, identical twins may have more similar experiences than fraternal twins. Of course it is really *experience* rather than environment as such that has the effect on the development of intelligence. This means that the greater similarity in the IQ of identical twins could conceivably be due to their more similar experiences than to their identical genes. However, there is little hard evidence to support this view. When Baker and Daniels (1990) observed pairs of identical and fraternal twins together they saw no difference in the way they were treated, and moreover the twins who were judged to be treated the most similarly were no more similar in IQ than those who were treated distinctly differently.

Adoption studies

The most direct way to isolate the influences of genes and environment involves adoption. If children are adopted into a different environment from that of their birth family we have a situation where the children have the genes of the biological parents and the environment created by the adoptive parents. Any similarity between child and biological parents suggests a role for genes, while any similarity between child and adoptive parents suggests a role for environment. The first adoption study involving both the comparison of children's IQ with that of biological and adoptive parents was by Skodak and Skeels (1949). They found a signif-icant relationship between child and biological parent's IQ, suggesting genetic influence, and also a difference between the typical IQ of adopted and non-adopted children, suggesting the importance of environment.

An adoption study by Plomin *et al.* (1997) provides particular support for the role of genes in the development of intelligence and further suggests that genetic influences increase throughout childhood. We can look at this study in detail.

research now

do adopted children grow up to be like their adoptive parents?

Plomin, R., Fulker, D.W., Corley, R. and DeFries, J.C. (1997) Nature, nurture and cognitive development from 1–16 years: a parent–offspring adoption study. *Psychological Science 8, 442–7.*

Aim: Previous adoption studies have shown that adopted children resemble both their biological and adoptive parents, thus indicating the importance of both genes and environment. The aim of this study was to see whether with age children come to resemble their adoptive parents more in their IQ as they get older or whether in fact they become more like their biological parents with age. Common sense would predict that the longer children spend with their adoptive parents the more they will become like them.

Method: The study was longitudinal, running over 20 years. A matched pairs design was used in which 245 children adopted in the first year and 245 non-adopted children were matched for a number of variables including age, sex and socio-economic status, and then followed up from birth to 16 years of age. A range of IQ tests were given to all the biological and adoptive parents and to the children at 1, 2, 3, 4, 7, 12 and 16 years. It was then possible to compare the children's IQ with that of the biological and adoptive parents, and to see whether with age the children came to resemble more the adoptive or the biological parents.

Results: In early childhood the IQ of the adopted children was related to that of both the biological and adoptive parents. However, with age the IQ of the adopted children became increasingly like that of their biological parents. By adolescence there was no correlation between children's IQ and that of their adoptive parents. Moreover, there was no difference between the extent to which the adopted children resembled their biological parents in the children who were adopted and the control group who had always lived with their biological parents.

Conclusion: The results provide strong support for the role of genes in affecting IQ. It is particularly interesting that, contrary to what common sense would predict, children came to resemble their biological parents more and their adoptive parents less with age. This *does not* suggest that environment is unimportant in the development of intelligence. It does, however, suggest that, as children get older, they choose the nature of their environment and experiences to a greater extent, and that their choice of type of environment and experiences may be genetically influenced. The study also suggests, contrary to common sense, that the intelligence of parents does not necessarily have a particularly strong influence on the aspects of the environment they provide for children that influence their intellectual development.

Adoption studies are useful in highlighting the role of genes in the development of intelligence. What is perhaps more interesting, however, is what studies like this tell us about the effect of environment. We cannot assume that children's environment is related to the IQ of their parents. Also, it appears that as children get older and encounter a range of environments and, critically, as they exert a greater degree of choice in their environment, the influence of the family environment appears to decrease.

Adoption studies, like twin studies, have their problems. One issue concerns the *representativeness* of adopted children in relation to the population. Clearly most children are not adopted and the factors affecting adoption may conceivably have an impact on intellectual development. A further problem with some adoption studies is *selective placement*. When children are adopted they are frequently placed in a family as similar as possible to their biological family. This means that it is difficult to see whether apparent similarities to the biological family are in fact caused by the influence of the similar adoptive family. With regard to the Plomin *et al.* study, it is worth adding that not all adoption studies have found similar results. In a recent review of the evidence Howe (1998) has pointed out that some studies have found differences as great as 20 IQ points between adopted children and their biological parents.

what's new?

molecular genetics and intelligence and abilities

We have already seen that twin and adoption studies have fairly serious methodological weaknesses. They are of course still practised and more recent studies tend to have rather fewer flaws than older ones. It may be that the future of separated twin and adoption studies is not a rosy one – considerably fewer twins are now separated and adoption has become much rarer with a growing acceptance of single parenthood (these are of course positive developments!). We may in time simply run out of participants for these studies. However, technological developments have allowed a new line of research – *molecular genetics*. Molecular genetics looks at the association between particular genes and psychological characteristics. Genetic material is extracted from individuals, or in some cases whole families, and associations are calculated between variations in particular genes and the psychological characteristics of the individuals or families.

The simplest way to establish that a particular gene may be implicated in affecting a characteristic is to look at whether people who exhibit that characteristic are more likely to have the gene. A study by Chorney *et al.* (1998) has attracted much attention. They claim to have, for the first time, isolated a gene linked to intelligence. In this study, two matched groups of children were established, a 'superbright' group (average IQ=136) and a matched group of children the same age but with an average IQ (average IQ=103). The researchers extracted DNA from the cells of members of the two groups and analysed their genetic makeup. The aim of the analysis was to see whether particular genetic variations were associated with the 'superbright' group. There was a significant difference between the two groups in the frequency of a single gene, situated on Chromosome 6. Twice as many (33 per cent) of the 'superbrights' as opposed to 17 per cent of the control group had a particular allele of the gene IGF2R. This indicated that IGF2R is one of the genes associated with cognitive ability. The researchers have suggested that IGF2R accounts for about 2 per cent of the variance in intelligence.

Other studies have linked specific genes with the development of specific mental abilities. Berman and Noble (1995) have isolated a particular gene called DRD2 that appears to be associated with spatial abilities but not with general intelligence. The Apolipoprotein E gene also appears to associated with memory and speed of processing in older people, but not with general intelligence or verbal ability (Henderson *et al.*, 1995). Molecular genetics is very much in its infancy, but these exciting findings are further evidence for a role for genes in the development of intelligence and abilities.

for and against

the role of genes

+ Twin and adoption studies have shown that children resemble in IQ those with whom they share a large proportion of genes, even if they have grown up in different environments.

− There are fairly serious methodological weaknesses in both twin and adoption studies, and not all psychologists accept that their findings demonstrate the importance of genes.

+ Molecular genetic studies have begun to isolate some genes that appear to have an effect on intelligence and abilities.

− Molecular genetics is a relatively new field, and many findings have not been replicated enough times to accept them as 'facts'.

where to now?

The following are good sources of further information regarding the role of genes in the development of intelligence:

▶ **Plomin, R., DeFries, J.C., McClearn, G.E. and Rutter, M. (1997)** *Behavioural Genetics*. **New York: Freeman** – an excellent advanced account of the study of genes in psychology with two chapters devoted to intelligence and cognitive abilities.

▶ **Cooper, C. (1999)** *Intelligence and Abilities*. **London: Routledge** – a good general account of issues around intelligence and abilities, including an informative chapter on the role of genes in development.

The role of environment in intelligence and abilities

Having read the last section on the importance of genes in the development of intelligence and abilities you may be tempted to think that environment is not important. Actually nothing could be further from the truth. At least half the variance in individual IQ can be explained by environmental influences – or more strictly speaking by individuals' *experiences*. Remember also that general cognitive ability as measured by IQ tests is fairly far removed from performance in real-life tasks, and the environment is probably considerably more important than genes in performance in education and the workplace.

The shared and non-shared environment

When we speak of environment, we need logically to distinguish between two ideas, firstly that growing up in the same environment will make two children develop alike, and secondly that raising two children in different environments will make them different. At first, you might think this is a silly distinction, but actually the two ideas are rather different. Remember, as we have already said, it is really children's *experiences* that affect their development. If children grow up in quite different environments then they are very likely to have quite different experiences, and so their environment will cause them to develop differently. However, just because two children are raised in the same environment – for example in the same home with the same family – this does not necessarily mean that they will have similar experiences. Parents may bring up a second child quite differently from the first, and two children with different interests and personalities may seek out different environments and be treated quite differently by adults. Generally, psychologists believe that the non-shared environment, i.e. an individual's unique experience, is rather more important than the shared environment in the development of intelligence and abilities.

So what aspects of a person's experience influence that person's intelligence and abilities? One important distinction is between the biological environment and the psychological environment. Let us first consider the effects of the biological environment.

The biological environment

A number of biological factors can impact upon children's development. One of the best-known environmental factors that can damage children's developing intelligence is lead, which is present in car exhausts and old paint. In a recent study Sinha and Vibha (1998) assessed IQ and lead exposure in 960 Indian children aged 9 to 14 years. Lead exposure was measured by the amount of lead present in the children's hair. IQ was assessed using the Wechsler test for children. It was found that there was a negative correlation between lead levels and IQ, i.e. the more lead the children had been exposed to the lower their IQ.

Environmental factors affecting children's intellectual development can begin before birth. Loganovskaja and Loganovsky (1999) assessed the IQ of Russian children exposed prenatally to radiation during the Chernobyl catastrophe. Fifty irradiated children were compared to 50 matched control children. There were significantly fewer high IQ children in the irradiated group and significantly more children with below average scores and borderline retardation. Other circumstances that can inhibit intellectual development prior to birth include parental drug and alcohol abuse during pregnancy.

We can see then that severe problems in the biological environment can have a powerful negative impact on the development of intelligence. This in itself does not answer the more interesting question of whether *normal* variations in aspects of the biological environment have much effect on children's IQ. An epidemiological study by Gale and Martyn (1996) suggests that breastfeeding is one biological factor that gives children an advantage. Epidemiologists look at trends in large populations and can tell whether certain independent variables, in this case breastfeeding, are associated with certain dependent variables, in this case IQ. The Gale and Martyn study also looked at the use of dummies in relation to IQ. We will look at this study in detail.

research
now

is breast best for bright babies?

Gale, C.R. and Martyn, C.N. (1996) Breastfeeding, dummy use and adult intelligence. *The Lancet 347, 1072–5.*

Aim: Previous research had established a moderate but consistent advantage for breastfed babies over those who were bottlefed, perhaps due to the better nutritional value of breast milk. The aim of this study was to test whether two environmental variables in infancy, breastfeeding and dummy use are associated with IQ in adulthood. A further aim was to see whether being fed exclusively on breast milk gave children an advantage in IQ over those fed on both breast and bottle milk.

Method: Nine hundred and forty-four participants from Hertfordshire, born between 1920 and 1930, were assessed for their cognitive ability by the use of an IQ test called the AH4, administered by computer. The medical records of the participants were then examined in order to establish how they had been fed as babies and whether or not they had used dummies. Sixty-six per cent of the sample received breast milk only; 29 per cent had received both; and only 5 per cent had been exclusively bottlefed.

Results: The most dramatic finding was that the babies who did not use dummies were significantly higher in IQ than those who did use them. Breastfeeding also had an effect, the exclusively breastfed group tending to have the highest IQ and the exclusively bottlefed group the lowest. Although the effects were statistically significant the IQ difference was quite small, the largest difference being that the babies without dummies went on to have an average IQ 3.5 points higher than those who used dummies.

Conclusion: Two environmental variables were associated with IQ in adulthood, use of dummies and method of feeding in infancy. It was assumed that the effect of the breastfeeding was biological and that that of dummies was psychological.

It does seem then that normal variations in the biological environment of a young child can have an impact on the development of their intelligence. There are, however, good reasons to challenge the findings of this particular study. While the sample size seems quite large overall, when we are looking at the bottlefed group alone we are only talking about 53 people, quite a small number for a study of this type. The difference in IQ between the groups was also quite small. A further problem with this type of study is the difficulty in matching the groups that are being compared on all relevant variables. It may be that other differences between breast and bottlefed groups and between dummy and no-dummy groups accounted for the results.

The psychological environment

A number of aspects of the psychological environment also appear to be associated with the development of intelligence. Remember that we have already come across a number of studies in this chapter that show how variations in normal environment appear to impact on IQ. We have seen that the use of dummies is associated with reduced IQ (Gale and Martyn, 1996) and that higher IQ is associated with particular parenting styles, higher levels of maternal education and higher socio-economic status (Grigorenko and Carter, 1996).

A particularly socially sensitive line of research concerns studies showing that the experiences of children, including their access to intellectual stimulation, is different according to their socio-economic group. Hart and Risley (1995) looked at why this might be. They observed 3-year-old children in families categorised as either professional, working class or on benefits, counting the number of words that were directed towards each child in a week. The difference was enormous – children in professional families had up to 15,000 more words directed towards them in a week than did the children from families on benefits. Extrapolating from this week to the children's first 3 years Hart and Risley estimated that the children from professional homes had had 30 million words spoken to them as opposed to 20 million in the working class homes and 10 million in the benefits families.

It is also possible to reinterpret findings normally associated with biological environment as actually the results of psychological experiences. For example, Kolominsky *et al.* (1999) have suggested that the reduced IQ in children irradiated in the womb during the Chernobyl catastrophe is a result not of radiation damage but of the social disruption to families caused by large-scale bereavement and rehousing in the Chernobyl region. There is also a wealth of evidence to show that particularly poor psychological experiences (collectively known as environmental insults) can affect intelligence. We look here at the effects of child abuse and institutionalisation on the development of intelligence. We also review evidence for the changeability of intelligence and look at attempts to boost intelligence by improving the early environment.

The effects of child abuse

Children who have suffered abuse or trauma in childhood typically have lower IQ than their peers. In one recent study Carrey *et al.* (1996) compared the IQ as measured by the Wechsler test of 18 people aged between 7 and 23 who had been abused as children and 18 matched participants who had not suffered abuse. The abused group had significantly lower IQ than the control group and were particularly disadvantaged in verbal abilities. In a larger study Lane (1998) assessed 53 sexually abused boys aged 11 to 18 and compared them to a control group of non-abused boys. No overall difference in IQ was found between the two

Dummies may be associated with reduced IQ

groups, but the abused group did emerge as significantly lower in verbal ability. Cahill *et al.* (1999) reviewed studies of the relationship between several types of early maltreatment of children and concluded that there is ample evidence to say that neglect, physical abuse and sexual abuse are all associated with reduced intelligence.

Institutionalisation

In Chapter 3 you will have come across a series of classic studies (Hodges and Tizard, 1989a, 1989b) that investigated the effects of early institutionalisation on social and intellectual development. Adopted children consistently scored higher on IQ tests than those who were restored to their biological parents and those who remained in care throughout their childhood. This illustrates the negative impact of living in an institution and the positive impact of living in a stable family environment with experienced carers.

One of the difficulties with all studies looking at institutions is that many of the children in such institutions have already experienced serious trauma or deprivation prior to entering the institution, and that we can never be sure it is the institutionalisation itself that is having the effect. Furthermore, the regimes in different institutions and the standards of care experienced by children vary considerably from one institution to another. It is thus difficult to say what aspects of institutional care can be harmful. It is widely believed that one major problem with institutions is the lack of stimulation. One way to test whether it is lack of stimulation that has an effect on children would be to deliberately deprive children of a stimulating environment and see what effect this had on their development. Clearly this raises very serious ethical issues and such a study would not be permitted nowadays. However (you may be horrified to learn) it has been done in the past. We look here at one such study in detail.

classic research

the effects of deliberately understimulating babies

Dennis, W. (1941) Infant development under conditions of restricted and minimum social stimulation. *Genetic Psychology Monographs 23, 143–89.*

Aim: Dennis and colleagues had studied the effects of deprivation in institutional settings and observed that children who grew up in environments that lacked social and intellectual stimulation tended to suffer in their cognitive development. The aim of this study was to create a situation in which young children were deprived of stimulation in a controlled environment where researchers could be sure that other aspects of care were maintained.

Method: Two female fraternal twins were cared for from the age of 1 month to 14 months in the home of a husband and wife research team, the Dennises. The infants were kept in a room that was heated but which contained no pictures or toys and only minimal furniture. The girls were given good physical care, being fed and changed regularly, but social interaction with adults was kept to a minimum. Any behaviour that might be imitated by the children was avoided, and the children's behaviour was not rewarded or punished in any way. The total time spent in contact with adults was kept to approximately 2 hours per day. The twins were regularly given a selection of tests designed to measure their early intellectual development (IQ tests were not used as they are designed for older children). For the next few months the girls were given a programme of intensive stimulation designed to make up the intellectual deficits caused by their first 14 months.

Results: For the first 7 months the infants' scores of intellectual development remained within normal limits for their age, although slightly below average. However, in the second half of the experiment, from ages 7 to 14 months, development became more seriously impaired and at 14 months the twins were classified as seriously retarded. However, after a few months of intense stimulation their development returned to normal.

Conclusion: Even relatively mild understimulation (remember that the twins had contact with each other as well as 2 hours of adult contact per day – more than they might have received in a real institution) has serious effects on children's intellectual development. However, the effects of early understimulation are not necessarily permanent.

Institutionalisation *per se* has not been shown in all studies to be associated with poor intellectual development. In a comparison between 72 orphans and 72 children living with refugee parents in Eritrea, Wolff and Fesseha (1999) found that the orphans, who lived in institutions, scored higher on IQ tests than the children living in refugee camps. Unfortunately, however, on measures of emotional development the children in institutions did worse than those in refugee camps, showing that, although good quality institutions can provide better cognitive stimulation than poor family environments, it is much harder for them to provide a good social-emotional environment.

Can we increase IQ?

Clearly we think positively about having a high IQ and we see low IQ as a bad thing, despite the very modest relationship between IQ and real-life achievement. An interesting question concerns the extent to which we can manipulate our children's environment so as to increase their intelligence and abilities. If variations in children's experiences influence intellectual development – and it seems that they do – it should be possible to improve those experiences and so increase levels of intelligence and abilities. Howe (1998) has suggested that there are several sources of evidence to support the idea that we can increase a child's IQ:

Michael Howe emphasises the role of environment in changing children's IQ

- Adoption studies have shown that when adopted into a highly stimulating environment children's IQ increases and can become considerably higher than that of their biological parents.

- Deliberate attempts to boost the IQ of disadvantaged children have resulted in substantial increases.

- Education research has shown a relationship between amount of time spent at school and IQ.

- Medical research has shown that curing infections and improving nutrition can lead to increases in IQ.

- In countries where educational and social opportunities increase from one generation to the next, so does IQ.

Headstart programmes

The original Operation Headstart project began in 1965 in America. The aim was to target regions where poverty appeared to be affecting children's early environment and to compensate for this impoverished environment. For a year prior to entering kindergarten children received extensive intellectual and social stimulation accompanied by dietary supplements. After one summer the children in the Headstart group had an average of 10 IQ points advantage over their peers. Lazar *et al.* (1982) followed children up to primary education and found that the difference in IQ disappeared. Seitz (1990) set out to investigate why this might be. She followed up children from an earlier study (Zigler and Seitz, 1982), and found that the problem lay in the children's later education. The programme studied in the Zigler and Seitz study emphasised mathematical skills, and the children were simply not given enough later mathematical education to maintain their early gains. Interestingly however, Seitz (1990) found that the benefits to IQ had partially reappeared by adolescence, suggesting that early intervention did have a substantial long-term effect.

Despite the apparent success of the Headstart project there were problems. The programmes were implemented in several places and not all reported success. There was also considerable costs involved for relatively small gains. Since the original Headstart project, attempts have been made to refine the process. In the Milwaukee project infants with mothers with an IQ of less than 75 were given extra stimulation in daycare from 3 months. The mothers were also given help in work and parenting skills. Garber (1988) followed up the children to 14 years and found that they had an average IQ 10 points higher than their peers. Slaughter (1988) analysed a variety of Headstart programmes in an attempt to pick out the elements of a successful project and concluded that the most successful projects did not merely provide cognitive stimulation, but which also worked with families to improve family dynamics and/or develop interest and skills for children's education. Slaughter also proposed that different techniques worked with different client groups. With the very lowest socio-economic groups who could not become so involved with children's education the emphasis is best placed on providing stimulating day-care.

One methodological problem in researching Headstart programmes lies in comparing the development of children who were in the programme because their parents were motivated to enter them into it with a control group who were not in the programme because their parents were not motivated. You can see that if the children in the Headstart condition do better under these circumstances it may be due to the parental attitudes rather than the programme itself. One way around this is to randomly allocate children to two conditions, one of which receives the Headstart intervention but not the other. Ramey *et al.* (1999) reviewed ten studies that randomly allocated children to the two conditions and concluded that there was firm evidence that Headstart did boost IQ, and that the greater the deprivation suffered by the children the greater the gains achieved by Headstart.

Hothousing

Whereas the aim of Headstart projects is to enrich the environments of disadvantaged children in order to raise them to 'normal' levels of intellectual functioning, hothousing seeks to take 'normal' or bright children and boost them to a level of intellectual functioning *above* the norm. Sigel (1987) first used the term 'hothousing' as an analogy with the way in which vegetables are forced to ripen earlier than normal by placing them in a greenhouse.

Children who have very intensive early training have been compared to vegetables in greenhouses

There have been many case studies where children have been taught skills such as reading at a very young age and have later exhibited very high IQ. However, you can see that this type of case study has the problem that the children may have already been exceptionally intelligent and this may have enabled them to learn to read early. Some hothousing programmes involve segregating children into high ability classes. We have already looked at the effects of this in Chapter 5 (see p.92) and concluded that children develop a better self-image in mixed ability groups. There is, however, evidence to show that we can boost intellectual development by enhancing early experience.

One way of deciding whether exceptional skills can be developed by hothousing is to look at the early lives of particularly talented people. Howe (1988) has provided support for the principle that intensive early enrichment can enhance specific abilities. He reviewed biographical accounts of a wide variety of exceptionally talented and successful individuals, including the composer Mozart, the writer Dickens and the chemist Kekule. Howe found that in every case he studied, the early childhood of the individual was characterised by intensive training in their particular skill at an earlier age than is typical. Church (2000) has challenged Howe, suggesting that, just because intensive training and practice are *necessary* for the development of exceptional talents, this in itself does not mean that training and practice are *sufficient*. It may be that these individuals had innate talents that were developed by their hothousing, and it seems unlikely that we can hothouse just anyone and produce another Mozart or Dickens!

Some psychologists and parents are concerned that intensive early training may interfere with children's social and emotional development. Certainly the stereotyped view of hothousing in which a child is forced to stay in and practise a skill for untold hours when his or her friends are out playing may cause a child to suffer problems. However, there are now methods of enhancing intellectual development that do not involve enormous number of practice hours. Fowler (1990) devised a programme of accelerated language development in which parents were trained and taught their children at home. Parents were trained to spend more time and at more regular intervals than is usual talking to their infants, to point to objects and speak names earlier than would normally be done and to frequently play games like peek-a-boo, which involve intensive and lively interaction with the child. Fifteen babies were followed up from 5 months and their development assessed. The results were dramatic. By 24 months all the children could use 5-word sentences, although typically this becomes possible for children at around 32 months. The average language quotient for the group was 139 (remember that the average for the population is always 100). At 5 years follow-up the advantage for the children who had had the Fowler programme was maintained.

media watch

Pay your children too much attention and you could do more harm than good

There has been much controversy in Britain about the benefits of 'hot-housing'. Many parents have turned to educational play to improve their children's verbal and cognitive skills to ensure they are accepted by good schools.

In a study conducted by Zero to Three, researchers found that 87 per cent of parents believed the more stimulation a baby received the better.

Mr Melmed said: 'This finding is of particular concern given the attention on early brain development. It may make some parents feel driven to do more to "stimulate" their baby's brain. The downside… is that some parents will push toddlers and babies much further than they are developmentally capable of going, often to the child's long-term detriment.

'This very parent-directed interaction can lower children's curiosity, competence and ability to deal with the world on their own terms,' he told the Parent Child 2000 conference in London organised by the National Family and Parenting Institute.

Spending 'quality time' with your child is not necessary either, he said, as children benefit more from 'unhurried time' even if it is doing chores, such as shopping or cleaning.

Elizabeth Howell, of Parenting Connections consultancy, said that over-stimulating children was a form of 'child abuse'. 'Parents are motivated by the best possible intentions but they are confusing the messages and are stimulating their children to the point where it is invasive.

'Children who are bombarded with stimuli become over-whelmed and they shut down,' she said.

The Independent, 13 April 2000

Questions

1 Why do you think hothousing is so popular at the moment?

2 What would you identify as the dangers in hothousing? Can it be done safely?

for and against

the role of environment

+ There is clear evidence that environmental insults, both biological and psychological, can adversely affect the development of intelligence.

+ There is also clear evidence that by removing children from poor environments and placing them in better environments boosts IQ.

+ There is further evidence from Headstart and hothousing studies that enriched environments can boost the abilities of children.

− Genes probably remain an important factor in the development of intelligence and abilities.

− The environment in which a child grows up does not necessarily predict their experiences that affect their intellectual development.

where to now?

The following are good sources of further information regarding the role of the environment in the development of intelligence:

▶ **Howe, M.J.A. (1998) Can IQ change?** *The Psychologist 11(2), 69–72* – a very readable article exploring different sources of evidence for the role of environment in changing IQ.

▶ **Howe, M.J.A. (1999)** *The Psychology of High Abilities***. Basingstoke: Macmillan** – a detailed view of the evidence for the role of the environment in the development of high IQ and a variety of mental abilities.

Gene–environment interaction

If we accept that both genes and environment influence individual differences in general intelligence and cognitive abilities, then the question becomes 'How do they interact and which is more important for the average child?'. Sandra Scarr (1992) has suggested that, while extremely good or bad environments may influence intelligence, for most children genetic differences are more important. We now look a little more closely at the ideas of Scarr.

Scarr's triarchic theory

Scarr (1992) proposed a theory that sees all variance in intelligence and other individual differences as coming ultimately from genes, although there is not a simple genetic basis to intelligence *per se*. This is possible because Scarr believes we tend to create our own environment, and the type of environment we create will be a product of our (genetically determined) personality. This is a radical departure from a common-sense view that would say that as young children we are at the mercy of the environment provided by others. Scarr explains this in three ways:

- *Gene–environment correlation* – Scarr proposed that the only reason we find correlations between environmental variables and later intelligence is because parents provide both the environment and the genes – so the quality of environment and genes inevitably correlate. It is however the genes and not the environment that leads to the intelligence.

- *Evocation of responses* – Scarr proposed that different children *evoke* different treatment from adults, thus creating their own social and intellectual environment. From a very early age, more sociable infants evoke more social interactions from caregivers, thus receiving more stimulation. This pattern continues at school, where bright children may attract more attention from teachers.

- *Choice of environment* – once past infancy, children have a degree of choice in what environment they seek out. As adults we select our environment in the form of education, occupation and leisure according to our preferences for certain levels and types of stimulation.

Scarr points out that very poor environments that fall outside the *average expectable environment* can still have negative effects on children because the opportunity to influence their environment is denied by neglect or abuse. However, provided parenting falls into the bounds of the average expectable environment, there is no reason why parenting styles should affect cognitive or social development.

Support for Scarr's position comes from adoption studies like that of Plomin *et al.* (1997) (see p.173), which have indicated that with age, the effects of genes appear to become greater and the influence of parental environment less. However, if Scarr is correct, we might expect there to be evidence for the effects of environmental insults on intelligence but no evidence that variations in children's normal experiences have an impact. In fact, as we have seen, there is some evidence that normal variations in environment have an impact on children's development. We have seen that socio-economic status, parenting style, breastfeeding and the use of dummies are all associated with IQ. Scarr is none the less probably correct that unusual environments have a greater impact than normal variations. A further problem with Scarr's theory is that if intelligence depends on personality we would expect lively, sociable children to be more intelligent than more introverted children; there is no evidence for this.

The social-emotional development of gifted children

Some children demonstrate exceptional mental abilities. We can call such children 'gifted'. Some gifted children display highly specific abilities, for example in maths or music, while others have particularly high general intelligence. We have already dealt with some of the major issues concerning gifted children. For example, we have examined the extent to which their abilities are innate (as is implied by the word 'gifted'), and to what extent these abilities are acquired by some kind of hothousing. We have also looked at the issue of whether to integrate or segregate gifted children in the school system in Chapter 5 (see p.92).

There is, however, a further issue that is worth spending some time exploring. This concerns the psychological well-being of gifted children. There are two stereotypical views of the gifted child in psychological literature; one of the highly resilient child whose social skills and emotional development mirror his or her intellectual development, and another of a very vulnerable and socially retarded child. Neihart (1999) reviewed the evidence and concluded that either stereotype can be true, depending on the nature of the 'gift', the appropriateness of the child's education and the child's temperament. There is no reason why children with a resilient temperament and who have positive educational experiences should be socially disadvantaged by their unusual abilities. However, you can imagine that an already vulnerable child who is then made to feel like a freak at school because of his or her abilities is likely to be scarred by the experience.

So how do gifted children perceive themselves and their 'gifts'? In a recent study Lewis and Knight (2000) investigated the self-concept of 368 gifted American children in both primary and secondary education. Interestingly it was found that the children's self-concept was positive in both primary school and high school (corresponding to our 6th form), but that it dipped during junior high (secondary school). Boys were reported as suffering more than girls, being lower on scores of perceived intelligence and social status at school, and higher on scores of anxiety. It seems likely then that gifted girls have a somewhat easier time fitting in during their early adolescence than gifted boys.

where to now?

The following is a good source of further information on gifted children:

▶ **Howe, M.J.A. (1999)** *The Psychology of High Abilities*. **Basingstoke: Macmillan** – contains sections on the origins of giftedness, genius and child prodigies as well as practical advice about how to develop the abilities of children.

Conclusions

There are good reasons for questioning whether intelligence as such really exists. People from different cultures often have different mental abilities, and intelligence tests cannot be used to compare individuals from different cultural backgrounds. Some psychologists have gone so far as to suggest that intelligence has been invented in order to perpetuate social inequalities. Another problem with the idea of intelligence is that we have a range of mental abilities and some of us might do particularly well in some and badly in others. It may therefore be wiser to think of different mental abilities rather than a single intelligence. However, broadly speaking, people who test high in one ability tend to do so in others as well. The role of genes and environment in the development of intelligence and mental abilities has been a major area of research. There is ample evidence for the importance of both genes and environment in the development of intelligence and abilities. Recently, geneticists have begun to isolate individual genes associated with general intelligence and some specific abilities. Environmental variables include both biological factors (e.g. radiation poisoning) and psychological factors (e.g. abuse). There has been some success in manipulating the environment in the form of Headstart and hothousing programmes so as to increase children's intelligence. We normally think of high intelligence and exceptional abilities as a positive thing; however gifted children can run into problems if they are initially vulnerable and are then given a hard time at school. However, although very high intelligence can create problems under these circumstances there is no reason why most gifted children cannot undergo normal social and emotional development.

what do you know?

1 Outline two reasons why we might question the existence of intelligence.

2 How closely related is IQ as measured by psychologists to real-life achievement?

3 Describe one twin study and one adoption study. What do they suggest about the role of genes in the development of intelligence?

4 What criticisms can be levelled at these types of study?

5 Why is the non-shared environment more important than the shared environment in the development of intelligence?

6 Outline research into one aspect of the psychological environment that may be associated with the development of intelligence.

7 Assess the success of programmes that have aimed deliberately to improve children's intelligence and/or mental abilities.

10

The development
of moral reasoning

In this chapter we can apply our knowledge of cognitive development to understanding how children develop their grasp of morality. We begin with Piaget's approach to children's understanding of rules and lies, and go on to look at the work of Laurence Kohlberg, whose ideas have dominated the field for many years. We will also look at alternative approaches to moral development, such as that of Carol Gilligan, who made a sharp distinction between the ways in which boys and girls make moral judgements, and Nancy Eisenberg, who thought of moral development as a shift from selfishness towards selflessness. In *What's new?* we look at some very up-to-date research linking moral reasoning to the quality of family relationships.

What is morality?

One of the major tasks of every human society is to communicate to its children a set of standards by which they can make judgements about what is right and wrong (Hetherington and Parke, 1993). Of course different societies have different moral rules about what is considered right and wrong, but the existence of such rules is universal. Morality can be divided into three components: moral reasoning, moral behaviour and moral feelings. In this chapter we are mainly concerned with the development of children's moral reasoning in line with their cognitive development, although later we will look briefly at the importance of moral behaviour.

Piaget's theory of moral development

Piaget (1932) proposed that children's understanding of moral reasoning develops in line with their cognitive development, and that as children get older their moral reasoning becomes increasingly sophisticated. Piaget developed several interesting ways of researching moral development. For example, he looked at children's ability to take a person's *intentions* into account when judging the moral status of their actions. He did this by presenting children with pairs of scenarios, one of which involved minor harm caused by a deliberate action and the other which involved more serious harm being caused accidentally. One such pair of scenarios is shown in Box 10.1.

---

1 A boy called John is in his room. He is called to dinner, but when he opens the dining room door it knocks into a chair on which is a tray of cups. The tray falls and 15 cups are broken.

2 When his mother is out, a boy called Henry climbs on to a chair in order to steal some jam from a high cupboard. He knocks over a cup and it breaks.

Box 10.1 An example of the type of scenarios used by Piaget

It is clear that in the first scenario the child has done more damage, but that it is not the result of any naughty intentions on the part of the child. In the second scenario the child has done rather less damage, but has done so in the course of being naughty. Piaget found that children under 10 years of age tended to judge that John was more guilty than Henry because he broke more cups. However, children over the age of 10 tended to say that Henry was the more guilty because, whereas John was trying to obey his parents' instruction to come to dinner, Henry was engaged in stealing jam. From these results Piaget concluded that, from the age of 10, children are sufficiently intellectually developed to take a person's intentions into account when judging their actions.

In a closely related procedure Piaget (1932) investigated children's moral judgements about the telling of untruths. They were shown pairs of incorrect statements, one of which was slightly but deliberately incorrect and the other more seriously incorrect, but not deliberately so. For example, children under 10 years judged that it was naughtier accidentally to get someone's age wrong by 4 years than to deliberately lie about it by one year. However, children over 10 tended to judge the lie as more serious. Piaget called the tendency for under-10s to judge morality purely according to the seriousness of consequences *moral realism*.

Another way in which Piaget studied moral development was by observing children's co-operative play (see p.75 for a discussion of co-operative play) and noting how the children applied the rules of the game. He came to believe that play with rules is a major source of children's developing understanding of morality. Piaget also interviewed the children to find out what they believed about rules. It emerged that children under 10 years had rather different beliefs about rules than children over 10. Under-10s tended to think of rules as absolute and unchangeable, whereas over-10s saw rules as more flexible. When asked where the rules came from, under-10s typically cited God and their own parents. Children under 10 years also had a tendency to believe in *immanent* (inevitable) *justice*. This is the idea that people who break rules will inevitably be found out and receive some form of punishment.

According to Piaget children develop their understanding of moral rules during play

Based on his studies of rules and intentionality, Piaget (1932) proposed a theory of children's moral development, in which children progress from having a lack of any awareness of morality to a stage where they have a rigid moral understanding based on their understanding of 'the rules'. Finally they develop to a more advanced stage where moral decisions are based on respect for others.

- *The amoral stage (0 to 5 years)* – prior to around 5 years children are oblivious to moral issues. They have tightly regulated environments in which they have little opportunity to make moral decisions and do not in any case have sufficient reasoning ability to do so.

- *The stage of heteronomous morality (5 to 10 years)* – children now have a good awareness of rules, and make moral decisions based on these rules. Rules are seen as absolute and inflexible, and anyone breaking them will inevitably be caught and punished (immanent justice). In making moral judgements about people, the consequences of their actions are more important than their intentions.

- *The stage of autonomous morality (10 years+)* – children from around 10 years can begin to appreciate that rules are not absolute and that they can in fact be negotiated with peers. Punishment for breaking rules is no longer seen as inevitable, and children can make sensible judgements about whether rules should be broken in particular circumstances. In making moral judgements about people's actions it becomes possible to take into account their intentions.

The general idea that children's understanding of morality changes and becomes more sophisticated with age is generally supported by psychologists. This idea has proved useful in education where teachers have to teach morality in a form suitable to the age of the children. In a review of strategies for teaching morality at school Goodman (2000) has suggested that the approach has to be tailored to the cognitive development of the children, and that younger children will be moral realists and therefore benefit from firm rules. Negotiation and consideration of rules can begin when children are sufficiently developed to make rational decisions.

Research has also supported Piaget's idea that children develop their understanding of morals during interaction with their peers. Kruger (1992) tested whether children would learn more about morality from a peer or parent by presenting girls with two moral dilemmas to solve. In one condition the girls were paired with their mother while in the other they were paired with another girl of the same age. It was found that the peer pairs had much more sophisticated discussions than the mother–daughter pairs and that afterwards they displayed more advanced moral reasoning.

Although the general principles underlying Piaget's theory hold true, contemporary research findings have challenged some of the specifics. A number of studies have found that children considerably younger than 10 years can take account of people's intentions when making moral judgements. Cameron et al. (1999) presented Canadian and Chinese children aged 7, 9 and 11 years with stories in which someone told a lie in a politeness situation. For example, one friend tells another that an apple they have just given them is sour (when it is not) in order to offend them, or alternatively that it is sweet when it is in fact sour so as not to offend. The children of all ages and both nationalities clearly distinguished between the malicious and benevolent lies, and rated the malicious lies as more naughty. This suggests that Piaget underestimated the moral reasoning abilities of younger children, who can in fact take into account people's intentions when making moral judgements about them.

A further limitation of Piaget's theory was that his assumption that moral maturity is associated with a shift away from rigid rules and towards the freedom to make up one's own mind is bound up with the culture of Western Europe and America. The freedom of the individual is at the heart of European-American culture. However, Schweder (1991) has pointed out that this is not universal, and that in fact very religious cultures that base their moral codes on sacred books tend to become more rather than less inflexible with age.

for and against

Piaget's theory

+ It seems that children's moral understanding does become more sophisticated with age.

+ Research has supported Piaget's idea that moral understanding develops during interaction with peers.

− It does seem, however, that Piaget underestimated the abilities of younger children.

Kohlberg's theory

Kohlberg has perhaps been the most influential researcher in the area of moral development for many years. Like Piaget he believed that moral reasoning required both a certain level of cognitive development and life experiences. He believed, however, that Piaget had not taken enough account of moral development during adolescence, and set out to research this in more depth. Kohlberg (1958) investigated morality in boys aged 10 to 16 years, using a set of stories involving moral dilemmas. The best known of these is that of Heinz and the pharmacist. This is shown in Box 10.2.

Heinz's wife was very ill with a rare form of cancer, and was close to death. A local pharmacist had developed a drug that might save her but he was charging $2,000 for a small dose, ten times what it cost to make. Heinz managed to raise $1,000 and begged the pharmacist to sell the drug cheaply or allow him to pay in instalments. However the pharmacist refused and in desperation Heinz broke in to the pharmacy and stole the drug.

Box 10.2 Kohlberg's Heinz dilemma

Kohlberg asked boys whether Heinz was right to do so and why? On the basis of their answers to this and similar dilemmas Kohlberg classified moral reasoning into three broad levels of development:

- *Preconventional morality* – develops from approximately 5 to 12 years. This corresponds approximately to Piaget's heteronomous stage. Morality is based entirely on external influences. During this period there is a shift from deference to authority based on the avoidance of punishment – the earliest conception of morality – to a realisation that conformity brings rewards – a more advanced reasoning.

- *Conventional morality* – develops from approximately 13 to 15 years. Moral judgements can now be applied to others. Although the reactions of adults are still important, these are seen not in terms of reward and punishment but in terms of approval – being seen as 'good' is an important motivator. By the end of the conventional period morality is *internalised*, i.e. children make moral decisions based on their own judgements rather than the anticipated responses of others. By this point children have developed a respect for society and see the law as very important.

- *Postconventional morality* – develops from 16 to 20 years. This level is characterised by the awareness that people have a variety of values and opinions, and that rules are to some extent arbitrary. There is a shift during this period from a stage of general acceptance of rules for reasons of impartiality and because they constitute a social contract towards the highest moral state, that of *universal ethical principles*, i.e. equality and respect for individual dignity. This involves the realisation that although laws and conventions usually reflect moral principles, when they come into conflict the ethical principles rather than the rules must be upheld.

Kohlberg believed that only around 10 to 15 per cent of people achieved the highest moral state and acquired universal ethical principles. He named Jesus Christ, Martin Luther King, Mahatma Gandhi and himself as among the few. In his later writing Kohlberg stopped referring to universal principles as the endpoint of normal development and instead wrote of it as an ideal.

Kohlberg (1969) researched moral development in a number of countries and reported the same pattern of development in societies as diverse as America, Taiwan, Mexico and Turkey. A number of studies have supported Kohlberg's belief that his pattern of moral development is universal. Snarey (1985) reviewed 44 studies covering 26 countries and concluded that generally Kohlberg's theory could be applied to a wide variety of cultures. However, Burman (1994) has pointed out that people in some cultures do not shift to postconventional reasoning, and that if we start to classify whole cultures as 'morally immature' just because they tend to reach different moral decisions from our own, we become guilty of racism. Besides, as we have already discussed in relation to Piaget's theory, not all cultures place the same value on the freedom to make individual moral choices, so postconventional morality may not be the universal endpoint of

development. When Okwonko (1997) gave Kohlberg-type moral dilemmas to Igbo children in Nigeria she found that they often produced highly sophisticated answers that demonstrated advanced reasoning. However, because of Nigerian cultural values of obedience to parents, belief in a divine being and the close interdependence of all members of a community their answers did not fit neatly into Kohlberg's classification and they could not be classified as postconventional.

There are further problems with Kohlberg's research and theory. One important limitation lies with his choice of research method. His interviews centred on hypothetical situations, quite different from the types of moral dilemmas that his participants had ever faced. Millis (1999) demonstrated the importance of the context in which moral dilemmas are presented. She presented children with four moral dilemmas set in school and four set out of school. It was found that children were much more conventional when dilemmas were set in school, and that they were more likely to give responses classifiable as postconventional when the dilemmas were set in out-of-school situations.

Perhaps the acid test of a theory like Kohlberg's is to see whether children and young people classified at different levels of moral reasoning actually behave differently when it comes to making real-life moral decisions. One way of testing this idea is to look at the moral reasoning of criminals – Kohlberg's theory would predict that criminals would operate at a preconventional level. A recent study from Aleixo and Norris (2000) did just this. We now look at their study in detail.

research
now

are criminals just morally immature?

Aleixo, P.A. and Norris, C.E. (2000) Personality and moral reasoning in young offenders. *Personality and Individual Differences 28, 609–23.*

Aim: Kohlberg's theory of moral development would predict that criminals reason at a lower developmental level than do law-abiding citizens. However, few studies have set out to directly test this idea. An alternative explanation for criminal behaviour has been proposed by Eysenck (1987), who suggested, in contrast to Kohlberg, that criminality is associated with certain personality characteristics. The aim of this study was to assess young criminals for personality and moral reasoning, and to see whether Kohlberg's and Eysenck's theories hold true.

Method: The participants for this study were 101 convicted male offenders, aged between 16 and 21 years. As well as looking at their criminal records the researchers questioned the young men about their criminal activities, in order to get a fuller picture of the crime they had been involved in. They were then assessed for their level of moral reasoning using Kohlberg-type dilemmas and their personality characteristics were measured using a personality test called the Eysenck Personality Questionnaire (or EPQ), which measures three aspects of personality: *extraversion* – liveliness and sociability; *neuroticism* – emotional instability; and *psychoticism* – tough-mindedness. Results were analysed to see if there were any relationships between criminality, personality and moral reasoning. They were also given IQ tests.

Results: Overall the level of moral reasoning in the sample of young offenders was lower than is typical for the age group. However, there was no relationship between moral reasoning and type of crime reported. IQ was found on average to be lower than in the general population. The only personality characteristic found to differ in the criminal sample from the general population was psychoticism (tough-mindedness). This was significantly higher in the criminal group.

Conclusions: These results provide partial support for Kohlberg's theory. As expected, moral reasoning was at a lower level than is typical for the age group. However, Eysenck's theory is also supported. The authors suggested that the low level of moral reasoning in the criminal sample was due to a combination of psychoticism and low IQ.

We can see then that Kohlberg's theory seems to be a partial explanation for real-life moral reasoning, although he seems to have underestimated the importance of factors like personality and his methods of assessing stage of development have limited use in assessing individuals from a range of cultures. Kohlberg has been criticised for his exclusive use of boys and young men in his research – a criticism that also applies to much of the research that has supported his ideas. Carol Gilligan (1982) has suggested that the development of moral reasoning in girls is quite different from that in boys. We can examine this suggestion in some detail when we move on to look at Gilligan's theory.

for and against

Kohlberg's theory

+ Kohlberg's general principle that people's moral reasoning continues to change during adolescence, and that this involves a shift from conventional to postconventional reasoning, seems to be broadly correct.

– Although Kohlberg's stages do hold true for a variety of cultures they may not be universal. Okwonko (1997) has demonstrated that standard Kohlberg dilemmas do not capture the sophisticated reasoning in young Nigerians.

+ As predicted by Kohlberg's theory, convicted criminals do tend to have lower levels of moral reasoning than is typical for their age.

– Kohlberg may have underestimated differences in the moral reasoning of boys and girls, and it seems that his theory is less successful in explaining moral reasoning in girls.

where to now?

The following are good sources of further information about the theories of Piaget and Kohlberg:

▶ **Lee, K. (2000) Lying as doing deceptive things with words: a speech act theoretical perspective. In Astington, J.W. (ed.)** *Minds in the Making*. **Oxford: Blackwell** – an excellent, though quite advanced chapter that looks at Piaget's ideas and reviews relevant recent work in the area.

▶ **Shaffer, D.R. (1999)** *Developmental Psychology: childhood and adolescence*. **Pacific Grove: Brooks/Cole** – contains an excellent chapter on moral development, including in-depth coverage of Piaget and Kohlberg.

▶ **Durkin, K. (1995)** *Developmental Social Psychology*. **Oxford: Blackwell** – a very detailed but clear account of theories of moral development, including Piaget and Kohlberg. Particularly interesting in its coverage of cultural factors in moral development.

Gilligan's theory of female moral development

Carol Gilligan (1982) challenged Kohlberg's then widely supported theory of moral development by pointing out that he had not addressed differences in the development of moral reasoning in boys and girls. In his original studies Kohlberg only used male participants, and some early studies using male and female participants found that girls emerged as being at a lower level of moral development than boys of the same age. Gilligan investigated moral reasoning in women, and developed a theory of how their reasoning differed from that of men. We now look at her original study in detail.

classic research

how do women make moral choices?

Gilligan, C. (1977) In a different voice: women's conceptions of self and morality. *Harvard Educational Review 47, 481–517.*

Aim: Gilligan was concerned that Kohlberg's theory of moral development addressed morality in men but not in women. Having spoken to men and women about moral issues she developed the idea that women have a fundamentally different way of looking at moral issues. In this study Gilligan aimed to find out how adolescent girls and young women responded to a real-life moral dilemma.

Method: Participants in the study were 29 girls and women aged between 15 and 33 years. They were an opportunity sample of women facing the real-life dilemma of whether to continue with or terminate an unplanned pregnancy. All participants were recruited from pregnancy and/or abortion counselling services. Gilligan interviewed the women in order to gain an idea of what factors might underlie their decision as to whether to continue with their pregnancy. The interviews were relatively informal and there was no attempt to fit the participants' responses into pre-existing categories. However, once the interviews were complete Gilligan divided the responses into categories.

Results: Three levels of moral reasoning were identified from the interviews, all on a spectrum based on care, ranging from care of oneself to care for others. On level 1, the lowest level of moral reasoning, women's decisions were governed by self-interest. On level 2, decisions depended on self-sacrifice. Self-sacrifice might involve keeping an unwanted baby because of the belief that its rights outweighed her own, or aborting a foetus to please an unenthusiastic partner. On level 3, the highest level of moral reasoning, women reasoned according to the principle of 'universal care', balancing their own needs with those of the child.

Conclusion: Gilligan had identified three levels of moral reasoning which characterised women's moral decision-making. These appeared to be more appropriate for categorising women's reasoning than Kohlberg's system, because they were based not on the principle of justice but on that of caring.

Based on this study Gilligan (1982) proposed that men and women use different criteria when making moral judgements. Although Gilligan's three levels of female moral reasoning are roughly equivalent to Kohlberg's preconventional, conventional and postconventional levels, they are based on different principles. Gilligan suggested that whereas men's moral reasoning is based on their understanding of justice, women's reasoning is based on their understanding of caring. She referred to these two ways of thinking as the *justice orientation* and the *caring orientation*. We can see how Gilligan compared her own theory of female morality with Kohlberg's theory in Table 10.1.

	Male	Female
Level of reasoning 1	Preconventional	Self-interest
Level of reasoning 2	Conventional	Self-sacrifice
Level of reasoning 3	Postconventional	Universal care
General moral orientation	Justice	Caring

Table 10.1 Comparison of levels of moral reasoning in males and females

So where do males and females get their different moral orientations? In Chapter 6 on gender development, we looked at Nancy Chodorow's ideas on the development of female gender identity (see p.106). Gilligan was interested in Chodorow's idea that girls remain very close to their mothers and develop their gender identity directly from them while boys have to break away from the mother to develop a male gender identity. Gilligan suggested that this difference in girls' and boys' maternal relationship means that women retain a sense of *connectedness*, which characterises their reasoning. Boys, having had to detach themselves from the mother in order to develop a male gender identity, develop a sense of *separateness*, which characterises their later social development. It is this sense of separateness that leads boys to rely on logical decisions about justice.

Interactive angles

Gather some friends or classmates into a mixed-gender group, and discuss a moral issue of your choice. A suitable issue might include homelessness, for example. When each person has had his or her say, classify their views according to whether they fit a justice orientation or a care orientation.

Questions

1 Was there an association between gender and moral orientation, i.e. were boys more inclined to go for justice-oriented responses and girls for care-oriented responses?

2 Do your results support Gilligan's theory?

Do these boys and girls make moral judgements on different bases?

In her early work Gilligan believed that male and female moral reasoning were completely different, and that men based judgements purely on justice whereas women based theirs purely on care. However, researchers soon revealed this to be an oversimplification. Johnson (1988) presented moral dilemmas from classic fables to male and female adolescents, and assessed their responses as based on either justice and caring orientations. She found that both boys and girls made judgements based on an understanding of justice and caring, although responses based on caring were more common in girls and responses based on justice were more common in boys. Based on this type of research, Gilligan altered her original idea that men and women develop entirely different moral orientations. Instead she proposed that, although the judgements of both men and women are based on both types of moral reasoning, the justice orientation is dominant in men whereas the caring orientation is dominant in women.

Gilligan has been criticised for the small-scale nature of her research and for overstating the differences between women and men. However, her major contribution has been in challenging the assumption made by Piaget and Kohlberg that we make our decisions about moral issues based principally on our understanding of justice. Take a moment to think back to a moral decision you have made yourself, and the chances are that you took account of your feelings towards the people involved, as well as your opinion of the justice issue. Contemporary research tends to support Gilligan's more moderate view that women place more emphasis on care and men on justice when making moral decisions. In one recent study Garmon *et al.* (1996) tested the moral reasoning of 543 participants aged 9 to 18 using a standard interview called the *Sociomoral Reflection Measure* and found that female participants were more likely to refer to issues of care and idealism than males.

for and against

Gilligan's theory

+ Gilligan has added the dimension of care to that of justice in the study of moral reasoning.

– Gilligan's early research was very limited and she probably overstated the differences between male and female moral reasoning.

+ Research supports Gilligan's more moderate view that males rely more on justice and females more on care when making moral decisions.

where to now?

The following are good sources of further information about Gilligan's theory and research:

▶ Brannon, L. (1996) *Gender: psychological approaches*. Needham Heights: Allyn & Bacon – a quite detailed account of Gilligan's ideas.

▶ Gilligan, C. (1982) *In a Different Voice: psychological theory and women's development*. Cambridge: Harvard University Press – so much has been written about Gilligan's work from a number of perspectives, that it is well worth taking a look at the original.

Eisenberg's theory of prosocial development

Nancy Eisenberg (1986) proposed that in parallel to moral development there was a corresponding course of *prosocial* development, i.e. the development of personal social responsibility and altruism. Eisenberg believed that these values of responsibility and altruism were gradually internalised from society at large as the child develops an increasing capacity for *empathy* – the ability to appreciate the feelings of others.

Eisenberg investigated children's responses to prosocial dilemmas similar to those used by Kohlberg. One story of the type used by Eisenberg is shown in Box 10.3.

Eric is on his way to a friend's birthday party when he sees a boy who has fallen and hurt his leg. The boy asked if he could come back so he could call home and arrange to be picked up. If Eric agreed he would miss the food at the party.

Box 10.3 An example of a prosocial dilemma

On the basis of children's responses at different ages they were classified as attaining one of five levels of prosocial development:

- *level 1 (hedonistic)* – individuals are concerned with consequences to themselves. Decisions to perform prosocial acts are based on direct gain, future reciprocal gain and concern for those for whom affection exists. This is typical of pre-school-age children.

- *level 2 (needs-oriented)* – this level also typically exists in pre-school and primary age children. Concern can be expressed for others even when their needs conflict with their own.

- *level 3 (approval-oriented)* – typically found in primary, middle and secondary school children. There are stereotyped images of good and bad people and behaviours. When justifying pro or anti-social behaviour children tend to refer to the approval of others.

- *level 4 (empathic)* – present in some secondary school children. This stage is characterised by empathic responding to the feelings of others and concern for their feelings. Values and responsibilities are now internalised although the child has limited ability to describe them.

- *level 5 (internalised values)* – this level is attained by only a small minority of children of school age. Values and responsibilities are clearly understood and can be vocalised. Whether these standards are lived up to constitutes an important factor in self-respect.

The existence of pro-social development as distinct from moral development requires justification. One way of approaching this is to see whether children who score highly in pro-social development also score highly in the development of moral reasoning. This has been tested in a study by Eisenberg *et al.* (1997), who found only moderate correlations between children's levels as measured by Eisenberg's procedures and that measured by Kohlberg's procedures. Durkin (1995) reviewed studies of pro-social development and has confirmed the principle that, as cognitive development progresses, pro-social behaviour increases. However Eisenberg's explanation is not the only possible one. Lourenco (1993) has pointed out that with increasing age comes an increased awareness of gains to the actor. It could well be this, rather than internalisation of pro-social values, that may explain increases in pro-social reasoning with age.

what's new?

the development of moral reasoning in the family

Much of the contemporary research in the field of moral development is returning to an old idea, explored in the early days of psychology by Sigmund Freud, that children's moral development is centred in their family relationships. Freud proposed that we internalise an image of the same sex parent during Oedipal conflict (see p.3 for a discussion of Oedipal conflict) and that this literally forms our conscience. We have already looked at modern research into Oedipal conflict in Chapter 5 (p.105) and concluded that even if it exists, Freud greatly overestimated its importance in children's development. There is no evidence that same-sex parents or single parents produce children lacking in moral development (at least once poverty is eliminated as a confounding variable), as we would expect were Oedipal conflict an essential part of moral development. What does exist, however, is a body of research showing that the general family climate and the quality of relationships within the family do seem to have an impact on moral development.

Pratt *et al.* (1999) studied the relationship between moral reasoning in adolescence and interaction with parents. Forty Canadian families took part, with adolescents aged 12 to 16 at the start of the study. The adolescents were followed up and regularly assessed for moral reasoning. Family climate was assessed by measuring how much time was spent talking to the child and how responsive parents were to the child's voice. It was found that the time spent talking to the child by fathers and the responsiveness of the mothers to the young people's voices were associated with the level of moral reasoning. In another study of much younger children Hughes and Dunn (2000) followed up developments in moral reasoning of

40 hard-to-manage (hyperactive) children from 4 to 6 years and looked in detail at the characteristics of their primary carers. They found that the group as a whole had a lower level of moral reasoning than is typical for the age group. They also found that moral reasoning was associated with high levels of maternal warmth and low levels of maternal criticism, suggesting the quality of the child's relationship with the primary carer influences moral reasoning.

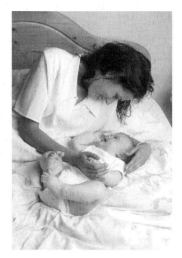

It seems likely that the quality of relationship between this mother and child will influence the child's moral development

There is thus solid evidence to suggest that the quality of family relationships influences moral reasoning. On a theoretical level, how can we explain this? We could approach this from a psychodynamic perspective. Van Ijzendoorn (1997) has proposed that quality of attachment is the major factor in moral development. Following on from Freud's idea of the internalised parent, it makes sense that an internalised warm, uncritical parent will give the child a sophisticated conscience, whereas a harsh, critical parent will leave the child with a cruder understanding of morality. An alternative approach to explaining the influence of family relationships on moral reasoning is to apply Vygotsky's theory. In Chapter 8 we saw that Vygotsky believed that we internalise our 'tools' of reasoning in childhood during interaction with adults. Haste (1999) has applied this approach to the internalising of moral reasoning. Because the frequency and success of child–adult interaction is associated with their quality of relationship, it makes sense that the better a child's relationship with its carers the more sophisticated 'tools' it can take on board. This means that we would expect children with good family relationships to have a more sophisticated moral reasoning.

where to now?

The following is a good source of further information about the importance of family context in the development of moral reasoning:

▶ **Shaffer, D. R. (1999)** *Developmental Psychology*. **Boston: ITP** – this excellent book has a particularly useful section on the role of the family in moral and pro-social development.

Conclusions

Piaget and Kohlberg have produced stage theories of moral reasoning. Both have suggested that moral reasoning requires both a minimum level of cognitive development and appropriate experiences. Kohlberg's theory differs from that of Piaget in that it focuses on higher levels of moral reasoning in adolescence. Both Piaget and Kohlberg have been criticised for the limited applicability of their theories across a range of human societies and for failing to account for gender differences in style of moral reasoning. Gilligan has researched moral decision-making in women and produced an alternative theory of moral development in women. A further alternative to the dominant approach of Kohlberg comes from Eisenberg, who emphasised the shift during childhood from selfishness to selflessness as the influence of society on the child increases. A major line of research into moral development concerns the importance of family relationships. This is not easily explained by major cognitive-developmental theories of moral development, but can be understood with reference to psychodynamic and Vygotskian theories.

what do you know?

1. Outline one way in which Piaget investigated moral development.

2. Suggest one way in which Piaget's theory has proved useful and provide one criticism of it.

3. Comment on Kohlberg's procedures for assessing moral development.

4. How well has Kohlberg's theory applied to a range of cultures?

5. Describe in detail one study of female moral reasoning. To what extent do you think men and women think differently about moral issues?

6. How important is the family in the development of moral reasoning? How might we explain this?

11

Autism

what's
ahead?

In this chapter we concentrate on typical autism as described by Kanner (1943). It is important to remember that autism is as varied as the individuals with such a diagnosis. It is also predominantly found in males and so 'he' is used throughout the chapter to refer to specific examples. We will discuss the most common symptoms of autism, including social impairments, a lack of imagination and difficulties with communication. After describing some of the most frequently observed symptoms, we will see how these issues contribute to the diagnostic criteria currently used. We will assess a range of possible causes, including biological and psychological theories, and some of the major therapies used to treat autism such as behavioural techniques and educational intervention.

What is autism?

Autism is a *pervasive developmental disorder*; that is, a disorder that is part of the individual, starting in early childhood and continuing as the child matures. It is usually seen to emerge between 0 and 3 years of age, has an incidence of approximately 0.05 per cent and is more common in males. It is important to remember that when talking about a developmental disorder we are discussing someone's entire personality and therefore it is much more complex than most people would consider.

Kanner (1943) was the first to document autism as a disorder. One of the major symptoms he noticed was that of self-absorption and it is from this that the name 'autism' is derived; the Greek word for 'self' is '*autos*'. Kanner then went on to describe five behavioural elements that he felt made up this newly christened disorder. He placed particular emphasis on:

- impaired social interaction

- impaired communication

- a strong resistance to change

- a preference for objects rather than people

- an occasional demonstration of a high level of intelligence.

This child with autism shows intense absorption in response to light and sound. Such self-containment is characteristic of the disorder

It is important to differentiate between characteristics and diagnostic criteria. *Characteristics* are features of the disorder that have been observed to be present in the majority of those with autism, whereas *diagnostic criteria* are features that must be present for a medical diagnosis of autism to be made. It is this fine line that marks the difference between definition and diagnosis. Kanner provided a definition of autism but it is interesting to note that the first four of his observations are found in the diagnostic scales used today.

A year later Asperger (1944) also published a paper that described the symptoms seen by Kanner. However, he described a greater span of individuals, ranging from those who were profoundly affected, to those who demonstrated mild symptoms only. He gave his name to a different form of an autistic-type disorder, now known as Asperger's syndrome. Simplistically, this can be described as a high-functioning version of autism. However, this should not be taken as a definition of Asperger's syndrome, because this stands alone from autism in the diagnostic scales. It is beyond the scope of this chapter to discuss Asperger's syndrome but those who are interested may refer to books recommended in *Where to now*.

Following the initial flurry of interest in the 1940s, there was little consideration given to the definition of autism until Creak (1961)

published a paper describing further characteristics, the presence of which would demonstrate autism. In addition to Kanner's points, Creak noted the following:

● People with autism often demonstrated a lack of awareness of their own body; that is, they knew it was *a* body, just not *their* body.

● There is evidence of abnormal perception in those with autism. This could take the form of abnormal sensitivity or insensitivity to various stimuli such as light, sound or pain.

● They may also show acute, and often apparently irrational, anxiety and it is possible that the last two points are related, although this link was not made within Creak's nine characteristics.

● Individuals with autism may show distorted mobility patterns such as walking on their toes or avoiding specific features of a floor or pavement.

In addition to these points, Creak extended Kanner's comment regarding levels of intelligence to say that those with autism often show unusual 'pockets' of intelligence and ability, and may have unusual skill patterns that allow them to achieve tasks that someone without autism would find challenging, while a simple task like tying their shoelaces would be impossible for them.

A drawing of Canary Wharf, London, by Stephen Wiltshire, an extraordinarily talented artist who has autism

You can see how the spectrum of defining characteristics started to widen and incorporate more of the 'autistic personality'. Creak's points have been further refined, as research into autism has revealed more about the characteristics of the disorder.

One of the most simple but useful definitions was proposed by Wing and Gould (1979) as a triad of characteristics which they felt were essential to autism. This is shown below.

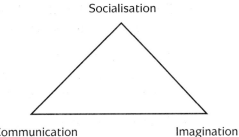

The triad of impairments (Wing and Gould, 1979). These three elements capture the main types of behaviours that are commonly seen in, and are specific to, autism

The triad clearly shows the interaction of the three most common domains of deficit seen in autism. Although this is far too simplistic to be used in a diagnostic manner it is still evident in extended revised scales that are being created today.

where to now?

The following are good sources of information about autism generally and Asperger's syndrome in particular:

▶ **Attwood, T. (1998)** *Asperger's Syndrome: a guide for parents and professionals.* **London: Jessica Kingsley Publishers** – a good text to read for a comprehensive exploration of Asperger's syndrome.

▶ **Wing, L. (1996)** *The Autistic Spectrum: A guide for parents and professionals.* **London: Constable and Co. Ltd** – a practical, accessible discussion of autism, covering many factors including treatment and cause.

Symptoms of autism

Definitions of autism focus on the shared characteristics exhibited by people with autism. The usual age at which the symptoms of autism become apparent is around 18 months, although it is likely that they will have been there since birth. Below we will describe these symptoms and discuss how they are detected and measured.

Theory of mind deficit

There is some argument as to whether a lack of a theory of mind is a cause or a symptom of autism. In this chapter it will be predominantly classified as a symptom, as it is easier to consider it as such, although it is important to keep this ambiguity in mind.

The phrase *theory of mind* means literally what it says; a theory or belief about someone else's mind, a concept of the world that allows us to predict their behaviour. A lack of a theory of mind would mean that social interaction would become virtually impossible as it prevents the individual from assessing how other people are feeling.

If we consider socialisation to be a developmental process, we may get a clue as to why this is impaired in autism as this is a pervasive developmental disorder. By their second year, a normally developing child can appreciate that someone may be pretending, by the age of 3 they appreciate the possession of private knowledge and by the age of 4 they are starting to grasp the idea that a complicated social interaction occurs when different people are faced with the same situation. In essence they become aware of the opinion of others. Wimmer and Perner (1983) first explored this in children unaffected by autism. They observed that children of 4 years old could grasp that other people may have a different, and possibly false, perception of a situation. Baron-Cohen *et al.* (1985) used this idea to look at children with autism and their perception of the world. He found that children who have autism may be *mind-blind*, that is they are unable to see the world from the point of view of somebody else.

Further evidence for the mind-blindness theory came from later studies (Perner *et al.*, 1989) that investigated the ability of those with autism to attribute false beliefs to other people. They found that the majority of those with autism failed to do this successfully, even though they were of an age group where it would be possible. Even those who did show success on these tests failed more complicated tests of false belief comprehension (Baron-Cohen, 1989). Such studies have led to the suggestion that the vast majority of people with autism show a significant delay in the development of a theory of mind. Happé (1995) analysed the results of such studies and concluded that the mental age at which a child with autism was successful, was likely to be higher than in a control group without autism.

A young boy with autism could not understand that he could not just take what he wanted. He had a language deficit and so could not ask for things. To try and prevent him taking things inappropriately his parents taught him to point to whatever he wanted, such as a biscuit, and they would give it to him. This worked well but sometimes they would come into a room and find him in a state of extreme distress. They were at a loss to explain this until his father caught sight of him through the kitchen window one day. The child was standing alone pointing towards a cupboard. He continued to stand like this for 5 minutes before he started to become a little distressed. After 10 minutes he was crying and 15 minutes later he was in hysterics; he could not understand that in order for the scheme to be effective there had to be someone else in the room to respond to his request.

Source: Baron-Cohen (2000)

Baron-Cohen *et al.* (1992) went on to suggest that such mind-blindness may cause the strange behaviours associated with autism. A child who runs away from a social situation, apparently without reason, may actually do so because they do not understand the interactions and behaviours of others. This in itself is frightening; imagine yourself in a situation where you are in a foreign country, you do not speak the language or understand the customs and then you are offered a platter of dubious looking food. You would quite likely run away at this point! In a way this is exactly what a child who is autistic has to deal with on a regular basis. They may also cope with the confusion of their environment by counteracting it with repetitive behaviours and an obsession with order. Thus they bring constancy to their world making it a little more stable and familiar. This would explain why a change of routine, such as an altered route to school, can be so distressing to a child who is autistic. We return to this topic later in the chapter (p.222), when we discuss Baron-Cohen's ideas about the causes of mind-blindness.

classic
research

does the autistic child have a theory of mind?

Baron-Cohen, S., Leslie, A.M., Frith, U. (1985) Does the autistic child have a theory of mind? *Cognition 21, 37–46.*

Aims: To try to establish whether children with autism were able to demonstrate the mental state that allows them to entertain a representation of reality that is not true.

Method: The participants were 20 able children with autism between 6 and 16 years with a verbal age of $5^1/2$ years; 14 Down's syndrome children of a similar age but decreased verbal ability; and 27 'typical' children with a mean age of $4^1/2$ years.

A scenario was presented to the participants using two dolls, Sally and Anne. Sally had a basket and Anne had a box. Sally placed a marble in her basket and then left the scene. Anne then moved the marble from Sally's basket to her box, thereby hiding it out of sight. Sally then returned to the scene and the experimenter asked the children 'Where will Sally look for her marble?'

To ensure that the children understood the language of the question and the events that had taken place, two control questions were asked: 'Where is the marble really?' and 'Where was the marble in the beginning?'.

Results: All children answered the control questions correctly. However, 85 per cent of the normal and Down's syndrome children responded that Sally would look in her basket, compared with 20 per cent of children with autism. All 80 per cent of incorrect children with autism pointed to the box (the actual location of the marble).

Conclusion: Despite the higher verbal age of those with autism, the majority of that group were unable to disregard their correct knowledge and perceive Sally's incorrect belief. This suggests that those children with autism do not have a theory of mind.

1.

Sally   Anne

2.

Anne watches while Sally puts a marble in the basket

3.

Sally leaves the room

4.

Anne moves the marble from the basket to the box

5. Where will Sally look for her marble?

The Sally and Anne dolls

Impaired responsiveness and social interaction

One of the earliest signs of autism to be identified was the apparent withdrawal from interactions with others. Children with autism often appear to be ambiguous about parental contact and may become actively frightened when cuddled. They tend to appear happiest when left on their own. A high level of withdrawal from siblings and peers is also common, although this behaviour may be less noticeable with other children who also have autism suggesting that it may be a response to fear of social and emotional interactions. Wing (1996) talks about 'socially aloof' children who fail to respond when called, pull away from physical contact and may be devoid of facial expression except at the extremities of the scale. Other people seem to be sought out for a purpose rather than pleasure, for example, to provide an object out of the child's reach. As soon as this is achieved the child once again ignores the other person.

Another sign of social aversion relates to eye contact. A child may either look 'through you' or may demonstrate a reluctance to make eye contact. Donna Williams, a well-known author who has autism, provides some insight into this in her description of a young boy with autism (Williams, 1996). When a task was demonstrated to him he would very quickly start gazing around the room or simply walk away. Williams's explanation for this was that he was 'emotionally hypersensitive' and could not cope with the eye contact required for such interaction; holding someone's gaze made him feel vulnerable and exposed. Such accounts are plentiful in the literature on autism: for example, Waterhouse (2000) quotes the experience of a young girl who described eye contact as a painful attack from which she required protection. This may arise from a lack of a theory of mind. A child without autism quickly develops the concept that another person cannot see into your head when they look at you. Without this implicit belief, eye contact suddenly becomes very threatening.

An alternative explanation for the lack of eye contact maintained by children with autism could be their hypersensitivity to light. There is now increasing evidence that the autistic experience often encompasses abnormal sensory experiences. Such hyper and hyposensitivities are discussed later in this chapter (p.217), but in this context it is perfectly possible to imagine that if a child experiences a high level of visual stimulation when making eye contact, they are going to try to avoid it. It may be that by moving around and changing what they can see, the amount of stimulation is reduced. It is also possible, of course, that when a child walks away from a situation, he is trying to find somewhere that has a lower light level.

Children who are autistic may show aversion to tactile stimulation. This makes hugging, washing, dressing and a multitude of other ordinary actions extremely difficult both for the child and for the carer. As a consequence a child may resist social contact, avoid situations such as shaking someone's hand or being patted by well-meaning strangers. In such instances the child is likely to respond negatively, often attracting the unfair label of a rude, badly behaved child. Such avoidance strategies, although effective for the child, are considered to be socially anomalous and so make the lives of such individuals even more difficult. This is one of the reasons that behavioural programmes have been developed to teach the child appropriate responses. This will be discussed in more detail later in the chapter (p.225). Given time, a child with autism will become attached in his own way to his family and other carers. This may be because they become familiar and therefore reassuring in their actions (Wing, 1996). Although this affection does not manifest itself in a universally recognisable way, it is still as genuine and emotionally compelling as any child's love.

Self-absorption and repetitive behaviours

Children with autism are seen to spend time sitting alone, apparently oblivious to others. They often have an 'inward' look about them and will not respond to outside stimuli such as conversation or music. This state of self-exclusion may be accompanied by repetitive behaviours such as rocking, or the covering of ears or eyes. Children with autism often seem oblivious when called and ignore simple instructions, apparently because they simply have not heard. They also become intensely absorbed in a particular object or action in a way that seems peculiar to most people. Spinning objects seem to hold a fascination for some children with autism. They will watch a ceiling fan or spin a plate for hours in apparent contentment. Again this may be to do with their sensory perception of such objects, in that the sight, sound or tactile sensation may be pleasurable to them. Alternatively it could be a manifestation of another symptom frequently observed in autism, that of the desire for regularity.

A child with autism may withdraw into himself and try to block all external stimulation. This posture appears to be that of someone who is distressed and may show fear

Individuals of all ages who have autism demonstrate an obsessive need for continuity and stability. They may be particularly interested in train timetables or other discrete pieces of information. A child with autism may line up toys such as Lego blocks and become distressed if anyone moves them. This need extends into daily life in many ways. Unfamiliar situations are frightening simply because they are unknown. A changed route to school may throw the whole day into confusion because regularity is a coping mechanism; take this away and the child with autism is unable to cope. This need for structure manifests itself in many ways. For instance, when asked to make a pizza in an art class, a student could not overlap the different ingredients but insisted that they were laid out in separate layers with no overlapping edges. Heaping the 'ingredients' on top of each other broke his regularity and caused significant distress. Such examples show how a child's day-to-day life can be affected by autism.

Central coherence weakness

Frith and Happé (1994) proposed the theory that people with autism have a weak drive for central coherence. This means that they process information at a local level rather than a global level so they may, for example, focus on the wheels of a car rather than the vehicle as a whole. In other words, someone with autism seems to have difficulty integrating separate pieces of information to produce an overall picture. Their experiences are effectively 'fragmented'; they perceive the individual pieces of the puzzle rather than the whole picture. This is demonstrated by the infrequency with which children with autism are fooled by visual illusions, for example Titchener's circles (see p.218). They are much faster at perceiving the constituent parts of the picture rather than being confused by the illusion, suggesting that they are experiencing the visual elements of the image separately.

research now

is there a relationship between lack of theory of mind and weak central coherence?

Jarrold, C., Butler, D.W., Cottington, E.M., and Jimenez, F. (2000) Linking theory of mind and central coherence bias in autism and in the general population. *Developmental Psychology 36(1), 126–38.*

Aim: Baron-Cohen *et al.* (1997) established that, in the general population, performance on the 'Eyes-test' (a measure of theory of mind) is inversely related to success on the Embedded Figures test (a measure of central coherence). The aim of this study was to compare autistic children to norms for theory of mind and central coherence.

Method: In Experiment 1, 20 schoolchildren aged 5 (mean age 67.63 months) were presented with a series of tests of varying difficulty to assess theory of mind. These included inferred belief, not own belief, explicit false belief, other's false belief and second order false belief. Central coherence bias was assessed using a pre-school version of the Embedded Figures test in which the target figure is always a triangle and the search figure is less complicated than in the adult version. The second test used was the Pattern Construction subtest of the Differential Ability Scales (Elliot, 1990), in which children were presented with a two-dimensional black-and-yellow segmented figure. They were then asked to recreate it using blocks with faces made up of different arrangements of yellow-and-black patterns. Performance was judged on the number of correctly completed tasks and the time in which this was achieved.

In Experiment 2, the same tests were presented to 13 boys and 4 girls (a ratio consistent with the incidence ratio of autism in boys and girls) with formally diagnosed autism. The group had a mean age of 9 years and 11 months. The children's version of the Embedded Figures test was used, in which a triangle was the target figure in the first 11 test items, followed by a house shape for the remaining 14 items.

Results: Experiments 1 and 2 showed that poor theory of mind performance is linked to weak central coherence in children both with and without autism when verbal mental age and age were accounted for. Comparatively high correlations were achieved across two separate groups of participants with two different tests of central coherence.

Conclusions: There is a relationship between a lack of theory of mind and weak central coherence, that is, in children with autism a failure to understand the perspective of others is related to an inability to take a global view.

Limited imaginative or pretend play

Another deficit seen in autism is a lack of imaginative or pretend play (see p.69 for a discussion of play). The tendency of children to invent complicated stories when playing with toys is familiar, but this tends to be absent in children with autism. Leslie (1987) suggested that this may be due to a theory of mind deficit in that pretence may require the same representational processes as are needed effectively to predict the behaviour of others. For example, a child may pretend to be a prince or princess. To do this they have to imagine both how they would be and how other people would behave towards them. This requires a knowledge of other people's feelings or theory of mind. As the ability to understand the thoughts of others is largely absent in those with autism this may explain the scarcity of pretend play seen in such children.

Language and communication deficits

A large proportion of children with autism demonstrate language and communication difficulties. Communication can be thought of as an umbrella that encompasses language. In this section we will focus on a few specific language deficits seen in autism. These may take many forms including a complete lack of speech or, more frequently, unusual, stereotyped speech. *Echolalia* (*echo* – repeat; *lalia* – speak) is the name given to the meaningless repetition of a word or phrase. A child with autism may initially repeat a phrase that is appropriate to the conversation, but will then continue to say it inappropriately. The child's intonation and inflection are often perfect reproductions of the original phrase. Such use of language is non-communicative as the phrase very rarely relates to the context.

Children with autism often show another language deficit known as *pronominal reversal*; literally the reversal of pronouns such as 'I' or 'you'. When asked when he has his dinner, a child with pronominal reversal would respond 'You have your dinner at 7 o'clock', but when referring to someone else will use 'I'. He does not understand the use of pronouns and will use that which he hears applied to him, namely, 'you'. This may be due to a lack of theory of mind, as an individual with autism cannot perceive language from the point of view of someone else. To the autistic individual, repetition is a form of communication.

A further deficit is that of *nominal aphasia*; the inability to name things. Although a child may be able to name his glove in the morning, by the evening the name will elude him. Often there is a pattern to misnomers; gloves become hands, shoes are feet and so on.

The speech of those with autism is may be very literal. Sarcasm has little place in a world with autism as the statement is quite likely to be taken at face value. As with children, this can be endearing, such as when a little boy with autism announced to his mother who had left him in the bath 'Mummy, hurry up, I'm going rusty!' (Waterhouse, 2000). However, it can also be upsetting to the child as for him the concept is real and therefore potentially very distressing.

Conversation is often notable by its absence. A child with autism will answer a question he is asked but not offer any more information. For example, 'Do you have a favourite toy'? will be answered with 'Yes'. If this question was asked of a child without autism you would expect all the details of the toy, why it is their favourite, who gave it to them and so on. Again this may contribute to the appearance of social aloofness associated with autism.

Hypersensitivity and hyposensitivity

Imagine that you are being tickled so much it hurts. You will probably be distressed, possibly crying and trying to get away. Now consider feeling like that if you did not understand what tickling was or why someone was doing it to you. Such a high level of stimulation is unpleasant to everybody, but it seems that in some cases of autism an individual may be exquisitely sensitive to light, sound, touch, taste or, more rarely, smell; a breeze may feel like being mercilessly tickled. Delacato (1974) studied the sensory experiences of children with autism and found that they may be hyposensitive (less) or hypersensitive (more) to all or any of the senses.

Sensitivity to sound was investigated by Metz (1967) who demonstrated that children with autism will consistently select a higher level of auditory stimulation than will a child with schizophrenia or a normally developing child, suggesting that some children with autism may be hyposensitive to sound. The experience of sensation is a complex but little researched area of autism, which is just starting to receive more attention. It may be a possible explanation for some of the behaviours and difficulties associated with autism such as self-stimulatory and self-injurious behaviours. Activities such as rocking or hand flapping are thought to be stimulatory behaviours. It is likely that these actions occur in those individuals who are hyposensitive to stimuli, and therefore find stimulatory behaviours pleasant and rewarding. Self-injurious behaviours are a little more difficult to explain. They often occur in children who appear to be hypersensitive to most stimuli but strangely insensitive to pain. This means that a child with autism may not appear to notice cuts and scrapes that would make another child scream but may get extremely distressed over someone cuddling him. Sometimes this insensitivity to pain leads to such behaviours as headbanging or picking of fingers and thumbs until they bleed. The reasons behind this are not entirely clear; is it pleasurable or rebellious? Regardless of the explanation this is another facet of autism that results in confusing and alien behaviours, thus isolating autistic individuals further.

Dustin Hoffman as Raymond, a young man with autism who shows unusual mathematical ability and a desire for sameness, in the film *Rainman*

Autistic savants

A number of individuals who are autistic are particularly highly skilled in certain areas such as art, music and maths. This is the symptom of autism with which people are familiar, made accessible by films such as *Rainman*, in which Dustin Hoffman played a man with autism who was a talented mathematician.

Another example is provided by Stephen Wiltshire (1987), who published a collection of his breathtakingly detailed drawings as shown on p.208. His ability to produce astonishingly accurate reproductions of a scene, particularly buildings, is well known.

Heaton (1999) found that absolute pitch is unusually common in children with autism even when they have not been musically trained in any way. The reason for such abilities is not known but Happé (1999) discussed the possibility that this was due to weak central coherence. If autism means that information is processed in parts rather than as a whole it may be that those with autism can readily break a melody down into its constituent notes. This was also investigated in relation to visual illusions (Happé, 1996). When tested on the Titchener circles test (see below) participants without autism were liable to say that the central circles were of different sizes while those with autism correctly identified that the circles were the same size. This would be expected if perception in autism is based on zooming in on features rather than zooming out to view the whole.

Titchener circles. The varying sizes of the surrounding circles affect the ability to perceive the relative size of the central circles.

where to now?

The following are good sources of further information on the theoretical approaches to autism:

Baron-Cohen, S. (1995) *Mindblindness: An essay on autism and theory of mind*. **London: MIT** – provides a detailed description of theory of mind development and the implications for autism.

Happé, F. (1994) *Autism: an introduction to psychological theory*. **Hove: Psychology Press** – an accessible text for those who wish to go into more theoretical detail of autism.

Diagnosis

Autism is usually described as a *spectrum disorder*; a condition in which symptoms may be experienced to a greater or lesser degree. The use of this term can be viewed as an attempt to acknowledge the highly subjective nature of diagnosis in this disorder. Obviously diagnosis is essential if an individual is to obtain the help and treatment that they need. There are many cases of autistic individuals being dismissed as mentally retarded and placed in institutions even as recently as the middle of the 20th century. Thankfully this no longer occurs but it does demonstrate the importance of an accurate (and sympathetic) diagnosis. This, unfortunately, is easier said than done! Usually when we discuss diagnosis we look for the presence of a specific set of symptoms and, if found, agree that the individual has the disease characterised by that pattern. The difficulties of diagnosis are compounded because it may be hard to decide which of the symptoms can be directly attributed to autism and which are simply personal experiences that may be affected by, rather than due to, autism. To try to overcome these variations, standard scales have been compiled that require a minimum number of symptoms to be present before a diagnosis can be confirmed.

The two scales that are predominantly used by practitioners today are the DSM-IV (Diagnostic and Statistical Manual of Mental Disorders, revision IV) and ICD-10 (International Classification of Diseases, revision 10). These both describe a set of similar symptoms, a number of which must be present to diagnose autism. A summary of these features can be seen on page 220:

■   **Autistic Disorder**

A.   A total of six (or more) items from (1), (2), and (3), with at least two from (1), and one each from (2) and (3):

  (1)   qualitative impairment in social interaction, as manifested by at least two of the following:

    (a)   marked impairment in the use of multiple nonverbal behaviors such as eye-to-eye gaze, facial expression, body postures, and gestures to regulate social interaction.

    (b)   failure to develop peer relationships appropriate to developmental level

    (c)   a lack of spontaneous seeking to share enjoyment, interests, or achievements with other people (e.g., by a lack of showing, bringing or pointing out objects of interest)

    (d)   lack of social or emotional reciprocity

  (2)   qualitative impairments in communication as manifested by at least one of the following:

    (a)   delay in, or total lack of, the development of spoken language (not accompanied by an attempt to compensate through alternative modes of communication such as gesture or mime)

    (b)   in individuals with adequate speech, marked impairment in the ability to initiate or sustain a conversation with others

    (c)   stereotyped and repetitive use of language or idiosyncratic language

    (d)   lack of varied, spontaneous make-believe play or social imitative play appropriate to developmental level

  (3)   restricted repetitive and stereotyped patterns of behaviour, interest, and activities, as manifested by at least one of the following:

    (a)   encompassing preoccupation with or more stereotyped and restricted patterns of interest that is abnormal either in intensity or focus

    (b)   apparently inflexible adherence to specific, nonfunctional routines or rituals

    (c)   stereotyped and repetitive motor mannerisms (e.g., hand or finger flapping or twisting, or complex whole-body movements)

    (d)   persistent preoccupation with parts of objects

B.   Delays or abnormal functioning in at least open of the following areas, with onset prior to age 3 years: (1) social interaction, (2) language as used in social communication, or (3) symbolic or imaginative play.

C.   The disturbance is not better accounted for by Rett's Disorder or Childhood Disintegrative Disorder.

A summary of diagnostic scale
DSM-IV-R

It is worth remembering that these scales are not exhaustive but provide little more than an educated guess! There are no tests that confirm the presence or absence of autism, although both physical tests such as blood tests and EEGs (electroencephalograms), and psychological tests may be used in the diagnostic procedure. Results from all these may be abnormal but the tests are not specific to autism and so must be considered to be aids to diagnosis rather than diagnostic tests.

We will now consider two psychological scales in a little more detail at this point because they are purely diagnostic aids and do not consider treatment options. CHAT was created by Baron-Cohen *et al.* (1992) and is used to assess young children, often at their routine check-up at 18 months. It is used to establish normal development and so highlights any unusual behavioural features. Similarly, DISCO is used for early stage diagnosis and confirmation of previous, tentative diagnoses. However, it focuses on social and communicative developmental problems and is much more comprehensive, interviewing parents and carers as well as the individual concerned. This is particularly important when working with high-functioning individuals as the signs may not be obvious at first assessment.

Causes

The cause or causes of autism are not known. In this section we will consider some of the most common theories but it is worth remembering that the ideas discussed are hypothetical approaches to the possible causes of autism and not definitive answers.

Psychological causes

A behavioural explanation was suggested by Kanner in his 1943 paper on autism. He proposed that the cold, rigid personalities of the parents resulted in an undesirable atmosphere for development, thus contributing to the manifestation of autism, particularly the social aspects. It was from here that the label 'refrigerator mother' was derived. The concept of 'cold parenting' was taken up by Bettleheim (1967) who believed that a precipitating factor in the development of autism was that the parents seemed to wish that the child did not exist. The media focused on the negative aspects of Bettleheim's work, despite the fact that he did successfully treat some children with autism. This biased reporting reinforced the concept that autism is the fault of the parents. Such claims are based on the belief that a high level of stress early in life shapes development; early negative experiences may therefore cause withdrawal and lack of communication, two significant symptoms of autism. Children who have been abused often show a high degree of withdrawal, a lack of social interaction and severely retarded linguistic development – all similar symptoms to those found in autism (see Chapter 3 for a discussion of reduced verbal ability in abused children). Observations such as this add weight to the concept that poor parenting may be, at least in part, responsible for autism.

Whilst early socialisation clearly can affect later development (see Chapters 2 and 3), research has not supported the concept of cold parenting as an explanation for the causation of autism. The case of Genie (Curtiss, 1977) is frequently cited to illustrate the effects of early deprivation (see p.54). She was kept in severely deprived conditions until the age of 13. She showed particular retardation in her language development and social interaction. The difference between her and a child with autism was that as soon as Genie was put into a safe and caring environment, her symptoms improved, whereas the same effect has not been observed in children with autism. This serves to illustrate that parental behaviour does not cause autism. It has a role in the development of a child with autism, as it does with all children, but professionals in the field will say that the majority of parents of children with autism have been among the most loving, sensitive and caring parents they have met. To say that autism is caused by parents is both inaccurate and hurtful. This view was reinforced by Roazen (1992), who failed to find any evidence that the parents of children with autism were cold, rejecting or rigid. Although it is generally agreed that early experience shapes later life, the developmental consequences of autism are no longer attributed to parental behaviour.

Another psychological perspective of the causation of autism is that of a cognitive or perceptual deficit. The most well-known theory in this category is that of a lack of theory of mind. As discussed in the section on symptoms above, a lack of theory of mind may act as a type of 'sub-cause'. Although such mind-blindness may be due to a biological or cognitive cause, it in turn may be the source of such symptoms as a lack of social interaction and withdrawal. It seems to take a place along the blurry line of cause or effect and it is outside the scope of this chapter to debate it definitively. A final point regarding mind-blindness is that of its cause. Baron-Cohen suggests that it may be due to a genetic fault. In terms of evolution being able to 'mind-read' is a strong strategy. It allows you to assess others and avoid dangerous or unpleasant people. It also means that you can spot those you like; rather important if the species is to continue! This would suggest that a lack of a theory of mind is to be avoided and thus is likely to cause abnormal behaviours and difficulties with socialisation. Although this is still hypothetical there is evidence for a genetic component in autism and the study of theory of mind remains a major area of research.

Biological causes

There is some suggestion that children with autism are more likely to have suffered peri-natal (at birth) difficulties than those without. What is not known is whether this is a cause or an effect; is autism the result of problems at birth or is it the presence of autism before birth that causes the difficulties at birth? At present the more popular view is the latter.

The reason that a foetus with autism may undergo a difficult birth is unclear. It might be that exposure to environmental insults, such as drugs or stress *in utero*, resulting in abnormal development but there is increasing evidence of a genetic component in autism.

Familial and twin studies reveal complex patterns of inheritance in autism, suggesting that more than one gene is affected. This would be unsurprising considering the range of symptoms associated with autistic spectrum disorders. It has also been observed that autism is more prevalent in boys than girls, again suggesting genetic influences. If one member of a family is autistic then the chance of other siblings demonstrating some degree of autistic spectrum symptoms is increased. Bolton *et al.* (1994) observed that in their sample, around 3 per cent of siblings of children with typical autism also had typical autism and a further 3 per cent had other pervasive developmental disorders. This was compared to a control group of siblings of children with Down's syndrome in whom no such trend was apparent. Bailey *et al.* (1998) have identified specific chromosomes that may be implicated in the development of, or susceptibility to, autism. These are located on chromosome 7 and there is some evidence for the possible involvement of chromosome 16. The exact mechanism for the genetic effect is unknown, but it may be that children who have a genetic predisposition for autism respond to environmental triggers or insults and develop an autistic spectrum disorder.

The way in which such environmental triggers affect the brain is not known, nor is the time at which they are influential. There is also some debate over whether different degrees of autism are due to different types of brain dysfunction. At present the favoured areas of the brain implicated in the causation of autism are the limbic system and the cerebellum (Courchesne *et al.*, 1994). These have been investigated using MRI (magnetic resonance imaging) and autopsies, and have revealed microscopic abnormalities that probably originated before birth and may be associated with symptoms such as social difficulties and weak central coherence. The limbic system is predominantly involved in the processing of emotion, while the cerebellum processes and assimilates sensory and motor information and that required for learning, all areas that are commonly deficient in autism.

Finally, there is the possibility that there is a fault in the neurotransmission of signals in the brain (Yuwiler and Freedman, 1987). This may occur either because of problems with receptors or with the chemical signallers themselves, including neurotransmitters and hormones such as oxytosin.

Environmental causes

Environmental causes can include any factors contributing to the development of autism, which arise externally to the child. We have already discussed such factors as peri-natal stress. Another possible cause of autism is that of the effect of vaccines, in particular MMR. MMR (measles, mumps and rubella) was introduced as a combined vaccine in 1988. It has been suggested that this vaccine causes encephalitis, which could result in autism by damaging the blood-brain barrier. Wakefield *et al.* (1998) undertook a study into the effect of MMR and found that after receiving the vaccine, children who had previously been developing normally developed diarrhoea, behavioural problems and lost learned skills. Further investigation showed that the average time of onset of symptoms was 6.3 days post vaccination. Those with intestinal symptoms were diagnosed as having ileal-lymphoid-nodular hyperplasia, which is characterised by swelling of intestinal lymph nodes, inflammation and constipation. There are increasing numbers of cases with such symptoms. Wakefield *et al.* demonstrated an apparent link between the intestinal disorder and autism, but no conclusive link between autism and MMR. It may be that the vaccine triggers autism-like symptoms in individuals who are already susceptible but this has not been established with any certainty. Clearly more research is needed to confirm or refute the link.

Treatment

Pharmaceutical intervention

There are no drugs available to treat autism *per se*. This is largely because we do not know what causes autism and therefore cannot use drugs to counteract it. Some drugs are given to help to control the symptoms of autism, such as hyperactivity or insomnia. These are often tranquillising agents or beta-blockers, which work on the autonomic nervous system to reduce heart rate, breathing rate and so on. In some cases other conditions are present in addition to autism such as epilepsy or manic depression, in which case drugs appropriate to the additional condition can be given, but these only treat the symptoms not the cause.

Secretin therapy has been one of the most recent sources of hope for a 'cure' for autism. Secretin is a synthetic version of a hormone normally found in the pancreas. There is some evidence that individuals with autism have difficulties with their digestive systems and indeed it was through just such a case that the therapy was discovered. A young boy was given the hormone to try and investigate the functioning of his pancreas. His parents rapidly noticed a change in his behaviour and an improvement in his language skills. This led to a number of studies that gave secretin or a placebo to children with autism to see what effect it would have. Unfortunately, as yet there is little success.

Sandler *et al.* (1999) studied 60 children with autism but found no significant change in a group taking the secretin as opposed to those taking a placebo. Similar results were found by Chez *et al.* (2000) who investigated secretin therapy using a two-part clinical trial. Fifty-six patients between the ages of approximately 2 and 18 years were given an injection of secretin. When these patients were followed up there was some improvement in their symptoms, including language function and social interactions. The second part of the study used 17 of the most responsive patients from the previous trial and 8 additional patients. This time the trial was structured as a double-blind trial. They concluded that both investigations showed that treatment with secretin caused some changes in speech and behaviour in some of the participants, but that the differences were not significant when compared to a control group who received a placebo.

Behavioural techniques

Techniques that are based on the teaching of new, appropriate behaviours and reduction of undesirable ones are not a new idea. They are usually based on modelling and operant conditioning. One of the most well-known programmes was developed by Lovaas (1974) who used progressive behavioural interaction to bridge the gap between those with and without autism. Operant conditioning is used to reinforce desired behaviours, while modelling consists of demonstration and then encouragement to emulate that behaviour (for a more detailed discussion of operant conditioning and modelling see *Angles on Psychology* in this series).

Lovaas (1987) noted that behaviours must be broken down into their constituent parts and that reinforcement must be consistent and clear. This is because changes in routine are often distressing to those with autism. They also have difficulty associating rewards with the appropriate behaviour. Ideally, such intervention should occur as early as possible, not least to reduce the distress caused by the symptoms of autism. It is interesting to consider how actions need to be broken down into individual parts; this is possibly evidence for poor central coherence, in that autism seems to prevent people from processing things as a whole.

Family therapy

This is becoming more widespread with schemes such as the National Autistic Society's 'Early-Bird' programme in which both young children and their families are taught behavioural techniques to make life with autism easier. Family therapy also allows parents and siblings to express distress, look for reassurance and learn to understand autism to make family life less stressful. Such a scheme means that techniques taught by professionals can be continued throughout daily life, thus improving the integration of the child with autism.

Educational measures

The course of education for children with autism largely depends on how severely they are affected. Those with higher functioning autism are often placed in mainstream schools to try to improve their level of social integration. Those who are more severely affected may be placed in special units within mainstream schools or specialist institutions that are fully equipped to help the individual child. Similar schemes are implemented regardless of the situation. Behavioural techniques are used as previously described to improve socialisation, language skills and so on.

Communication systems are frequently employed because the majority of those with autism show some degree of linguistic impairment. In many cases this is characterised by a complete loss of language. Therapists may then use symbolic communication, which could take the form of standard sign language, a composite communication system utilising both speech and sign or a system based entirely on visual symbols. Makaton is an example of such a system. Different words are assigned arbitrary symbols chosen by the user. Communication is then achieved by using symbolic keyboards to create words. Both words and pictures are displayed on the screen and so the individual can associate words with actions. Facilitated communication is a similar system in which a facilitator supports the child's hand, allowing them to select words, letters or symbols on a board or keyboard. They can thus create sentences but there is some question over whether or not the facilitator is unconsciously influencing the child's choice. Obviously if this is the case then the value of the communication achieved this way is called into question.

Some specialist schools and centres also have equipment for treating behavioural distress. This may be caused by sensory overload. This can be reduced by the use of sensory rooms (also known as 'Snoezelen rooms'), which consist of rooms with carefully controlled visual, auditory and tactile stimuli. These allow 'time out' from the world and are often very effective at combating the negative symptoms of hypersensitivity to stimuli.

where to now?

The following are good sources of information about autism:

www.nas.org.uk – National Autistic Society web-page – accessibly pitched general information about many aspects of autism. Designed for those with autism and their carers but an interesting academic source also.

Williams, D. (1996) *Autism, an inside-out approach.* **London: Jessica Kingsley Publishers** – a well-written first-hand account giving a fascinating and revealing insight into autism.

Waterhouse, S. (2000) *A Positive Approach to Autism.* **London: Jessica Kingsley Publishers** – a detailed and thoroughly readable general text about autism. All the major points discussed in this chapter are covered in much more detail. A good text for those who wish to extend their knowledge.

conclusion

In this chapter we have considered the way in which the characteristics used to define autism have changed very little over time. The main types of impairment were summarised by Wing and Gould (1979) (see p.209) and these are reflected in the diagnostic criteria used today. We also looked at the symptoms of autism such as social aloofness and communicative difficulties. Additionally the main theories of autism such as central coherence theory were discussed to provide a theoretical basis for this disorder. The influence of the symptoms was discussed with relation to the criteria required for a clinical diagnosis of autism. The main scales used in diagnosis are the DSM-IV and ICD-10 (see p.220 for a summary of DSM-IV). They both have limitations and the difficulties of testing were considered.

The cause of autism is unknown but some of the major biological, psychological and environmental influences were discussed and evaluated. It is unlikely that any one cause will be found to be responsible for such a complicated disorder so it is important to consider all the options. Finally, treatment options were discussed. Pharmaceutical therapies can be used to treat the symptoms of autism but not the cause, because this is not known. The potential of Secretin therapy was also discussed. Behavioural programs are effective in the control of symptoms in children with autism and educational measures were considered. There are also programmes that help with the communicative problems associated with autism and such measures were included in the section on treatment. The overall aim of this chapter was to provide an overview of the complicated pervasive developmental disorder of autism. More detailed accounts of the aspects mentioned here can be found in 'Where to Now?' on p.226.

what do you know?

1 How has autism been defined?

2 Discuss the evidence for the absence of theory of mind in children with autism.

3 Describe one explanation for the causes of autism and provide evidence for this theory.

4 Describe how behavioural techniques have been applied to alleviating the symptoms of autism, and discuss the advantages and disadvantages of these techniques.

5 What is family therapy and how has it been used in cases of autism?

Glossary

Accommodation (in Piagetian theory) The formation of a new **schema** to accommodate new information.

Animism The attribution of emotions and motives to inanimate objects.

Assimilation (in Piagetian theory) The incorporation of new information into an existing **schema**.

Attachment A two-way bond between two individuals (humans or some other animal species), in which each individual gains a sense of security from the other.

Attachment theory A **psychodynamic** approach to developmental psychology, which places a lot of emphasis on the formation of a secure **attachment** between infant and **primary carer**(s).

Average expectable environment (in psychoanalytic and behavioural genetic theory) The normal range of quality of competent child rearing.

Castration anxiety The anxiety that boys suffer during the Oedipus complex that their rivalrous father may castrate them.

Child-centred An approach to teaching characterised by children learning independently and at their own pace.

Collectivist society A society characterised by a high level of mutual interdependence between individuals.

Constructivism An approach to cognitive development, which emphasises children's construction of a mental representation of the world.

Culture A shared system of beliefs, values and ways of seeing the world, characterising a group of people such as a regional or ethnic group.

Day care Any form of care of an infant or child that does not involve the **primary carer**. Ranges from care from other family members to nursery care.

Delinquency Criminal/antisocial activity.

Deprivation The separation of an infant from its **primary carer**. Can be short-term as in **day care** or long-term as occurs in family **re-ordering**.

Ethnic identity The sense of being a member of a particular ethnic group.

Ethnocentrism The practice of researching or theorising from the perspective of a particular ethnic or national group.

Evolutionary psychology An approach to explaining human behaviour based on the principles of evolution, thus typical human behaviours are explained as having evolved because they convey an evolutionary advantage on that individual or others.

Gender constancy The awareness that a person's gender is permanent.

Gender schema A mental structure containing all of our knowledge, beliefs and feelings about gender.

Genes Functional units of DNA, the material that controls the inheritance of biological characteristics.

Giftedness The possession of very high IQ or particularly highly developed specific mental abilities.

Hothousing The practice of giving children intense stimulation in an attempt to boost their general intelligence or particular mental abilities.

Individualist society A society characterised by a low level of mutual interdependence between individuals.

Instinct A predisposition to behave in a certain way, present from birth rather than acquired by experience.

Learning The acquisition of knowledge and skills from the environment.

Learning theory The collective term given to explanations of psychological phenomena based on the assumption that they are characterised by one or more forms of learning.

Meta-analysis A statistical technique that involves combining the results of previous studies in order to be able to analyse data from a large number of participants.

Metacognition Awareness of one's own mental processes.

Molecular genetics The study of genetic processes on a molecular level. In psychology the term is used to describe the study of the relationship between psychological characteristics and particular genetic material.

Neo-Piagetian The term given to current theory and research that has retained some of Piaget's central ideas.

Object relations theory A loose collection of psychoanalytic theories characterised by their emphasis on the importance of the first relationship.

Operations (from Piagetian theory) Understanding of the principles by which the world works.

Personality A set of characteristics, including patterns of thinking, emotion and behaviour that distinguish one individual from another.

Primary carer The individual or individuals that take primary responsibility for the care of an infant. The primary carer is often the biological mother, but many psychologists prefer to only use the term 'mother' when referring to the biological mother.

Primary femininity (from psychoanalytic theory) The idea that all children who have a female **primary carer** begin life with a female identity because they acquire their initial sense of identity from the primary carer.

Privation The failure to form a normal infant-carer **attachment**.

Prosocial Behaviour that is judged to be beneficial to other individuals.

Prospective study A study in which participants are followed up following a particular period or event to see whether or not that period or event appears to impact on later development. This is a superior, although more time-consuming method than the alternative **retrospective study**.

Psychoanalysis A body of theory and therapeutic technique based on a **psychodynamic** understanding of human behaviour, cognition and emotion. Psychoanalysis exists mostly outside psychology, although psychoanalytic ideas are very useful in many areas of child psychology.

Psychodynamic A broad approach to explaining human behaviour, cognition and emotion based on the assumption that adults are influenced by unconscious processes that relate to childhood experience. A psychodynamic understanding of child development draws heavily on **psychoanalysis** but is not synonymous with it.

Psychological defences Mental strategies that serve to protect the individual from experiencing unpleasant emotional states.

Re-ordering Changes to structure of a family, for example divorce, separation and re-marriage.

Resilience The capacity of the individual to withstand the effects of less than optimum environments.

Retrospective study A study in which the impact of early experience on later development is assessed by looking back from the time of the alleged effect to the early experience.

Scaffolding (in social constructivist theory) The ways in which adults help children learn.

Schema A unit of memory containing all the information pertaining to one object, idea or skill.

Self-esteem The emotional component of our self-concept, i.e. the extent to which we like ourselves.

Sensitive responsiveness (in attachment theory) The success with which a **primary carer** picks up and responds to the signals of an infant. Widely believed to be a major determinant of the quality of infant-carer **attachment**.

Social comparison The tendency to judge our own behaviour against that of others.

Social constructionism An approach to psychology that emphasises the social construction of psychological ideas. Thus ideas like intelligence can be seen not so much as real things but more as ideas that have served the interests of society or groups within society.

Social constructivism An approach to cognitive development that emphasises the role of other people in constructing the child's mental representation of the world.

Sociometry The study of the interactions between a group of children.

Temperament The aspects of a child's personality that are present at birth and generally believed to be genetic in origin.

Theory of mind The child's understanding of the emotions and motives of other people.

Therapeutic Having a positive effect on mental health.

Unconscious Mental processes of which we are not aware. In Freudian theory, mental processes of which we are not aware but which have a powerful effect on our behaviour, thinking and emotional states.

references

Adams, G.R., Gullotta, T.P. and Markstrom-Adams, C. (1994) *Adolescent Life Experiences*. Pacific Grove: Brooks/Cole.

Ainsworth, M.D.S. (1967) *Infancy in Uganda: Infant care and the growth of love.* Baltimore: Johns Hopkins University Press.

Ainsworth, M.D.S. (1985) Patterns of infant–mother attachments: antecedents and effects on development. *Bulletin of the New York Academy of Medicine* 61, 771–91.

Ainsworth, M.D.S. and Wittig, B.A. (1969) Attachment theory and the exploratory behaviour of one-year-olds in a strange situation. In Foss, B.M. (ed.) *Determinants of Infant Behaviour, vol. 4.* London: Methuen.

Ainsworth, M.D.S., Blehar, M.C., Waters, E. and Wall, E. (1978) *Patterns of Attachment.* Hillsdale: Erlbaum.

Albers, S.M. (1998) The effect of gender-stereotyped clothing on children's social judgements. *Child Study Journal* 28, 137–59.

Alex, J.A. and Ritchie, M.R. (1992) School-aged children's interpretation of their experience with acute surgical pain. *Journal of Pediatric Nursing* 7(3), 171–80.

Aleixo, P.A. and Norris, C.E. (2000) Personality and moral reasoning in young offenders. *Personality and Individual Differences* 28, 609–23.

Andersson, B.E. (1996) Children's development related to day care, type of family and other home factors. *European Child and Adolescent Psychiatry* 5, 73–5.

Asher, S.R., Parkhurst, J.T., Hymel, S. and Williams, G.A. (1990) Peer rejection and loneliness in childhood. In Asher, S.R. and Coie, J.D. (eds) *Peer Rejection in Childhood.* Cambridge: Cambridge University Press.

Asperger, H. (1944) Die 'aunstisehen Psychopathen' im Kindesalter. *Archiv fur psychiatrie und Nervenkrankheiten* 117, 76–136.

Astington, J.W. (1998) Theory of mind, Humpty Dumpty and the ice box. *Human Development* 41, 30–9.

Attwood, T. (1998) *Asperger's Syndrome: a guide for parents and professionals.* London: Jessica Kingsley Publishers.

Avis, J.S. and Harris, P.L. (1991) Belief-desire reasoning among Baka children: evidence for a universal conception of mind. *Child Development* 62, 460–7.

Axline, V.M. (1947) *Dibs in Search of Self*. London: Penguin.

Bailey, A., Luthert, P., Dean, A., Harding, B., Janota, I., Montgomery, M., Rutter, M. and Lantos, P. (1998) A clinicopathological study of autism. *Brain* 121(5) 889–905.

Baillargeon, R. and DeVos, J. (1991) Object permanence in young infants: further evidence. *Child Development* 62, 1227–46.

Baker, L.A. and Daniels, D. (1990) Nonshared environmental influences and personality differences in adult twins. *Journal of Personality and Social Psychology* 58, 103–10.

Bancroft, D. and Carr, R. (eds.) (1995) *Influencing Children's Development*. Milton Keynes: Open University Press.

Bandura, A. (1977) *Social Learning Theory*. Englewood Cliffs: Prentice Hall.

Bandura, A. (1986) *Social Foundations of Thought and Action: a social cognitive theory*. Englewood Cliffs: Prentice Hall.

Bandura, A., Ross, D. and Ross, S.A. (1961) Transmission of aggression through imitation of aggressive models. *Journal of Abnormal and Social Psychology* 63, 575–82.

Barnes, P. (1995) *Personal, Social and Emotional Development of Children*. Milton Keynes: Open University Press.

Barnett, M.A. (1984) Similarity of experience and empathy in preschoolers. *Journal of Genetic Psychology* 145, 241–50.

Baron-Cohen, S. (1989) The autistic child's theory of mind: a case of specific developmental delay. *Journal of Child Psychology and Psychiatry* 30, 285–97.

Baron-Cohen, S. (1995) *Mindblindness: An essay on autism and theory of mind*. London: MIT.

Baron-Cohen, S., Leslie, A.M. and Frith, U. (1985) Does the autistic child have a theory of mind? *Cognition* 21, 37–46.

Baron-Cohen, S., Allen, J. and Gillberg, C. (1992) Can autism be detected at 18 months: the needle, the haystack, and the CHAT. *British Journal of Psychiatry* 161, 839–43.

Baron-Cohen, S., Joliffe, T., Mortimore, C. and Robertson, M. (1997) Another advanced test of theory of mind. Evidence from very high functioning adults with autism or Asperger syndrome. *Child Psychology and Psychiatry and Allied Disciplines* 38, 813–22.

Baron-Cohen, S., Tager-Flusberg, H. and Cohen, D.J. (2000) *Understanding Other Minds*. Oxford: Blackwell.

Bateman, A. and Holmes, J. (1995) *Introduction to Psychoanalysis*. London: Routledge.

Baydar, N. and Brooks-Gunn, J. (1991) Effects of maternal employment and child care arrangements on pre-schoolers' cognitive and behavioural outcomes. *Developmental Psychology* 27, 932–45.

Belsky, J., Steinberg, L. and Draper, P. (1991) Childhood experience, interpersonal development and reproductive strategy: an evolutionary theory of socialisation. *Child Development* 62, 647–70.

Bem, S.L. (1985) Androgyny and gender schema theory: a conceptual and theoretical integration. In Sonderegger, B. (ed.) *Nebraska Symposium on motivation 1984: Psychology and Motivation* 179–226.

Benenson, J.E., Morash, D. and Petrakos, H. (1998) Gender differences in emotional closeness between preschool children and their mothers. *Sex Roles* 38, 975–85.

Berman, S.M. and Noble, E.P. (1995) Reduced visuospatial performance in children with the D2 dopamine receptor A1 allele. *Behaviour Genetics* 25, 45–58.

Berndt, T.J. (1979) Developmental changes in conformity to peers and parents. *Developmental Psychology* 15, 662–3.

Bernstein, B. and Branner, J. (eds.) (1996) *Children, Research and Policy*. London: Taylor & Francis.

Bettleheim, B. (1967) *The Empty Fortress*. New York: Free Press.

Bifulco, A., Brown, G.W. and Alder, Z. (1991) Early sexual abuse and clinical depression in later life. *British Journal of Psychiatry* 159, 115–22.

Bjorkland, D.F. and Brown, R.D. (1998) Physical play and cognitive development: integrating activity, cognition and education. *Child Development* 69, 604–6.

Bjorkvist, K., Osterman, K. and Kaukiainen, A. (1992) The development of direct and indirect aggressive strategies in males and females. In Bjorkvist, K. and Niemala, P. (eds) *Of Mice and Women: aspects of female aggression*. San Diego: Academic Press.

Blos, P. (1962) *On Adolescence: A psychoanalytic interpretation*. New York: Free Press of Glencoe.

Blos, P. (1967) The second individuation process of adolescence. *Psychoanalytic Study of the Child* 22, 162–86.

Blos, P. (1968) Character formation in adolescence. *Psychoanalytic Study of the Child* 23, 245–63.

Bolton, P. *et al.* (1994) A case-control family history study of autism. *Journal of Child Psychology and Psychiatry* 35, 877–900.

Borich, G.D. and Tombari, M.L. (1997) *Educational Psychology, a contemporary approach*. New York: Longman.

Bosacki, S. and Astington, J.W. (1999) Theory of mind in preadolescence: relations between social understanding and social competence. *Social Development* 8, 237–55.

Bouchard, T.J.J. (1993) The genetic architecture of human intelligence. In

Vernon, P.A. (ed.) *Biological Approaches to the Study of Human Intelligence*. New York: Ablex.

Bouchard, T.T.J. (1995) Longitudinal studies of personality and intelligence: a behaviour genetic and evolutionary psychology perspective. In Saklofske, D.H. and Zeidner, Z. (eds) *International Handbook of Personality and Intelligence*. New York: Plenum.

Bowlby, J. (1946) *Forty Four Juvenile Thieves*. London: Balliere, Tindall & Cox.

Bowlby, J. (1951) *Maternal Care and Mental Health*. Geneva: World Health Organisation.

Bowlby, J. (1957) Symposium on the contribution of current theories to an understanding of child development. *British Journal of Medical Psychology* 30, 230–40.

Bowlby, J. (1958) The nature of the child's tie to his mother. *International Journal of Psychoanalysis* 39, 350–73.

Bowlby, J. (1969) *Attachment and Loss, vol. I*. London: Pimlico.

Bowlby, J. (1988) *A Secure Base*. London: Routledge.

Bradmetz, J. (1999) Precursors of formal thought: a longitudinal study. *British Journal of Developmental Psychology* 17, 61–81.

Brannon, L. (1996) *Gender: psychological perspectives*. Boston: Allyn & Bacon.

Brazleton, T.B. (1979) Behavioural competence in the newborn infant. *Seminars in Perinatology* 3, 35–44.

Brazleton, T.B., Tronick, E., Adamson, L., Als, H. and Wise, S. (1975) Early mother–infant reciprocity. Parent–infant Interaction. *Ciba Symposium* 33, 137–54.

Brody, L. and Hall, J. Gender and emotion. In Lewis, M. (ed.) *et al. Handbook of Emotions*. New York: Guilford Press.

Brooks-Gunn, J. and Reiter, E.O. (1990) The role of pubertal processes. In Feldman, S. and Elliott, G.R. (eds) *At the Threshold: the developing adolescent*. Cambridge: Harvard University Press.

Brown, B.B. (1990) Peer groups and peer cultures. In Feldman, S. and Elliott, G.R. (eds) *At the Threshold: the developing adolescent*. Cambridge: Harvard University Press.

Brown, D. and Pedder, J. (1991) *Introduction to Psychotherapy*. London: Routledge.

Bruner, J.S. (1964) The course of cognitive growth. *American Psychologist* 19(1), 1–15.

Bruner, J.S. (1966) *Towards a Theory of Instruction*. New York: Norton.

Bruner, J.S. (1971) The course of cognitive growth. In Richardson, K. and Sheldon, D. (eds) *Cognitive Development to Adolescence*. Hove: LEA.

Bruner, J.S. (1986) *Actual Minds, Possible Worlds*. Cambridge: Harvard University Press.

Bruner, J.S. and Kenney, H. (1966) *The Development of the Concepts of Order and Proportion in Children.* New York: Wiley.

Bryant, P. (1998) Cognitive development. In Eysenck, M. (ed.) *Psychology, an integrated approach.* Harlow: Longman.

Burman, E. (1994) *Deconstructing Developmental Psychology.* London: Routledge.

Cahill, L.T., Kaminer, R.K. and Johnson, P.G. (1999) Developmental, cognitive and behavioural sequellae of child abuse. *Child and Adolescent Clinics of North America* 8, 827–43.

Cameron (1999) Self-esteem changes in children enrolled in weight management programs. *Issues in Comprehensive Pediatric Nursing* 22, 75–85.

Cameron, C.A., Xu, F. and Fu, G. (1999) Chinese and Canadian children's concept of lying and their moral judgement: similarities and differences. *Paper presented at the Biennial Meeting of the Society for Research in Child Development,* Albuquerque.

Carlo, G., Roesch, S.C. and Meltby, J. (1998) The multiplicative relations of parenting and temperament to prosocial and antisocial behaviours in adolescence. *Journal of Early Adolescence* 18, 266–90.

Carlson, V., Cicchetti, D., Barnett, D. and Braunwald. K. (1989) Disorganised/disoriented attachment relationships in maltreated infants. *Developmental Psychology* 25, 525–31.

Carrey, N.J., Butter, H.J., Persinger, M.A. and Bialik, R.J. (1996) Physiological and cognitive correlates of child abuse. *Journal of the American Academy of Child and Adolescent Psychiatry* 34, 1067–75.

Case, R. (1985) *Intellectual Development: from birth to adulthood.* New York: Academic Press.

Cash, T.F. (1995) Developmental teasing about physical appearance: retrospective descriptions and relationships with body image. *Social Behaviour and Personality* 23, 123–9.

Cernovsky, Z.Z. (1997) A critical look at intelligence research. In Fox, D. and Prilleltensky (eds) *Critical Psychology, an introduction.* London: Sage.

Chapman, J.W. and Tunmer, W.E. (1997) A longitudinal study of beginning reading achievement and reading self-concept. *British Journal of Educational psychology* 67, 279–91.

Chez, M.G., Buchanan, C.P., Bagan, B.T., Hammer, M.S., McCarthy, K.S., Ovrutskaya, I., Nowinski, C.V. and Cohen, Z.S. (2000) Secretin and autism: A two-part clinical investigation. *Journal of Autism and Developmental Disorders* 30(2), 87–98.

Child, D. (1997) *Psychology and the Teacher.* London: Cassell.

Chodorow, N.J. (1994) *Femininities, Masculinities, Sexualities: Freud and beyond.* Lexington: University of Kentucky Press.

Chorney, M.J., Seese, K., Owen, M.J., Daniels, J., McGuffin, P., Thompson, L.A.,

Detterman, D.K., Benbow, C.P., Lubinski, D., Eley, T.C. and Plomin, R. (1998) A quantitative trait locus (QTL) associated with cognitive ability in children. *Psychological Science* 9, 159–66.

Church, M. (2000) Understanding genius. *The Psychologist* 13, 445–6.

Clarke, A.M. and Clarke, A.D.B. (1992) How modifiable is the human life path? *International Review of Research in Mental Retardation* 18, 137–57.

Clarke, A.D.B. and Clarke, A.M. (1998) Early experience and the life path. *The Psychologist* 11, 433–6.

Cockett, M. and Tripp, J. (1994) Children living in re-ordered families. *Social Policy Research Findings 45*, Joseph Rowntree Foundation.

Coie, J.D. and Dodge, K.A. (1983) Continuities and changes in children's social status: a five-year longitudinal study. *Merrill-Palmer Quarterly* 29, 261–82.

Coie, J.D. and Dodge, K.A. (1988) Multiple sources of data on social behaviour and social status in the school: a cross-age comparison. *Child Development* 59, 815–29.

Coleman, J.C. (1974) *Relationships in Adolescence*. London: Routledge.

Coleman, J.C. (1990) *Teenagers and Divorce*. Brighton: Trust for the Study of Adolescence.

Coleman, J.C. and Hendry, L.B. (1999) *The Nature of Adolescence*. London: Routledge.

Connolly, J.A. and Doyle, A. (1984) Relation of social fantasy play to social competence in preschoolers. *Developmental Psychology* 20, 797–806.

Coon-Carty, H.M. (1998) The influence of subject-specific academic self-concepts on academic achievement from a Vygotskian developmental perspective: a longitudinal investigation. *Dissertation Abstracts International* 59, 3091.

Cooper, C. (1999) *Intelligence and Abilities*. London: Routledge.

Coopersmith, S. (1967) *The Antecedents of Self-esteem*. San Francisco: Freeman.

Cote, J.E. and Levine, C.G. (2000) Attitude vs attitude: is intelligence or motivation more important for positive higher-educational outcomes. *Journal of Adolescence Research* 15, 58–80.

Courchesne, E., Townsend, J. P. and Saitoh, O. (1994) The brain in infantile autism: Posterior fossa structures are abnormal. *Neurology* 44, 214–23.

Cowie, H. (1995) Child care and attachment. In Barnes, P. (ed.) *Personal, Social and Emotional Development of Children*. Oxford: Blackwell.

Creak, M. (1961) The schizophrenic syndrome in childhood. *British Medical Journal* 2.

Crook, C. (1994) *Computers and the Collaborative Experience of Learning*. London: Routledge.

Cross, T.L. (1998) Understanding family resiliency from a relational world view. In McCubbin, H.I. (ed.) *Resiliency in Native American and Immigrant Families. Resiliency in families series. vol.2*. Thousand Oaks: Sage Publications.

Csikszentmihalyi, M. and Larson, R. (1984) *Being Adolescent: conflict and growth in the teenage years.* New York: Basic Books.

Curry, N.E. and Arnaud, S.H. (1984) Play in developmental preschool settings. In Yawkey, T.D. and Pellegrini, A. (eds) *Child's Play: developmental and applied.* Hillsdale: Lawrence Erlbaum.

Curtiss, S. (1977) *Genie: a psycholinguistic study of a modern day 'wild child'.* London: Academic Press.

Cush, D. (1993) *Bhuddism.* London: Sage.

Damon, W. (1983) *Social and Personality Development.* New York: Norton.

Das Gupta, P. (1995) Growing up in families. In Barnes, P. (ed.) *Personal, Social and Emotional Development of Children.* Milton Keynes: Open University Press.

Delacato, C.H. (1974) *The Ultimate Stranger. The Autistic Child.* Arena Press: California.

Dennis, W. (1941) Infant development under conditions of restricted and minimum social stimulation. *Genetic Psychology Monographs* 23, 143–89.

Diamond, M. (1982) Sexual identity, monozygotic twins reared in discordant sex roles and a BBC follow-up. *Archives of Sexual Behaviour* 11, 181–6.

Diamond, M. (1997) Sexual identity and sexual orientation in children with traumatised or ambiguous genitals. *Journal of Sex Research* 34, 199–211.

Dinnerstein, D. (1990) Sometimes you wonder if they're human. In Zanardi, C. (ed.) *Essential Papers on the Psychology of Women.* New York: New York University Press.

Dunn, J. (1988) *The Beginnings of Social Understanding.* Oxford: Blackwell.

Dunn, J. and Kendrick, C. (1982) The speech of 2 and 3 year-olds to infant siblings: baby talk and the context of communication. *Journal of Child Language* 9, 579–95.

Dunn, J. and Munn, P. (1985) Becoming a family member: family conflict and the development of social understanding in the first year. *Child Development* 50, 306–18.

Dunn, J., Hughes, C. and Omotoso, S.G.D.P. (1999) Violent fantasies and anti-social behaviour in hard to manage preschoolers' dyadic peer play. *Proceedings of the British Psychological Society* 7, 97.

Durkin, K. (1995) *Developmental Social Psychology.* Oxford: Blackwell.

Eisenberg, N. (1986) *Altruistic Emotion: cognition and behaviour.* Hillsdale: Erlbaum.

Eisenberg, N., Losoya, S. and Guthrie, I.K. (1997) Social cognition and prosocial development. In Hala, S. (ed.) *et al. The Development of Social Cognition Studies in developmental psychology.* Hove: Psychology Press.

Elder, G.H., Modell, J. and Parke, R.D. (1993) Studying children. In Modell, J. and Parke, R.D. (eds) *Children in Time and Space.* Cambridge: Cambridge University Press.

Elliot, A. (1990) Adolescence and early adulthood 2: the needs of the young adult with severe difficulties. In Ellis, K. (ed.) *Autism: professional perspectives and practice. Therapy in Practice Series* 17, 105–22. London: Chapman Hall.

Erikson, E.H. (1959) *Identity and the Life Cycle*. New York: Norton.

Erikson, E.H. (1968) *Identity Youth and Crisis*. New York: Norton.

Erwin, P. (1998) *Friendships in Childhood and Adolescence*. London: Routledge.

Eysenck, H.J. (1987) Personality theory and the problem of criminality. In McGurk, B. and Thornton, D.M. (eds.) *Applying Psychology to Imprisonment: theory and practice*. London, HMSO.

Faigenbaum, A., Zaichkowsky, L.D., Wescott, W.L., Long, C.J., LaRosa-Loud, R., Micheli, L.J. and Outerbridge, A.R. (1997) Psychological effects of strength training on children. *Journal of Sport Behaviour* 20, 164–75.

Faulkner, D. (1995) Play, self and the social world. In Barnes, P. (ed.) *Personal, Social and Emotional Development of Children*. Oxford: Blackwell.

Faulkner, D., Littleton, K. and Woodhead, M. (1998) *Learning Relationships in the Classroom*. London: Routledge.

Fein, D. (1975) A transformational analysis of pretending. *Developmental Psychology* 11, 291–6.

Fergusson, D.N., Horwood, L.J. and Lynskey, M.T. (1992) Family change, discord and early offending. *Journal of Child Psychology and Psychiatry* 33, 1059–75.

First, E. (1994) The leaving game, or I'll play you and you play me: the emergence of dramatic role play in 2 year-olds. In Slade, A. and Wolf, D.P. (eds) *Children at Play*. Oxford: Oxford University Press.

Fisher, S. and Greenberg, R.P. (1996) *Freud, Scientifically Reappraised: testing the theories and the therapy*. New York: Wiley.

Flanagan, C. (1999) Early privation and developmental catch-up. *Psychology Review* 6(1), 24–5.

Flanagan, C. (1999) *Early Socialisation*. London: Routledge.

Fonagy, P. and Target, M. (1994) The efficacy of psychoanalysis for children with disruptive disorders. *Journal of the American Academy of Child & Adolescent Psychiatry* 33(1).

Fonagy, P., Steele, M., Moran, G., Steele, H. and Higgitt, A. (1993) Measuring the ghost in the nursery: an empirical study of the relation between parents' mental representations of childhood experiences and their infants' security of attachment. *Journal of the American Psychoanalytic Association* 41, 957–89.

Fonagy, P., Steele, H., Steele, M. and Holder, J. (1997) Attachment and theory of mind: overlapping constructs? In Forrest, G. (ed.) *Bonding and Attachment: current issues in research and attachment*. Occasional Papers 14. London: Association for Child Psychology and Psychiatry.

Foot, H., Morgan, M. and Shute, R. (1990) *Children Helping Children*. Chichester: Wiley.

Fowler, W. (1990) Early stimulation and the development of verbal talents. In

Howe, M.J.A. (ed.) *Encouraging the Development of Exceptional Abilities and Talents*. Leicester: British Psychology Society.

Fox, N.J., Joesbury, H. and Hannay, D.R. (1991) Family attachments and medical sociology: A valuable partnership for student learning. *Medical Education* 25(2), 155–9.

Frankel, K.A. and Bates, J.E. (1990) Mother–toddler problem solving: antecedents in attachment, home behaviour and temperament. *Child Development* 61, 810–19.

Freeman, N., Lloyd, S. and Sinha, C. (1980) Hide and seek is child's play. *New Scientist* 304–5.

Freud, A. (1936) *The Ego and the Mechanisms of Defence*. London: Hogarth Press.

Freud, S. (1905) *Three Essays on the Theory of Sexuality*. London: Hogarth.

Freud, S. (1909) Analysis of a phobia in a five year-old boy. *Collected papers*, vol. III, 149–295.

Freud, S. (1921) The psychology of day-dreams. London: *Standard Edition* 18, 271.

Freud, S. (1922) Author's abstract of a congress address. *International Journal of Pychoanalysis* 8, 486.

Freud, S. (1924) *Neurosis and Psychosis*. Harmondsworth: Penguin.

Frith, U. and Happé, F. (1994) Autism: beyond theory of mind. In Messer, D. and Dockrell, J. (1999) *Developmental Psychology: a reader*. London: Arnold.

Gale, C.R. and Martin, C.N. (1996) Breastfeeding, dummy use and adult intelligence. *The Lancet* 347, 1072–5.

Garber, H.L. (1988) *The Milwaukee Project: preventing mental retardation in children at risk*. Washington, DC: American Association of Mental Retardation.

Gardner, H. (1993) *Frames of Mind*. London: HarperCollins.

Garmon, L.C., Basinger, K.S., Gregg, V.R. and Gibbs, J.C. (1996) Gender differences in stage and expression of moral judgement. *Merrill-Palmer Quarterly* 42, 418–37.

Geertz, C. (1984) From the natives' point of view. On the nature of anthropological understanding. In Schweder, R. and LeVine, R.A. (eds) *Culture Theory: essays on mind, self and emotion*. Cambridge: Cambridge University Press.

Gildea, J.H. and Quirk, T.R. (1977) Assessing the pain experience in children. *Nursing Clinics of North America* 1, 631–7.

Gilligan, C. (1977) In a different voice: women's perspectives on self and morality. *Harvard Educational Review* 47, 481–517.

Gilligan, C. (1982) *In a Different Voice: psychological theory and women's development*. Cambridge: Harvard University Press.

Goldsmith, H.H. and Alansky, J. (1987) Maternal and infant temperamental predictors of attachment: a meta-analytic review. *Journal of Consulting and Clinical Psychology* 55, 805–16.

Goodman, J.F. (2000) Moral education in early childhood: the limits of constructivism. *Early Education and Development* 11, 37–54.

Goossens, L. and Marcoen, A. (1999) Relationships during adolescence: Constructive vs. negative themes and relational dissatisfaction. *Journal of Adolescence* 22(1), 65–79.

Goossens, L. and Marcoen, A. (1999) Relationships during adolescence: Constructive vs. negative themes and relational satisfaction. *Journal of Adolescence* 22, 49–64.

Goossens, L., Marcoen, A., van Hees, S. and van de Woestijne, O. (1999) Attachment style and loneliness in adolescence. *European Journal of Psychology of Education* 13, 529–42.

Gottman, J.M. (1986) The world of coordinated play: Same- and cross-sex friendship in young children. In Gottman, J.M. (ed.) *et al. Conversations of friends: Speculations on affective development. Studies in emotion and social interaction.* Cambridge: Cambridge University Press.

Greenfield, P.M. (1966) On culture and conversation. In Bruner, J.S., Olver, R.R. and Greenfield, P.M. (eds) *Studies in Cognitive Growth*. Chichester: Wiley.

Griffith, C.T. (1999) A study of stress and cognitive distortions in adolescent male offenders and non-offenders. *Dissertation Abstracts International* 59, 5083.

Grigorenko, E.L. and Carter, A.S. (1996) Co-twin, peer and mother–child relationships and IQ in a Russian adolescent twin sample. *Journal of Russian and East European Psychology* 34, 59–87.

Gross, R. (1997) Attachment theory; extensions and applications. *Psychology Review* 4, 10–13.

Grossman, K.E. and Grossman, K. (1990) The wider concept of attachment in cross-cultural research. *Human Development* 33, 31–47.

Guiney, K.M. and Furlong, N.E. (1999) Correlates of body satisfaction and self-concept in third and sixth-graders. *Current Psychology: Developmental, Learning, Personality, Social* 18, 353–67.

Haight, W.L. and Miller, P.J. (1993) *Pretending at Home: early development in a socio-cultural context*. Albany: SUNY Press.

Hall, G.S. (1904) *Adolescence: its psychology and relation to physiology, anthropology, sociology, sex, crime, religion and education*. New York: Appleton.

Happé, F. (1995) The role of age and verbal ability in the theory of mind task performance of subjects with autism. *Child Development* 66(3), 843–55.

Happé, F. (1998) *Autism – An Introduction to Psychological Theory*. Cambridge: Harvard University Press.

Happé, F. and Frith, T. (1996) The neuropsychology of autism. *Brain* 119, 1377–400.

Harr, G.A.R. (1999) The impact of maternal employment on the academic attainment and social adjustment of school-age children. *Dissertation Abstracts International* 60, 0333.

Harrison, A.O., Stewart, R.B., Myambo, K. and Teveraische, C. (1995) Perceptions of social networks among adolescents from Zimbabwe and the United States. *Journal of Black Psychology* 21, 382–407.

Hart, B. and Risley, T. (1995) *Meaningful Differences in Everyday Parenting and Intellectual Development in Young Children*. Baltimore: Brooks.

Hartley, J. (1998) *Learning and Studying*. London: Routledge.

Haste, H. (1999) Moral understanding in socio-cultural context: lay social theory and a Vygotskian synthesis. In Woodhead, M., Faulkner, D. and Littleton, K. (eds) *Making Sense of Social Development*. Milton Keynes: Open University Press.

Hayes, N. (1994) *Foundations of Psychology*. London: Routledge.

Hayes, N. (1998) *Foundations of Psychology*. London: Nelson.

Hayes, N. (2000) *Foundations of Psychology*. London: Thomson Learning.

Hazan, C. and Shaver, P. (1987) Romantic love conceptualised as an attachment process. *Journal of Personality and Social Psychology* 52, 511–24.

Hazan, C. and Shaver, P. (1990) Love and work: an attachment-theoretical perspective. *Journal of Personality and Social Psychology* 59, 270–80.

Heaton, M.K. (1999) The use of the Rorschach in the assessment of PTSD among child victims of sexual abuse: a validity study. *Dissertation Abstracts International* 60, 3001.

Heaven, P.C.L. (1994) *Contemporary Adolescence*. Basingstoke: Macmillan.

Helman, D. and Bookspan, P. (1992) In Big bird's world, females are secondary. *Albany Times Union* E2.

Henderson, A.S., Easteal, S., Jorm, A.F., Mackinnon, A.J., Korten, A.E., Christensen, H., Croft, L. and Jacomb, P.A. (1995) Apolipoprotein Allele e4, dementia and cognitive decline in a population sample. *Lancet* 346, 1387–90.

Hendry, L., Shucksmith, J., Love, J. and Glendinning, A. (1993) *Young people's leisure and lifestyles.*London: Routledge.

Herrnstein, R.J. and Murray, C. (1994) *The Bell Curve: intelligence and class structure in American life*. New York: Free Press.

Hetherington, E.M. and Parke, R.D. (1993) *Child Psychology: a contemporary viewpoint*. New York: McGraw-Hill.

Hinde, R.A., Titmus, G., Easton, D. and Tamplin, A. (1985) Incidence of friendship and behaviour toward strong associates versus nonassociates in preschoolers. *Child Development* 68, 234–45.

Hobson, R. (1985) *Forms of feeling*. London: Routledge.

Hodges, J. (1996) The natural history of non attachment. In Bernstein, B. and Branner, J. (eds.) *Children, Research and Policy*. London: Taylor & Francis.

Hodges, J. and Tizard, B. (1989a) IQ and behavioural adjustment of ex-institutional adolescents. *Journal of Child Psychology and Psychiatry* 30, 53–76.

Hodges, J. and Tizard, B. (1989b) Social and family relationships of ex-institutional adolescents. *Journal of Child Psychology and Psychiatry* 30, 77–98.

Holmes, J. (1993) *John Bowlby and Attachment Theory*. London: Routledge.

Honess, T.M. and Charman, E.E. (1998) Adolescent adjustment, social systems and parental separation. *European Journal of Psychology of Education* 13, 557–67.

Howe, M.J.A. (1988) Hot house children. *The Psychologist* 1, 356–8.

Howe, M.J.A. (1997) *IQ in Question: the truth about intelligence*. London: Sage.

Howe, M.J.A. (1998) Can IQ change? *The Psychologist* 11, 69–72.

Howe, M.J.A. (1999) *The Psychology of High Abilities*. Basingstoke: Macmillan.

Hsueh, W.C. (1998) A cross-cultural comparison of gifted children's theories of intelligence, goal orientation and responses to challenge. *Dissertation Abstracts International* 58, 3416.

Hughes, C. and Dunn, J. (2000) Hedonism or empathy? Hard to manage children's moral awareness and links with cognitive and maternal characteristics. *British Journal of Developmental Psychology* 18, 227–46.

Hurley, A. and Whelan, E.G. (1988) Cognitive development and children's perception of pain. *Pediatric Nursing* 14(1), 21–4.

Hyde, J.S. (1990) *Understanding Human Sexuality*. New York: McGraw-Hill.

Hyde, J.S. and Linn, M.C. (1988) Gender differences in verbal ability: a meta-analysis. *Psychological Bulletin* 104, 53–69.

Hyde, J.S., Fennema, E. and Lamon, S.J. (1990) Gender differences in mathematics performance: A meta-analysis. *Psychological Bulletin* 107(2), 139–55.

Idle, T., Wood, E. and Desmarais, S. (1993) Gender role socialisation in toy play situations: mothers and fathers with sons and daughters. *Sex Roles* 28, 679–91.

Ijzendoorn van, M.H. and Kroonenberg, P.M. (1988) Cross-cultural patterns of attachment: a meta-analysis of the strange situation. *Child Development* 59, 147–56.

Inhelder, B. and Piaget, J. (1958) *The Growth of Logical Thinking from Childhood to Adolescence*. London: Routledge & Kegan Paul.

Isaacs, S. (1929) *The Nursery Years*. London: Routledge & Kegan Paul.

Jacobs, M. (1992) *Sigmund Freud*. London: Sage.

James, W. (1892) *A Text Book of Psychology*. London: Routledge & Kegan Paul.

Jarrold, C., Butler, D.W., Cottington, E.M. and Jiminez, F. (2000) Linking theory of mind and central coherence bias in autism and in the general population. *Developmental Psychology* 36(1), 126–38.

Jarvis, M. (1994) Attention and the information processing approach. *Psychology Teaching* 3, 1–20.

Jarvis, M. (2000) Empirical studies of psychodynamic phenomena. *Paper delivered to the annual conference of the Association for the Teaching of Psychology*, Edinburgh University.

Jarvis, M., Russell, J., Flanagan, C. and Dolan, L. (2000) *Angles on Psychology*. Cheltenham: Stanley Thornes.

Jekielek, S.M. (1998) Parental conflict, marital disruption and children's emotional well-being. *Social Forces* 76, 905–36.

Johnson, D.K. (1988) Adolescents' solutions to difficult dilemmas in fables: two moral orientations-two problem solving strategies. In Gilligan, C., Ward, J.V. and Taylor, J.M. (eds.) *Mapping the moral domain: a contribution of women's thinking to psychological theory and education*. Cambridge: Harvard University Press.

Jones, W.H., Hobbs, S.A. and Hockenbury, D. (1982) Loneliness and social skills deficits. *Journal of Personality and Social Psychology* 42, 682–9.

Juffer, F., Hoksbergen, R.A.C., Rene, A.C., Riksen-Walraven, J.M. and Kohnstamm, G.A. (1997) Early intervention in adoptive families: supporting maternal sensitive responsiveness, infant–mother attachment and infant competence. *Journal of Child Psychology and Psychiatry and Allied Disciplines* 38, 1039–50.

Kagan, J. (1997) Temperament and the reactions to unfamiliarity. *Child Development* 68(1), 139–43.

Kail, R. (1991) Developmental change in speed of processing during childhood and adolescence. *Psychological Bulletin* 109, 490–501.

Kamin, L.J. (1995) Lies, damned lies and statistics. In Jacoby, R. and Glauberman, N. (eds) *The Bell Curve Debate: history, documents, opinions*. New York: Times Books.

Kanner, L. (1943) Autistic disturbances of affective contact. *Nervous Child* 2, 217–50.

Kenyetta, J. (1965) *Facing Mt Kenya*. New York: Vintage Books.

Kerns, K.A. (1994) A longitudinal examination of links between mother–infant attachment and children's friendships. *Journal of Personality and Social Relationships* 11, 379–81.

Kerns, K.A. and Stevens, A.C. (1996) Parent–child attachment in late adolescence. *Journal of Youth and Adolescence* 25, 323–42.

Kimura, D. (1996) Sex, sexual orientation and sex hormones influence human cognitive function.*Current Opinion in Neurobiology* 6, 259–63.

Kirchler, E., Pombeni, M.L. and Palmonari, A. (1991) Sweet sixteen: Adolescents' problems and the peer group as a source of support. *European Journal of Psychology of Education* 6(4), 393–410.

Kirkby, R.J. and Whelan, R.J. (1996) The effects of hospitalisation and medical procedures on children and their families. *Journal of Family Studies* 2, 56–77.

Kloep, M. (1999) Love is all you need? Focusing on adolescents' life concerns from an ecological point of view. *Journal of Adolescence* 22(1), 49–63.

Kohlberg, L. (1966) A cognitive-developmental analysis of children's sex role concepts and attitudes. In Maccoby, E.E. (ed.) *The Development of Sex Differences*. Stanford: Stanford University Press.

Kohlberg, L. (1969) Stage and sequence: the cognitive developmental approach to socialisation. In Goslin, D.A. (ed.) *Handbook of Socialisation Theory and Research*. Chicago: Rand–McNally.

Kolominsky, Y., Igumnov, S. and Drozdovith, V. (1999) The psychological development of children from Belarus exposed in the prenatal period to radiation from the Chernobyl atomic power plant. *Journal of Child Psychology and Psychiatry* 40, 299–305.

Koluchova, J. (1972) Severe deprivation in twins: a case study. *Journal of Child Psychology and Psychiatry* 13, 107–11.

Koluchova, J. (1991) Severely deprived twins after 22 years observation. *Studia Psychologica* 33, 23–8.

Kramarski, B. and Mevarech, Z.R. (1997) Cognitive-metacognitive training within a problem-solving based Logo environment. *British Journal of Educational Psychology* 67(4), 425–46.

Kroeger, J. (1996) *Identity in Adolescence*. London: Routledge.

Kruger, A.C. (1992) The effect of peer and adult-child transductive discussions on moral reasoning. *Merrill-Palmer Quarterly* 38(2), 191–211.

Lacan, J. (1966) *The Four Fundamental Concepts of Psychoanalysis*. London: Hogarth.

Ladd, G.W. and Golter, B.S. (1988) Parents' management of preschoolers' peer relations: is it related to children's social competence? *Developmental Psychology* 24, 109–17.

LaFreniere, P.J. (2000) *Emotional Development*. Belmont: Wadsworth.

LaFreniere, P.J. and Sroufe, L.A. (1985) Profiles of peer competence in the preschool: interrelations between measures, influence of social ecology and relation to attachment theory. *Developmental Psychology* 21, 56–69.

Lane, D.J. (1998) Cognitive and clinical implications of sexual victimisation on boys. *Dissertation Abstracts International* 59, 3064.

Langlois, J.H., Ritter, J.M., Casey, R.J. and Sawin, D.B. (1995) Infant attractiveness predicts maternal behaviours and attitudes. *Developmental Psychology* 31, 464–72.

Lanyado, M. and Horne, A. (1999) *The Handbook of Child and Adolescent Psychotherapy*. London: Routledge.

Larson, R., Richards, M., Moneta, G., Holmback, G. and Duckett, E. (1996) Changes in adolescents' daily interactions from ages 10–18: disengagement and transformation. *Developmental Psychology* 32, 744–54.

Lauer, C. (1992) Variability in the patterns of agonistic behaviour of preschool children. In Silverberg, J. and Gray, J.P. (eds.) *Aggression and peacefulness in humans and other primates*. New York: Oxford University Press.

Laursen, B. and Collins, W.A. (1994) Interpersonal conflict during adolescence. *Psychological Bulletin* 115, 197–209.

Lavallee, M. and Pelletier, R. (1992) Ecological value of Bem's gender schema theory explored through females' traditional and non-traditional occupational contexts. *Psychological Reports* 70, 79–82.

Lazar, L., Darlington, R., Murray, H., Royce, J. and Snippet, A. (1982) Lasting effects of early education: a report for the consortium for longitudinal studies. *Monographs for the Society for Research in Child Development* 47, 2–3.

LeBlanc, M. and Ritchie, M. (1999) Predictors of play therapy outcomes. *International Journal of Play Therapy.* 9(2), 19–34.

Lee, K. (2000) Lying as doing deceptive things with words: a speech act theoretical perspective. In Astington, J.W. (ed.) *Minds in the Making.* Oxford: Blackwell.

Lee, V. and Das Gupta, P. (1995) *Children's Cognitive and Language Development.* Oxford: Blackwell.

Leinbach, M.D. and Fagot, B.I. (1993) Categorical habituation to male and female faces: gender schematic processing in infancy. *Infant Behaviour and Development* 16, 317–32.

Lemma, A. (1996) *Introduction to Psychopathology.* London: Sage.

Lemma-Wright, A. (1995) *Invitation to Psychodynamic Psychology.* London: Whurr.

Leslie, A.M. (1987) Pretence and representation: the origins of 'theory of mind'. *Psychological Review* 94, 412–26.

Leslie, A.M. (1994) Pretending and believing: issues in the theory of ToMM. *Cognition* 50, 211–38.

Leslie, J.C. and O'Reilly, M.F. (1999) *Behaviour Analysis.* Amsterdam: Harwood.

Levaenan, M. and Silven, M. (2000) Does the mother's quality of attachment predict maternal sensitivity? *Psykologia* 35, 58–70.

Levinger, G. and Levinger, A.C. (1986) The temporal course of close relationships: some thoughts about the development of children's personalities. In Hartup, W.W. and Rubin, Z. (eds) *Relationships and Development.* Hillsdale: Erlbaum.

Levy, D.G. (1989) Relations among aspects of children's social environments, gender schematisation, gender role knowledge and flexibility. *Sex Roles* 21, 803–24.

Lewis, J.D. and Knight, H.V. (2000) Self-concept in gifted youth: an investigation employing the Piers-Harris subscales. *Gifted Child Quarterly* 44, 45–53.

Lewis, M. (1990) Social knowledge and social development. *Merrill-Palmer Quarterly* 36, 93–116.

Lewis, M., Young, G., Brooks, J. and Michalson, L. (1975) The beginnings of friendship. In Lewis, M. and Rosenblum, L. (eds) *Friendship and Peer Relations.* New York: Wiley.

Lightfoot, C. (1992) Constructing self peer and culture: a narrative perspective on adolescent risk-taking. In Winegar, L.T. and Valsiner, J. (eds) *Children's Development Within Social Context.* Hillsdale: Erlbaum.

Lips, H.M. (1989) Gender role socialisation: Lessons in femininity. In Freeman, J. (ed.) *Women: a feminist perspective*. Mountain View: Mayfield.

Loehlin, J.C. (1992) *Genes and Environment in Personality Development*, Newbury Park: Sage Publications.

Loganovskaja, T.K. and Loganovsky, K.N. (1999) EEG, cognitive and psychopathological abnormalities in children irradiated in utero. *International Journal of Psychophysiology* 34, 213–24.

Lourenco, O.M. (1993) Toward a Piagetian explanation of the development of prosocial behaviour in children: The force of negational thinking. *British Journal of Developmental Psychology* 11(1), 91–106.

Lovaas, I. (1974) After you hit a child, you can't just get up and leave him; You are hooked to that kid (A conversation with P. Chance). *Psychology Today* 7, 76–84.

Lovaas, O.I. (1987) Behavioral treatment and normal education and intellectual functioning in young autistic children. *Journal of Consulting and Clinical Psychology* 55, 3–9.

Luecke-Aleksa, D., Anderson, D.R., Collins, P.A. and Schmitt, K.L. (1995) Gender constancy and television viewing. *Developmental Psychology* 31, 773–80.

Luria, A.R. and Yudovich, F.I. (1971) *Speech and the Development of Mental Processes in the Child*. Harmondsworth: Penguin.

Lyons-Ruth, K., Bronfman, E. and Parsons, E. (1999) Maternal frightened, frightening or atypical behaviour and disorganised infant attachment patterns. In Vondra, J.I. and Barnett, D. Atypical attachment in infancy and early childhood among children at developmental risk. *Monographs of the Society for Research into Child Development*.

MacArthur, L.Z. and Eisen, S.V. (1976) Television and sex role stereotyping. *Journal of Applied Social Psychology* 6, 329–51.

Maccoby, E.E. and Jacklin, C.N. (1974) *The Psychology of Sex Differences*. Stanford: Stanford University Press.

Magnusson, D., Stattin, H. and Allen, V.L. (1985) Biological maturation and social development: a longitudinal study of some adjustment processes from mid-adolescence to adulthood. *Journal of Youth and Adolescence* 14, 267–83.

Mahler, M. (1968) *On Human Symbiosis and the Vicissitudes of Individuation: infantile psychosis*. New York: International Universities Press.

Main, M. and Solomon, J. (1986) Discovery of a disorganised disoriented attachment pattern. In *Affective Development in Infancy*. Norwood: Ablex.

Marcia, J. (1980) Identity in adolescence. In Adelson, J. (ed.) *Handbook of Adolescent Psychology*. Wiley: New York.

Marcia, J. (1993) *The Relational Roots of Identity*. Hillsdale: Lawrence Erlbaum.

Martin, C.L. (1991) The role of cognition in understanding gender differences. *Advances in Child Development and Behaviour* 23, 113–49.

Martin, C.L. and Halverson, C.F. (1983) The effects of sex-typing schemas on young children's memory. *Child Development* 54, 563–74.

Martin, C.L. and Little, J.K. (1990) The relation of gender understanding to children's sex-typed preferences and gender stereotypes. *Child Development* 61, 1427–39.

Martinez, R. and Dukes, R. (1997) The effects of ethnic identity, ethnicity and gender on adolescent well-being. *Journal of Youth and Adolescence* 26, 503–16.

Mbiti, J.S. (1970) *African Religions and Philosophy.* New York: Doubleday.

McCafferey, M. (1972) *Nursing Management of the Patient with Pain.* Philadelphia: Lippincott.

McCarthy, G. (1999) Attachment style and adult love relationships and friendships: a study of a group of women at risk of experiencing relationship difficulties. *British Journal of Medical Psychology* 72, 305–21.

McGarrigle, J. and Donaldson, M. (1974) Conservation accidents. *Cognition* 3, 341–50.

Meadows, S. (1993) *The Child as Thinker.* London: Routledge.

Meins, E. (1997) *Security of Attachment and the Development of Social Cognition.* Hove: Psychology Press.

Melhuish, E.C., Mooney, A., Martin, S. and Lloyd, E. (1990a) Type of childcare at 18 months I. Differences in interactional experience. *Journal of Child Psychology and Psychiatry* 31, 849–59.

Melhuish, E.C., Lloyd, E., Martin, S. and Mooney, A. (1990b) Type of childcare at 18 months II. Relations with cognitive and language development. *Journal of Child Psychology and Psychiatry* 31, 861–70.

Meltzoff, A.N. (1990) Foundations for developing a concept of self: The role of imitation in relating self to other and the value of social mirroring, social modeling and self practice in infancy. In Cicchetti, D (ed.) *et al. The Self in Transition: Infancy to childhood.* Chicago: University of Chicago Press.

Melzak, S. (1999) Psychotherapeutic work with child and adolescent refugees from political violence. In Lanyardo, M. (ed.) *et al. The Handbook of Child and Psychotherapy: Psychoanalytic approaches.* New York: Routledge.

Messer, D. and Dockerell, J. (eds.) (1999) *Developmental Psychology, A Reader.* London: Arnold.

Messer, D. and Millar, S. (1999) *Exploring Developmental Psychology.* London: Arnold.

Metz, J.R. (1967) Stimulation level preferences of autistic children. *Journal of Abnormal Psychology* 72(6), 529–35.

Mevarech, Z., Silber, O. and Fine, D. (1991) Learning with computers in small groups: cognitive and affective outcomes. *Journal of Educational Computing Research* 7(2), 233–43.

Miell, D. (1995) Developing a sense of self. In Barnes, P. (1995) *Personal, Social and Emotional Development of Children.* Milton Keynes: Open University Press.

Millis, L.A. (1999) Contextual effects on the development of children's sociomoral judgements: a comparison of public school and non-school dilemma contexts. *Dissertation Abstracts International* 60, 1923.

Modell, J. and Goodman, M. (1990) Historical perspectives. In Feldman, S.S. and Elliott, G.R. (eds) *At the Threshold: the developing adolescent*. Cambridge: Harvard University Press.

Money, J. and Erhardt, A.A. (1972) *Man and Woman, Boy and Girl*. Baltimore: Johns Hopkins University Press.

Montmayer, R. and Van Komen, R. (1985) The development of sex differences in friendship patterns and peer group structure during adolescence. *Journal of Early Adolescence* 5, 285–94.

Muller, D.J., Harris, P.J. and Wattley, L. (1986) *Nursing Children: psychology, research and practice*. London: Harper & Row.

Myers, L.B. and Brewin, C.R. (1994) Recall of early experiences and the repressive coping style. *Journal of Abnormal Psychology* 103, 288–92.

Myron-Wilson, P. and Smith, P.K. (1998) Attachment relationships and influences on bullying. *Proceedings of the British Psychological Society* 6(2), 89–90.

Nair, H. (1999) A study of the effects of divorce on maternal parenting and attachment security in preschool-aged children. *Dissertation Abstracts International* 59, 6517.

Neihart, M. (1999) The impact of giftedness on psychological well-being: what does the empirical literature say? *Roeper Review* 22, 10–17.

Neisser, U. (1988) Five kinds of self-knowledge. *Philosophical Psychology* 1(1), 35–59.

Newcomb, A.F. and Bagwell, C.L. (1995) Children's friendship relations: A meta-analytic review. *Psychological Bulletin* 117(2), 306–47.

Newman, H.H., Freeman, F.N. and Holzinger, K.J. (1937) *Twins: a study of heredity and environment*. Chicago: University of Chicago Press.

Nichols, J.D. (1996) Cooperative learning: a motivational tool to enhance student persistence, self-regulation and efforts to please teachers and parents. *Educational Research and Evaluation* 2, 246–60.

Nolen-Hoeksema, S., Wolfson, A., Mumme, D. and Guskin, K. Helplessness in children of depressed and nondepressed mothers. *Developmental Psychology* 31(3), 377–87.

Nowak-Fabrykowski, K. (1995) Can symbolic play prepare children for their future? *Early Child Development and Care* 102, 63–9.

O'Brien, S.F. and Bierman, K.L. (1988) Conceptions and perceived influence of peer groups: Interviews with preadolescents and adolescents. *Child development* 59(5), 1360–5.

Okami, P., Olmstead, R., Abramson, P.R. and Pendleton, L. (1998) Early exposure to parental nudity and scences of parental sexuality ('primal scenes'): an 18-year longitudinal study of outcome. *Archives of Sexual Behaviour* 27, 361–84.

Okwonko, R. (1997) Moral development and culture in Kohlberg's theory: a Nigerian (Igbo) evidence. *Ife Psychologia: an International Journal* 5, 117–28.

Olmstead, R.E., Guy, S.M., O'Mally, P.M. and Bentler, P.M. (1991) Longitudinal assessment of the relationship between self-esteem, fatalism, loneliness and substance use. *Journal of Social Behavior and Personality* 6(4) 749–70.

Palmonari, A., Pombeni, M.L. and Kirchler, E. (1989) Peer groups and the evolution of the self-system in adolescence. *European Journal of the Psychology of Education* 4, 3–15.

Parker, J.G. and Asher, S.R. (1987) Peer relations and later personal adjustment: are low-accepted children at risk? *Psychological Bulletin* 102, 357–89.

Parsons, M. (1999) The logic of play in psychoanalysis. *International Journal of Psychoanalysis* 80, 871–84.

Parten, M. (1932) Social participation among pre-school children. *Journal of Abnormal and Social Psychology* 27, 243–60.

Patterson, C.J. (1997) Children of lesbian and gay parents. *Advances in Clinical Child Psychology* 19, 235–82.

Pellegrini, A.D. (1994) The rough play of boys of different sociometric status. *International Journal of Behavioural Development* 17, 525–40.

Pellegrini, A.D. and Melhuish, E.C. (1998) Friendship, individual differences and children's literacy. *Proceedings of the British Psychological Society* 6, 90.

Pellegrini, A.D. and Smith, P.K. (1998) Physical activity play: the nature and function of a neglected aspect of play. *Child Development* 69, 577–98.

Pennington, D. (1986) *Essential Social Psychology*. London: Arnold.

Perner, J., Frith, U., Leslie, A.M. and Leekam, S. (1989) Exploration of the autistic child's theory of mind: Knowledge, belief and communication. *Child Development* 60, 689–700.

Peters, K. and Richards, P. (1998) 'Why we fight': voices of youth combatants in Sierra Leone. *Africa* 68, 183–210.

Phillips, J.L. (1975) *The Origins of Intellect: Piaget's theory*. San Francisco: Freeman.

Phinney, J. and Devitch-Navarro, M. (1997) Variations in bicultural identification among African-American and Mexican-American adolescents. *Journal of Research on Adolescence* 7, 3–32.

Piaget, J. (1932) *The moral judgement of the child*. London: Routledge and Kegan Paul.

Piaget, J. (1952) Logic and psychology. In *Series of lectures at Manchester University*, published Basic Books (1957).

Piaget, J. (1963) *The Origins of Intelligence in Children*. New York: Norton.

Piaget, J. (1972) Intellectual evolution from adolescence to adulthood. *Human Development* 15, 1–12.

Piaget, J. (1973) *The Child and Reality: Problems of genetic psychology*. New York: Grossman.

Piaget, J. and Inhelder, B. (1956) *The Child's Conception of Space*. London: Routledge & Kegan Paul.

Pierce, L.M. (1993) Effect of father-daughter relationship on traditional versus nontraditional career choice of adult women. *Dissertation Abstracts International* 54(3-B), 1695.

Pilgrim, D. (1992) Psychotherapy and political evasions. In Dryden, W. and Feletham, C. (eds) *Psychotherapy and its Discontents*. Milton Keynes: Open University Press.

Pillow, D.R., West, S.G. and Reich, J.W. (1991) Attributional style in relation to self-esteem and depression: Mediational and interactive models. *Journal of Research in Personality* 25(1), 57–69.

Plomin, R., DeFries, J.C., McClearn, G.E. and Rutter, M. (1997) *Behavioural Genetics*. New York: Freeman.

Plomin, R., Fulker, D.W., Corley, R. and DeFries, J.C. (1997) Nature, nurture and cognitive development from 1–16 years: a parent–offspring adoption study. *Psychological Science* 8, 442–7.

Pratt, M.W., Arnold, M.L., Pratt, A. and Diessner, R. (1999) Predicting adolescent moral reasoning from family climate: a longitudinal study. *Journal of Early Adolescence* 19, 148–75.

Radke-Yarrow, M., McCann, K., DeMulder, E., Belmont, B., Martinez, P. and Richardson, D.T. (1995) Attachment in the context of high risk conditions. *Development and Psychopathology* 7, 247–65.

Ramey, C.T., Campbell, F.A. and Ramey, S.S.L. (1999) Early intervention: successful pathways to improving intellectual development. *Developmental Neuropsychology* 16, 385–92.

Reznick, J.S., Corley, R. and Robinson, J. (1997) A longitudinal study of intelligence in the second year. *Monographs of the Society for Research in Child Development* 62, 1–154.

Richards, M.H., Boxer, A.M., Peterson, A.C. and Albrecht, R. (1990) Relation of weight to body image in pubertal girls and boys from two communities. *Developmental Psychology* 26, 313–21.

Roazen, P. (1992) The historiography of psychoanalysis. In Timms, E. and Robertson, R. (eds) *Psychoanalysis in its Cultural Context. Austrian Studies III*, 3–19.

Robert, M. (1990) Sex-typing of the water-level task: there is more than meets the eye. *International Journal of Psychology* 25, 475–90.

Robertson, J. and Bowlby, J. (1952) Responses of young children to separation from their mothers. *Courier Centre International d'Enfance* 2, 131–42.

Rogers, C. (1961) *On Becoming a Person: a therapist's view of psychotherapy*. Boston: Houghton-Mifflin.

Rose, S., Kamin, L.J. and Lewontin, R.C. (1984) *Not in our Genes*. Harmondsworth: Penguin.

Rubin, K. (1982) Social and social-cognitive developmental characteristics of young isolate, normal and sociable children. In Rubin, K. and Ross, H.S. (eds) *Peer Relationships and Social Skills in Childhood*. New York: Springer-Verlag.

Rubin, K.H., Fein, G. and Vandenberg, B. (1983) Play. In Hetherington, E.M. (ed.) *Handbook of Child Psychology*, vol 4. New York: Wiley.

Rushton, J.P. (1988) Race differences in behaviour: a review and evolutionary analysis. *Personality and Individual Differences* 9, 1009–24.

Russell, C.M. (1999) A meta-analysis of published research on the effects of nonmaternal care on child development. *Dissertation Abstracts International, A (Humanities and Social Sciences)* 59(9-A), 3362.

Rutter, M. (1979) *Changing Youth in a Changing Society*. London: Nuffield Provincial Hospitals Trust.

Rutter, M. (1981) *Maternal Deprivation Reassessed*. Harmondsworth: Penguin.

Rutter, M., Graham, P., Chadwick, D.F.D. and Yule, W. (1976) Adolescent turmoil: fact or fiction? *Journal of Child Psychology and Psychiatry* 17, 35–56.

Rutter, M. and the English and Romanian Adoptees Study Team (1998) Developmental catch up and deficit after severe global early privation. *Journal of Child Psychology and Psychiatry* 39, 465–76.

Salem, D.A., Zimmerman, M.A. and Notaro, P.C. (1998) Effects of family structure, family process and father involvement on psychosocial outcomes among African American adolescents. *Family Relations: Interdisciplinary Journal of Applied Family Studies* 47, 331–41.

Salois, K.A.N. (1999) A comparative study of the Wechsler Intelligence Scale for children 3rd edition (WISC III) test performance: Northern Cheyenne and Blackfeet Reservation Indian children with the standardisation sample. *Dissertation Abstracts International* 60, 1909.

Sandler, A., Sutton, K., DeWees, J., Girardi, M., Sheppard, V. and Bodfish, J.W. (1999) Lack of benefit of a single dose of synthetic human secretin in the treatment of autism and pervasive developmental disorder. *New England Journal of Medicine* 341(24), 1801–6.

Scarr, S. (1992) Developmental theories for the 1990s: development and individual differences. *Child Development* 63, 1–19.

Schafer, M. and Smith, P.K. (1996) Teachers' perceptions of play fighting and real fighting in a primary school. *Educational Research* 38, 173–81.

Schaffer, H.R. (1996) *Social Development*. Oxford: Blackwell.

Schaffer, H.R. and Emerson, P.E. (1964) The development of social attachments in infancy. *Monographs of the Society for Research into Child Development*.

Schiedel, D.G and Marcia, J.E. (1985) Ego identity, intimacy, sex role orientation, and gender. *Developmental Psychology* 21(1), 149–60.

Schultz, N.V. (1971) How children perceive pain. *Nursing Outlook* 3(6), 670–3.

Schweder, R.A. (1991) *Thinking through Cultures*. Cambridge: Harvard University Press.

Seitz, V. (1990) Intervention programmes for impoverished children: a comparison of educational and family support models. *Annals of Child Development* 7, 73–103.

Shaffer, D.R. (1999) *Developmental Psychology: childhood and adolescence*. Pacific Grove: Brooks/Cole.

Shaywitz, B.A., Shaywitz, S.E., Pugh, K.R., Constable, R.T., Skudlarski, P., Fulbright, R.K., Bronen, R.A., Fletcher, J.M., Shankweiler, D.P., Katz, L. and Gore, J.C. (1995) Sex differences in the functional organisation of the brain for language. *Nature* 373, 607–9.

Shields, J. (1962) *Monozygotic twins brought up apart and brought together*. Oxford: Oxford University Press.

Shultz, N.R. and Moore, D. (1989) Further reflections on loneliness research. In Hojat, M. and Crandall, R. (eds) *Loneliness: theory, research and applications*. Newbury Park: Sage.

Sigel, I.E. (1987) Early childhood education: Developmental enhancement or developmental acceleration? In Kagan, S.L. (ed.) *et al. Early Schooling: The national debate*. New Haven: Yale University Press.

Silver-Aylaian, M. (1999) The roles of prior stressful events and dyadic coping patterns in patients and spouses psychological adjustment to cancer. *Dissertation Abstracts International* 59, 5112.

Sinha, S. and Vibha, P. (1998) Intelligence and vigilance performance as related to exposure among children. *Indian Journal of Clinical Psychology* 25, 194–9.

Skodak, M. and Skeels, H.M. (1949) A final follow-up on one hundred adopted children. *Journal of Genetic Psychology* 75, 84–125.

Skuse, D.H. (1993) Extreme deprivation in early childhood. In Messer, D. and Dockerell, J. (1999) (eds.) *Developmental Psychology, A Reader*. London: Arnold.

Slade, A. and Wolf, D.P. (1994) *Children at Play*. Oxford: Oxford University Press.

Slaughter, D.T. (1988) Black children, schooling, and educational interventions. *New Directions for Child Development* 42, 109–16.

Sloan, S.A. (1999) Effects of aggressive therapeutic play: does it increase or diminish spontaneous aggression? *Dissertation Abstracts International* 59, 3677.

Smith, P. (1998) Social development. In Eysenck, M. (ed.) *Psychology, an integrated approach*. Harlow: Longman.

Smith, P.K., Cowie, H. and Blades, M. (1998) *Understanding Children's Development*. Oxford: Blackwell.

Snarey, J.R. (1985) Cross-cultural universality of social-moral development: A critical review of Kohlbergian research. *Psychological Bulletin* 97(2), 202–32.

Snarey, J.R., Reimer, R. and Kohlberg, L. (1985) Development of moral reasoning among Kibbutz adolescents: a longitudinal, cross-cultural study. *Developmental Psychology* 21, 3–17.

Solomon, J. and George, C. (1999) The development of attachment in separated and divorced families: effects of overnight visitation, parent and couple variables. *Attachment and Human Development* 1, 2–33.

Spurlock, J.C. and Magistro, C.A. (1998) *New and Improved: the transformation of American women's emotional culture*. New York: New York University Press.

Sroufe, L.A. (1985) Attachment classification from the perspective of infant–caregiver relationships and infant temperament. *Child Development* 56, 1–14.

Stangor, C. and Ruble, D.N. (1987) Development of gender role knowledge and gender constancy. In Liben, L.S. and Signorella, M.L. (eds) *Children's Gender Schemas*. San Francisco: Jossey-Bass.

Stern, W. (1911) *Differentielle psychologie*. Leipzig: J. A. Barth.

Stone, G.P. (1981) The play of little children. In Stone, G.P. and Faberman, H.A. (eds) *Social Psychology through Symbolic Interaction*. New York: Wiley.

Super, C.M. and Harkness, S. (1982) The development of affect in infancy and early childhood. In Wagner, D.A. and Stevenson, H.W. (eds) *Cultural Perspectives on Child Development*. Oxford: Freeman.

Super, C.M. and Harkness, S. (1986) The developmental niche: a conceptualisation at the interface of child and culture. *International Journal of Behavioural Development* 9, 545–70.

Sylva, K. (1994) The therapeutic value of play. *Psychology Review* 1.

Symons, D.K. and Clark, S.E. (2000) A longitudinal study of mother–child relationships and theory of mind in the preschool period. *Social Development* 9, 3–23.

Takahashi, K. (1990) Affective relationships and their lifelong development. In Baltes, P.B. (ed.) *et al. Life-span Development and Behavior*, vol. 10. Hillsdale: Lawrence Erlbaum Associates, Inc.

Tanner, J.M. (1989) *Foetus into Man*. Castlemead Publications.

Tarullo, L.B. (1994) Windows on social worlds: gender differences in children's play narratives. In Slade, A. and Wolf, D.P. (eds) *Children at Play*. Oxford: Oxford University Press.

Tasker, S.L. and Golombok, F. (1998) *Growing up in a Lesbian Family*. London: Guildford Press.

Terman, L.M. (1916) *The Measurement of Intelligence*. Boston: Houghton-Mifflin.

Thomas, A. and Chess, S. (1977) *Temperament and Development*, New York: Brunner/Mazel.

Tizard, B. and Hodges, J. (1978) The effect of early institutional care on eight year old children. *Journal of Psychology and Psychiatry* 19, 99–118.

Tizard, B. and Phoenix, A. (1993) *Black, White or Mixed Race?* London: Routledge.

Tizard, B. and Rees, J. (1974) A comparison of the effects of adoption, restoration to the natural mother and continued institutionalisation on the cognitive development of four-year old children. *Child Development* 45, 92–9.

Tobin, J.J., Wu, D.Y.H. and Davidson, D.H. (1989) *Preschool in Three Cultures: Japan, China and the United States*. New Haven: Yale University Press.

Tracy, R. and Ainsworth, M.D.S. (1981) Maternal affectionate behaviour and infant–mother attachment patterns. *Child Development* 52, 1341–3.

Tremblay-Leveau, H. and Nadel, J. (1996) Exclusion in triads: can it serve metacommunicative knowledge in 11 and 13 year-old children? *British Journal of Developmental Psychology* 14, 145–58.

Triandis, H.C. (1991) Cross-cultural differences in assertiveness/competing vs group loyalty/co-operation. In Hinde, R.A. and Groebel, J. (eds) *Co-operation and Social Behaviour*. Cambridge: Cambridge University Press.

Troy, M. and Sroufe, L.A. (1987) Victimisation among preschoolers: role of attachment relationship history. *Journal of the Academy of Child and Adolescent Psychiatry* 26, 166–72.

Twycross, A. (1998) Children's cognitive level and perception of pain. *Professional Nurse* 14, 35–37.

Unger, R.K. (1979) Towards a redefinition of sex and gender. *American Psychologist* 34, 1085–94.

Valsiner, J. (2000) *Culture and Human Development*. London: Sage.

Vandell, D.L. (1980) Sociability with peer and mother during the first year. *Developmental Psychology* 16, 355–61.

Van den Boom, D.C. (1994) The influence of temperament and mothering on attachment and exploration: an experimental manipulation of sensitive responsiveness among lower-class mothers with irritable babies. *Child Development* 65, 1457–77.

Van den Heuvel, H., Tellegen, G. and Koomen, W. (1992) Cultural differences in the use of psychological and social characteristics in children's self understanding. *European Journal of Social Psychology* 22, 353–62.

Van Ijzendoorn, M.H. (1997) Attachment, emergent morality and aggression: toward a developmental socioemotional model of antisocial behaviour. *International Journal of Behavioural Development* 21, 703–27.

Verkuyten, M. (1995) Self-esteem, self-concept stability and aspects of ethnic identity among majority and minority youth in the Netherlands. *Journal of Youth and Adolescence* 24, 155–76.

Vitaro, F., Brengden, M. and Tremblay, R.E. (2000) Influence of deviant friends on delinquency: searching for moderator variables. *Journal of Abnormal Child Psychology* 28, 313–25.

Vondra, J.I., Shaw, D.S. and Kevenides, M.C. (1995) Predicting infant attachment classification from multiple contemporaneous measures of maternal care. *Infant Behaviour and Development* 18, 415–25.

Vondra, J.I. and Barnett, D. (1999) Atypical attachments in infancy and early childhood among children at developmental risk. *Monographs of the Society for Research in Child Development*. Oxford: Blackwell.

Vygotsky, L.S. (1967) Play and its role in the mental development of the child. *Soviet Psychology* 12, 62–76.

Wakefield, A.J., Murch, S.H., Anthony, A., Linnell, J., Casson, D.M., Malik, M., Berelowitz, M., Dhillon, A.P., Thomson, M.A., Harvey, P., Valentine, A., Davies, S.E. and Walker-Smith, J.A. (1998) Ileal-lymphoid-nodular hyperplasia, non-specific colitis, and pervasive developmental disorder in children. *The Lancet* 351, 637–41.

Warren, S.L., Emde, R.N. and Sroufe, L.A. (2000) Internal representations: predicting anxiety from children's play narratives. *Journal of the Academy of Child and Adolescent Psychiatry* 39, 100–7.

Waterhouse, S. (2000) *A Positive Approach to Autism.* London: Jessica Kingsley Publishers.

Watson, M.W. (1994) The relation between anxiety and pretend play. In Slade, A. and Wolf, D.P. (eds) *Children at Play.* Oxford: Oxford University Press.

Wechsler, D. (1939) *The Measurement of Adult Intelligence.* Baltimore: Williams and Wilkins.

Wertsch, J. V. (1991) *Voices of the mind: a sociocultural approach to mediated action.* Cambridge: Harvard University Press.

Wertsch, J.V. and Tulviste, P. (1996) L.S. Vygotsky and contemporary psychology. In Woodhead, M., Faulkner, D. and Littleton, K. (eds) *Learning Relationships in the Classroom.* London: Routledge.

Whitbourne, S.K., Zuschlag, M.K., Elliot, L.B. and Waterman, A.S. (1992) Psychosocial development in adulthood: a 22-year sequential study. *Journal of Personality and Social Psychology* 63, 260–71.

Whiting, B.B. and Edwards, C.P. (1988) *Children of Different Worlds: the formation of social behaviour.* Cambridge: Harvard University Press.

Widdicombe, S. and Wooffitt, R. (1990) 'Being' versus 'doing' punk: on achieving authenticity as a member. *Journal of Language and Social Psychology* 9, 257–77.

Williams, D. (1996) *Autism, an inside-out approach.* London: Jessica Kingsley Publishers.

Wiltshire, S. (1987) *Drawings.* London: J.M. Dent and Sons Ltd.

Wimmer, H. and Perner, J. (1983) Beliefs about beliefs: representation and constraining function of wrong beliefs in young children's understanding of deception. *Cognition* 13, 103–28.

Wing, L. (1996) *The Autistic Spectrum. A guide for parents and professionals.* London: Constable.

Wing, L. and Gould, J. (1979) Severe impairments of social interaction and associated abnormalities in children: epidemiology and classification. *Journal of Autism and Developmental Disorders* 9, 11–29.

Wolff, P.H. and Fesseha, G. (1999) The orphans of Eritrea: A five-year follow-up study. *Journal of Child Psychology & Psychiatry & Allied Disciplines* 40(8), 1231–7.

Woodhead, M., Faulkner, D. and Littleton, K. (1998) *Cultural Worlds of Early Childhood*. London: Routledge.

Young, W.C., Goy, R.W. and Phoenix, C.H. (1964) Hormones and sexual behaviour. *Science* 143, 212–9.

Yuwiler, A. and Freedman, D.X. (1987) Neurotransmitter research in autism. In Schopler, E. and Gary, B. (eds) *Neurobiological Issues in Autism*. New York: Plenum.

Zahn-Waxler, C., Cole, P.M., Richardson, D.T., Friedman, R.J., Michel, M.K. and Belouad, F. (1994) Social problem-solving in disruptive preschool children; reactions to hypothetical situations in conflict and distress. *Merrill-Palmer Quarterly* 40, 98–119.

Zeidner, M. and Schleyer, E.J. (1999) The big-fish-little-pond effect for academic self-concept, test anxiety and school grades in gifted children. *Contemporary Educational Psychology* 24, 305–29.

Zigler, E. and Seitz, V. (1980) Measure for measure? *American Psychologist* 35(10), 939.

Zucker, K.J. and Bradley, S.J. (1998) Adoptee over-representation among clinic-referred boys with gender identity disorder. *Canadian Journal of Psychiatry* 43, 1040–3.

index

Page numbers in **bold** indicate where the term has been defined in the text